COLLEGE AND CAREER READINESS:

Writing

Level 11

Common Core State Standards Edition

Writers:
Bill McMahon and Douglas Grudzina

Senior Editor:
Paul Moliken

Cover and Text Design:
Maria J. Mendoza

Layout and Production:
Jeremy Clark

Prestwick House

P.O. Box 658

Clayton • Delaware 19938

Tel: 1.888.932.4593

Fax: 1.888.718.9333

Web: www.prestwickhouse.com

ISBN: 978-0-9823096-6-7

TABLE OF CONTENTS

Standards-Based Scoring Rubric for Grade 11.. v

PART I: Personal Writing [*conveying what students have experienced, imagined, thought, and felt*] 1

    Assignment 1: Evaluate a Significant Experience....................................... 3

        Mini-lesson 1: Journal Writing.. 19

    Assignment 2: Describe a Comic or Unfortunate Event.......................... 27

    Assignment 3: Fictional Narrative... 41

PART II: Informative Writing [*showing what students know about a subject*] 57

    Assignment 1: Interview or Personal Profile... 58

    Assignment 2: Book or Article Report... 75

        Mini-lesson 1: The Reading Check Essay: Summary 96

    Assignment 3: Literary Analysis—Fiction 101

    Assignment 4: Literary Analysis—Nonfiction 137

        Mini-lesson 2: The Reading Check Essay: Interpretation.................. 157

PART III: Persuasive Writing [*asserting and defending claims*] 161

    Assignment 1: The Initial Argument 162

    Assignment 2: The Rebuttal... 187

        Mini-lesson 1: The Test or Exam Essay (Support, refute, or qualify the thesis that…) 220

    Assignment 3: The Academic Thesis-Proof Essay 235

        Mini-lesson 2: The Test or Exam Essay (Develop a thesis and support it.) 261

PART IV: The Research Projects 277

    Assignment 1: Research Project—Non-English Language Arts 279

    Assignment 2: Research Project—English Language or Literature Topic... 307

APPENDIX: Samples of APA and MLA Citation and Documentation 346

STANDARDS-BASED SCORING RUBRIC FOR GRADE 11

	TOPIC	
5	Topic is **clear and sufficiently narrow** for the nature of the writing.	Topic is **sufficiently complex** and is **suitable to** fulfilling **the purpose** of the writing (e.g., persuasive versus informational).
4	Topic is **clear and sufficiently narrow** for the nature of the writing.	Topic is **sufficiently complex** and is **suitable to** fulfilling **the purpose** of the writing (e.g., persuasive versus informational).
3	Topic is **clear and sufficiently narrow** for the nature of the writing.	Topic is **sufficiently complex** and is **suitable to** fulfilling **the purpose** of the writing (e.g., persuasive versus informational).
2	Topic is **clear but either too broad or too narrow** for the nature of the writing.	Topic is **sufficiently complex** and is **suitable to** fulfilling **the purpose** of the writing (e.g., persuasive versus informational).
1	Topic is **clear but either too broad or too narrow** for the nature of the writing.	Topic either **lacks complexity**, or it is **unsuitable to the purpose** of the writing (e.g., persuasive versus informational).

CRAFTSMANSHIP		
5	Writing is competent and confident. Tone and style seem natural and appropriate to the topic, purpose, and audience of the piece.	• All claims or points being explored are expressed clearly. • The distinctions between the student's ideas and those from other sources are evident. • A strong attempt to present all claims (both the student's and others') accurately, objectively, and fully (as appropriate to the topic, audience, and purpose) is evident. • If appropriate to the topic, audience, and purpose, narrative techniques enhance the overall impact of the piece.
4	Writing is competent and reveals careful attention to technique. Tone and style are appropriate to the topic, purpose, and audience of the piece.	• All claims or points being explored are expressed clearly. • The distinctions between the student's ideas and those from other sources are evident. • An attempt to present all claims (both the student's and others') accurately, objectively, and fully (as appropriate to the topic, audience, and purpose) is evident. • A strong attempt to use narrative devices appropriate to the topic, audience, and purpose enhances the overall impact of the piece.

CRAFTSMANSHIP (CONT.)		
3	**Writing** is **strong** and reveals **careful attention to technique. Tone and style** are, for the **most part, appropriate** to the topic, purpose, and audience with a **few minor lapses** into **overly formal or conversational.**	• **Most claims** or points being explored are **expressed clearly,** while **some** may be **suggested or implied.** • The **distinctions** between the student's ideas and those from other sources are **usually apparent.** • The writing exhibits **uneven attempts to present all claims** (both the student's and others') **accurately** and **objectively.** • **Some omissions** in either strengths or limitations **may suggest bias** and/or **faulty reasoning.** • **A strong attempt** to **use narrative devices** appropriate to the topic, audience, and purpose **enhances** the **overall impact** of the piece.

CRAFTSMANSHIP (CONT.)		
2	Writing is strong and reveals some attention to technique. Tone and style are consistently maintained, but are generally overly formal or conversational for the topic, purpose, and audience.	• Most claims or points being explored are specified, but some are implied or are stated ambiguously. • The distinctions between the student's ideas and those from other sources are suggested. • The writing suggests tentative attempts to present all claims (both the student's and others') accurately, and objectively. • Obvious omissions in either strengths or limitations suggest bias and/or faulty reasoning. • When appropriate to the topic, audience, and purpose, some narrative techniques may be used with limited effectiveness. Devices that would make the writing clearer or more powerful may be missing or whatever narrative techniques are used are unnecessary or distracting.

CRAFTSMANSHIP (CONT.)	
1	**Writing** reveals **some attention to technique.** **Tone and style** tend to be **inconsistent or inappropriate** to the topic, purpose, and audience.	• **Most claims** or points being explored **are specified**, but **some are implied** or are **stated ambiguously.** • There is **minimal to no clear distinction** between the student's ideas and those from other sources. • The writing suggests **minimal or flawed attempts to present all claims** (both the student's and others') **accurately.** • There is **minimal to no attempt to use narrative devices** (when appropriate to the topic, audience, and purpose). **Devices** that would make the writing clearer or more powerful **are missing.** Whatever **narrative techniques** are used **are unnecessary and distracting.**

ELABORATION, DEVELOPMENT, AND SUPPORT		
5	**All claims**, inferences, and analyses are **supported with evidence** from literary or informational texts, as appropriate to the topic, audience, and purpose.	• **Facts**, examples, and/or details are **relevant and help to establish the purpose** of the writing and meet the needs of the audience. • When appropriate to the topic, audience, and purpose, **strong descriptive language** contributes to applicable **images and impressions**.
4	**All claims**, inferences, and analyses are **supported with evidence** from literary or informational texts, as appropriate to the topic, audience, and purpose.	• **Facts**, examples, and/or details are **relevant and help to establish the purpose** of the writing and meet the needs of the audience. • When appropriate to the topic, audience, and purpose, **strong descriptive language** contributes to applicable **images and impressions**.
3	**For the most part, claims**, inferences, and analyses are **supported with evidence** from literary or informational texts, as appropriate to the topic, audience, and purpose.	• **Facts**, examples, and/or details are **generally relevant and help to establish the purpose** of the writing and meet the needs of the audience. • A strong attempt to create appropriate **images and impressions** is evident.

ELABORATION, DEVELOPMENT, AND SUPPORT (CONT.)		
2	**Lack of adequate support** for one or more claims, inferences, or analyses **weakens the overall impact** of the writing.	• **Facts**, examples, and/or details are generally **relevant, but** are **insufficient to establish the purpose** of the writing and/or meet the needs of the audience. Some **irrelevancies cloud the topic** or **weaken some claims**. • A strong attempt to create appropriate **images and impressions** is evident.
1	**Lack of adequate support** for one or more claims, inferences, or analyses **weakens the overall impact** of the writing.	• Impact is weakened by **trivial or irrelevant** facts or details. Examples may be **tangential**. • An attempt to create appropriate **images and impressions** is apparent.

ORGANIZATION		
5	**Introduction**, thesis, lead, etc., **engages and orients** the reader to the **nature and purpose** of the piece to follow.	• **Conclusion follows from and supports** the information presented and provides a **satisfying sense of completeness** to the writing. • **Order** of ideas and the use of **transitional elements** establish the **relationships** between **claims and reasons**, between **reasons and evidence**, and between **claims and counterclaims**.
4	**Introduction**, thesis, lead, etc., **engages and orients** the reader to the **nature and purpose** of the piece to follow.	• **Conclusion follows from and supports** the information presented and provides a **strong sense of completeness** to the writing. • **Order** of ideas and the use of **transitional elements** establish the **relationships** between **claims and reasons**, between **reasons and evidence**, and between **claims and counterclaims**.
3	**Introduction**, thesis, lead, etc., **engages and orients** the reader to the **nature and purpose** of the piece to follow.	• **Conclusion follows from and supports** the information presented and provides a **sense of completeness** to the writing. • **Order** of ideas and the use of **transitional elements** suggest the **relationships** between **claims and reasons**, between **reasons and evidence**, and between **claims and counterclaims**.

ORGANIZATION (CONT.)		
2	**Introduction**, thesis, lead, etc., **orients the reader** to the **nature and purpose** of the piece to follow.	• **Conclusion follows from and supports** the information presented and provides an **adequate sense of closure** to the writing. • The **relationships** between **claims and reasons**, between **reasons and evidence**, and between **claims and counterclaims are suggested** but **not established** by the **order** of ideas or the use of **transitional elements**.
1	**Introduction**, thesis, lead, etc., is **accurate but unengaging**.	• **Conclusion follows from and supports** the information presented and provides a **sense of closure** to the writing. • The **relationships** between **claims and reasons**, between **reasons and evidence**, and between **claims and counterclaims can be inferred** but **are not necessarily supported** by the **order** of ideas or the use of **transitional elements**.

	FORMS AND CONVENTIONS	
5	Word choice is **precise** and conveys the student's **specific meaning**. **Strong attempts** at using language to add **variety and interest** are **evident**.	• When appropriate, **academic and domain-specific words and phrases** are used **accurately and effectively**. • **Writing** is **free of** spelling and/or typographical **errors**. • **Writing** is **free of** grammatical and **mechanical errors**. • The piece **clearly reflects the student's own thinking** and writing, with **all material** or ideas derived **from outside sources clearly identified** and **carefully cited**. • **All citations** and notations **conform** to the teacher's or school's prescribed style manual (MLA, APA, Turabian, etc.).
4	Word choice is **precise** and conveys the student's **specific meaning**. **Strong attempts** at using language to add **variety and interest** are **evident**.	• When appropriate, **academic and domain-specific words and phrases** are used **accurately and effectively**. • **Writing** is **free of** spelling and/or typographical **errors**. • **Writing** is **free of** grammatical and mechanical **errors**. • The piece **clearly reflects the student's own thinking** and writing, with **all material** or ideas derived **from outside sources clearly identified** and **carefully cited**. • **All citations** and notations **conform** to the teacher's or school's prescribed style manual (MLA, APA, Turabian, etc.).

FORMS AND CONVENTIONS (CONT.)		
3	Word choice is **precise** and conveys the **student's meaning. Some attempts** at using language to add **variety** and **interest** are **evident.**	• The use of **academic and domain-specific words and phrases occasionally reflects a misunderstanding** of the term's meaning or appropriate application. • **Writing** is **free of** spelling and/or typographical **errors.** • **Writing** is **free of** grammatical and mechanical **errors.** • The piece **clearly reflects the student's thinking** and writing, with **all material** or ideas derived **from outside sources clearly identified** and **carefully cited.** • **All citations** and notations **conform** to the teacher's or school's prescribed style manual (MLA, APA, Turabian, etc.).

FORMS AND CONVENTIONS (CONT.)

2	Word choice is **strong** and conveys the student's **meaning**.	• **Academic and domain-specific words** and phrases are used **unnecessarily** or **incorrectly**. • Spelling and/or typographical **errors** are **infrequent** and **do not interfere** with the reader's ability to understand the writing. • Grammatical and mechanical **errors** are **infrequent** and **do not interfere** with the reader's ability to understand the writing. • The piece **clearly reflects the student's own thinking** and writing, with **all material** or ideas derived **from outside sources clearly identified** and **carefully cited**. • **All citations** and notations **conform** to the teacher's or school's prescribed style manual (MLA, APA, Turabian, etc.).
1	Word choice is **adequate** to convey the student's **meaning**.	• **Academic and domain-specific words** and phrases are used **unnecessarily** or **incorrectly**, or they are **not used when** their application is **indicated**. • Spelling and/or typographical **errors** are **noticeable** and **distracting**. • Grammatical and mechanical **errors** are **noticeable** and **distracting**. • Material and/or ideas derived from **outside sources are not identified or cited**. • **Citations** and notations **generally conform** to the teacher's or school's prescribed style manual.

PART I:

Personal Writing

[conveying what students have experienced, imagined, thought, and felt]

By now, you know that "Personal Writing" is not the same as "Private Writing." More than anything else you will write in high school, college, or your career, personal essays will have the most notable impact on what schools you attend, what opportunities are offered to you, and what job you end up landing. Your personal writing, whether you write it as part of an application or as an introduction to a prospective employer, does more than represent you.

It should reveal you.

Remember the necessary elements of good personal writing:

- **A point**: Your answer to your reader's question, *Why are you telling me this*?

- **An angle**: What makes your account of your day at the beach, your first job, the day you got cut from the team, etc., unique—*more meaningful, moving, or memorable* than those of the hundreds of other teenagers who visited beaches, worked first jobs, or got cut from teams?

- **A voice**: Confident…Respectful…Witty…along with your angle, this is what will give your reader a sense of you beyond the mere facts of your narrative.

- **Substance**: Vague generalities and abstract concepts might suggest ideas to your reader, but they will do little to recreate the physical, psychological, emotional, and spiritual effects that will make the reader take notice of your account.

And always remember your writing process:

STEP 1: Select a Topic

STEP 2: Develop a Slant/Angle/Hook

STEP 3: Brainstorm, Discuss, Research

STEP 4: Outline

STEP 5: Write Your First Draft

STEP 6: Peer Edit

STEP 7: Final Draft

POSSIBLE STEP 8: Second Edit and Final Revision

ASSIGNMENT 1:

Evaluate a Significant Experience

This is a popular writing prompt on college applications. The key to a notable and effective essay lies in paying close attention to the verb—*evaluate*, not "narrate" or "describe."

> Evaluate a significant experience, achievement, risk you have taken, or ethical dilemma you have faced and its impact on you.

"**Chandra**" is a first-semester 11th grader in a large, urban magnet high school. Her ambition is to be the first member of her immediate family to attend college and graduate with a four-year degree. Her ultimate aspiration is law school.

Here is a re-creation of the process Chandra used when she was given the prompt to evaluate a significant experience, achievement, or risk:

STEP 1: Select a Topic

First, Chandra considered the prompt at length, and brainstormed on the most significant experiences that she felt might make an effective and affecting essay.

- Significant experiences: Mom's illness and death? Breaking my arm at soccer when I was fourteen? Encountering a bear in the woods when we went camping?

- Achievements: Winning at the debate finals? Organizing the fundraiser for the Lustgarten Foundation?

- Risks: Losing my Mom? Not having my arm heal properly? Getting eaten by the bear?

- Ethical dilemma: How to deal emotionally with Mom's death? Whether to kill the bear or not?

By considering each topic, she began to narrow her choices:

– Mom's illness and death—still the most significant event in my life. Might move the readers, make them sympathetic to me, but I might come off like a drama queen.

– Breaking my arm—painful, difficult, had to deal with being sidelined and temporarily disabled. But not very unique, not sure what slant to give it.

– Encountering the bear—dramatic at first, we realized not to run or move to attract its attention, then it went away, never even seeing us. But then what?

– Winning at the debate finals—I worked hard, it paid off, but I might come off as self-congratulating and conceited.

– Organizing the fundraiser for the Lustgarten Foundation—I did a good thing, I raised money for a fine cause, research on the disease that killed my mother. But wouldn't it be better to simply write about my Mom's death?

Chandra narrowed her possible topics to two, writing about her mother's illness and death, and organizing the fundraiser for the Lustgarten Foundation.

STEP 2: Develop a Slant/Angle/Hook

WHAT CAN MY ANGLE BE?

– Mom's death—How do I communicate how this affects me every day? Should this be about how a person deals with the death of a loved one? That's been done. Maybe I should show how this has changed my life forever, how it feels to be orphaned when you're not an adult yet, but everyone expects you to behave like one.

– Organizing the fundraiser—I could give this the slant of taking something back, or taking some revenge against the illness that killed my mother. That might work, or it might sound fake inspirational, phony like that Bette Davis movie.

WHERE DO I BEGIN MY EVALUATION?

– I think I'll begin with how I'm dealing with things now, then show how I got to that place.

Note: This is another early choice, and a strong one, but one that Chandra will need to re-evaluate in terms of how much her essay effectively conveys her point. She will find that, while her voice is strong and individual, she needs to guard against letting her emotional life overwhelm the piece, causing her to lose focus. While she wants to move the committee members and give them an effective window into who she is, she also needs to demonstrate discipline and skill as a writer.

WHAT TYPE OR TONE OF VOICE DO I WANT TO CREATE IN MY READER'S MIND?

— I want to stand out, show my ability to write about serious issues, but I want the essay to be unique, not just about something tragic but about how I react to something tragic, how it affects my point of view. So I'll try as much as I can to write it the way I would say it.

STEP 3: Brainstorm, Discuss, Research

Considering what her angle and tone would be, Chandra decided she was ready to write directly about her mother's death and how it has changed her. She also felt she had some strong ideas about how to convey her feelings and impressions and that she had the opportunity to capture the reader and get a strong evaluation of her writing skills.

Having made this choice, she started then to list the details and nuances that would color her essay emotionally and help make her experiences real to the reader.

— How hard Mom's death was, how much she suffered, what an awful disease cancer is.

— How beautiful she had been before, the silver-framed wedding picture.

— That dumb Bette Davis movie about the woman who dies, how ironic that is when I contrast it with how she herself died.

— The cigarettes I found hidden around the house after she died, how angry I was that she couldn't kick the habit.

— My sister's reaction to Mom's death, how different it seems from my own.

Chandra is not being as detailed as she should be in her brainstorming. She needs to take more time with this part of the process, listing more specific details about her mother, what kind of person her mother was, how she is both like and unlike her mother, the specific ways her sister's reaction differed from her own, etc. The deeper she makes her well, the more choices she will have in writing the first draft, and the stronger her choices will be.

STEP 4: Outline

Chandra has decided to tell her story not in chronological fashion, but to begin with the death of her mother, then proceed to outline its emotional impact on her and how it has changed her outlook.

1. I'll start with the big points in the first paragraph:

   A. how awful her death was,

   B. how she suddenly went from young and pretty to old and diseased, and

   C. how hard it was for me to witness.

2. Then I'll move on to the factual stuff:

   A. how useless the surgery was,

   B. how all it accomplished was to make her suffer more, and me as well.

3. Next I'll give my personal impressions:

   A. how stupid that Bette Davis movie she loved so much really is,

   B. how ridiculous it is to show death as glamorous and noble when it's really terrible and ugly.

4. That will give a good lead-in to talk about the wedding picture and how beautiful and young she had once been, if it hadn't been for the cigarettes.

5. Then I can tell how she was never able to quit, up to the last day she lived, how I found packs of the things hidden all over the house.

6. I'll end with how little people understand, even my sister, and how uncertain I am now about everything in life.

While Chandra clearly has a compelling story to tell, and an impassioned approach and angle, there are some risks she is taking here that could affect how well her reader will react. The sense of irony and her individual voice are already in evidence, but her emotional reactions seem likely to take her on tangents that might lose points for organization and focus. Also, while her point is to show how this event affected her, her singular focus on her own emotions without much reference to anyone else's might make her appear self-absorbed and self-pitying—which will not win her points with an evaluator.

STEP 5: First Draft

Now, read Chandra's first draft and evaluate its strengths and weaknesses. Consider how successfully she responds to the prompt and presents an essay that will be noticed by the selection committee of a large scholarship foundation.

My mother's death was the most horrible thing I have ever had to witness; she was only forty-eight years old, which seems old to a sixteen-year-old like me, but it's pretty young to be dying. You always think of your parents as old, so much older than you—until one of them isn't there, and you realize that a person can be young and old all in the same moment, and the moment passes very quickly.

The first paragraph grabs the reader's attention with a compelling situation and a distinct voice that helps define the viewpoint of the writer and the angle of the story.

It was cancer—pancreatic cancer, to be exact—that took her from me and my family. Not an easy death, by any means; she had intense, evil pain that almost never let up, she endured five hours of unbelievably invasive surgery that was supposed to extend her life and didn't, and I know that from the moment she was given her diagnosis, fear was a constant companion.

This paragraph effectively conveys needed information about the incident, as well as the emotional context for the author. Already, however, the essay begins to lose some focus on the main point, the impact of Chandra's mother's death on Chandra. There is also an instance of awkward usage— "...me and my family" would more properly be phrased "... my family and me."

One of my Mom's favorite movies was a really old black-and-white deal with Bette Davis, where she plays this woman who is dying from cancer. It's called Dark Victory. I can't watch it now, not because it makes me sad, but because it makes me angry. Bette Davis doesn't suffer the way my mother suffered; she doesn't scream out in pain

This section, while effective, may overemphasize the anger of the author; while it's giving a vivid account of the emotional impact of the event, it misses the opportunity to make the reader understand why the author's mother was important to her, so we can better understand the anger and grief she is feeling. The reference to the film as a "black and white deal" might come across as too flippant, also pushing the reader away from the author's viewpoint rather than causing the reader to embrace it.

or lose so much weight she starts to resemble a skeleton or lose control of her bodily functions. She suffers prettily, in furs and diamonds and satin; then she gets to die prettily, in a gauzy fadeout, talking about meeting death "bravely and finely." The whole thing actually looks glamorous. I can't remember anything brave or fine in how my mother died. I don't blame her for that; no one can be either brave or fine when they're being eaten alive by disease.

There is a silver-framed photo of my Mom on her Wedding Day, and she looks glamorous enough to make Bette pea-green with envy. She's in a beautiful lace dress, simple but elegant; her face is framed by a veil that might as well be a halo, and she holds a bouquet of gardenias. Her eyes shine and glow; the picture is so alive you feel she might start speaking to you from it. She would probably say how excited she is, how wonderful her wedding was, how she is looking forward to the life ahead of her. She doesn't know what's headed for her down the line. If she did, maybe she would have quit smoking.

The description of the wedding photo with the last sentence, effectively shocks and compels the reader and further defined the author's voice and viewpoint.

I can barely remember her without a cigarette, from the time I was little. She did try to quit several times, and even once went for several months without a single cigarette, after my sister and I begged her relentlessly, but she always relapsed. She even smoked after the diagnosis, secretly; she would sneak them behind our backs when no one was in the room with her. I found packs of the evil things stashed all over the house after she died, behind the computer, between the cushions on the sofa, in the kitchen cupboards behind the salt and sugar. I'd tear them up when I found them, destroy them one by one and drop them into the garbage can.

Again, while the passion and voice of the writing are compelling, she hasn't yet conveyed a fuller picture of the character of her mother, why she was important and loved, what made her special. We have heard only about the disease, the addiction, and a pretty picture.

My sister tells me I need to accept what's happened and move on, that I shouldn't dwell on my grief and work on remembering happier times with Mom, and all the good things about her. I know this is true, yet I can't help resenting the statement. It's easy for Deirdre to say that, since she's already moved on to college and the next phase of her life, and she missed much of the really rougher parts of Mom's illness because she had finals at school, and Mom insisted that took preference.

Now I have finals, and tests for college to study for, and Forensics and Drama Club, and basketball; Mom would tell me whenever I was having a tough time with anything to just "put your head down and barrel through." I bury myself in my routine and hope that I can do that. But every now and then, I catch a glimpse of Mom's wedding photo: the lace, the smile, and especially the eyes that can follow you wherever you are in the room. I find myself questioning things a lot more, like God, religion, the random nature of life, and just what it is that we're supposed to hold onto, if anything. I have no answers right now, but I have a lot of questions.

Here the author truly risks losing the empathy of the reader; she is allowing her anger to take her on a tangent, portraying her resentment of her sister and still not giving us a sense of who her mother was.

Chandra offers a bit more of a window on the character of her mother and effectively describes her emotional state and how the experience of her mother's death has changed her. But we are left wanting more of a distinct point, more of why this particular story is unique and important, what meaning it has to the reader, not just the author. While there is, indeed, the beginnings of a powerful essay here, the author needs to focus and refine her work, making sure she portrays not just her emotions, but what fuels those emotions.

Analysis of First Draft

What is this writer's point? The writer effectively shares her emotional journey in witnessing the illness and death of her mother, but *comes up short in terms of bringing the reader to a unique revelation about this experience*—we never get a satisfactory answer to the question *"Why this story?"*

What is her angle? The author is reaching for an unstinting portrayal of the emotional toll the loss of a parent takes on a teenager, how it changes her view and experience of everything around her, and the difficulty of reconciling oneself to loss.

What type or tone of voice has she created in her reader's mind? The author most definitely has a distinct voice, one that does not shy away from her anger and grief, while recognizing implicit irony and even absurdity. However, while her voice is commendably passionate and brave, *she allows her anger to dominate her writing at times and take the essay on tangents that detract from her point. Her style can also be overly conversational and flippant, which is a risky choice on a college entrance essay.*

What techniques has the writer used to create this voice? There is an unflinching directness, a refusal to pull any punches—as well as an ironic viewpoint—from the first sentence. The portrayal of pain and emotional distress is consistent throughout the piece, as is a strong, vital descriptive ability.

What specific details, facts, etc., make this narrative real? There are several potent examples of strongly observed details, such as the wedding portrait, the hiding of the cigarettes, and the author's reaction to the Bette Davis film. The portrayal of the mother's unsuccessful efforts to quit smoking, especially the hiding of the packs of cigarettes that are later found by the author, also ring true and effectively ground the essay in a recognizable reality.

NOW plan your own essay to the same prompt. You will probably find it helpful to follow the same process by which Chandra arrived at her first draft. Remember that Chandra brainstormed and took notes on several possible topics and developed each of them to see which one would yield the best essay.

> Evaluate a significant experience, achievement, risk you have taken, or ethical dilemma you have faced and its impact on you.

STEP 1: Select a Topic

What experiences lend themselves to a successful evaluation?

What point would you want to make in evaluating each of these potential topics?

> Go back and look at Chandra's thoughts in this step. Even in the selection of topics, you need to think about things like an interesting angle and providing sufficient and relevant details.

STEP 2: Develop a Slant/Angle/Hook

What will your angle be?

Where might you begin your evaluation?

What type or tone of voice do you want to create in your reader's mind?

STEP 3: Brainstorm, Discuss, Research

What specific details, facts, etc., will make this experience real and not merely hypothetical?

STEP 4: Outline

Notice that, although Chandra's outline was a bulleted list, the division of topics and the use of single, double, and triple bullets closely resembles a traditional formal, academic outline.

STEP 5: First Draft

> Be your own first editor. Go back and look at the scorer's notes and analysis of Chandra's first draft and see if you can avoid some of the first-draft blunders she has committed, especially those concerning clarifying the point early in the essay and selecting only the most relevant details.

STEP 6: Peer Edit

You and your partner might find it helpful to use the same questions Chandra and her peer editor used:

What is this writer's point?

What is this writer's angle?

What type or tone of voice has the writer created in his or her reader's mind?

What techniques has this writer used to create this voice?

What specific details, facts, etc., make this experience real?

STEP 7: Revised/Final Draft

Remember to consider all critiques on your draft from your peer editors and to consider seriously why you are taking or rejecting their suggestions. Validate all reasoning of your final revision decisions with clear, organized explanations. Once you understand your reasoning clearly enough to explain it in your own words, you will have the tools your essay needs to succeed.

Here are Chandra's peer editor's comments and analysis, as well as Chandra's responses. It is important that even if you disagree with a comment, you understand what your editor is saying. You must be able to articulate specifically why you disagree and choose not to make the suggested revision.

- The essay begins strongly, with a fine opening paragraph that quickly defines the significance of the event and tells its impact on Chandra. There is one instance of awkward usage, however: "*which seems old to a sixteen-year-old like me*" needs to be refined somehow, possibly "*which seems old to someone who's sixteen.*"

- The second paragraph remains strong, giving the reader the factual information, but in an effective, personal voice. There is, however, a missed opportunity to characterize Chandra's mother, to give us an idea of what kind of person she was and why she was important to her daughter. We're told she was afraid of her diagnosis, but anyone would be. The reader craves more details.

- The third paragraph, while it nicely defines Chandra's voice and point of view, again misses an opportunity to define her mother as a character. The detail of the Bette Davis film is nice, and the author's irony is effective, but Chandra allows her emotional response to drive the paragraph off topic, so that the focus becomes her anger, rather than the ways her mother was special. For instance, why was the Bette Davis movie one of her favorites? What does that say about Chandra's mother? This would make us feel Chandra's grief more than her criticism of a classic Hollywood tearjerker would.

- The fourth paragraph has a very fine description of the wedding photo in the silver frame, how beautiful her mother looks, and a nice use of irony in relating the photo to her mother's ultimate fate. But Chandra's description stays on the surface, rather than digging deep; once again, she misses the chance to define the person her mother was, beyond being a smoker with a penchant for old Bette Davis movies, who looks pretty in an old picture. Who was this woman to Chandra? What made her unique?

- The fifth paragraph mostly restates what we already know about the mother's addiction to cigarettes, and what is largely described here is Chandra's anger both with her mother and with her own circumstances. We would feel more for Chandra here if she focused less on her issues and instead made us feel her loss through well-observed details.

- The sixth paragraph seems entirely tangential, and could easily be excised. Chandra introduces her sister, who has not made an appearance in the essay until this very late point. The only information this paragraph relates is Chandra's annoyance with, and possible resentment of, her sister, apparently for not understanding Chandra's grief. At this point, she risks looking self-absorbed and losing the empathy of the reader.

- The final paragraph makes an attempt to bring us to a final point about Chandra's experience and how it has changed her, but it does so ineffectively. Again, she risks losing the reader's empathy, since she devotes a large section to a litany of all the things she must carry on with in the wake of her mother's death; for the first time, a self-pitying tone is implicit. Her final sentence, "I have no answers right now, but I have a lot of questions" is weak and unsatisfying.

Here is Chandra's reaction:

> I guess the biggest problem is that I write too much about myself and not enough about my Mom. I need to show who she was when she wasn't sick. I guess I show her only as a dying woman and a pretty picture in a frame and that's not enough.
>
> I should sit and do some free writing on some of the things we used to do together that I loved, like cooking together or taking a "mental health day" when she would call in sick to work and I'd stay home from school, and we'd spend the day together. I should talk about how funny she was, what a clown she could be when she wanted to.
>
> I suppose the last paragraph is pretty weak. I need to make more of a point, something more than just being uncertain about what's ahead. Everyone's uncertain about what's ahead. That doesn't make me special.

Analysis of First Draft

What is this writer's point? The writer effectively shares her emotional journey in witnessing the illness and death of her mother, but *comes up short in terms of bringing the reader to a unique revelation about this experience*—we never get a satisfactory answer to the question "*Why this story?*"

> My point was that my Mom's death was no ordinary death—it was way too awful, too early, and wrong in so many ways, and that having to witness it has made me a different person. I think I need to be more specific about my Mom, about why she was important and unique and special to me.

What is her angle? The author is reaching for an unstinting portrayal of the emotional toll the loss of a parent takes on a teenager, how it changes her view and experience of everything around her, and the difficulty of reconciling oneself to loss.

> Okay, so they like my angle. But I seem to lose them halfway in; maybe I need to be more consistent, not get lost in my own stuff, and concentrate more on Mom but show the positive along with the negative.

What type or tone of voice has she created in her reader's mind? The author most definitely has a distinct voice, one that does not shy away from her anger and grief, while recognizing implicit irony and even absurdity. However, while her voice is commendably passionate and brave, *she allows her anger to dominate her writing at times and take the essay on tangents that detract from her point. Her style can also be overly conversational and flippant, which is a risky choice on a college entrance essay.*

> I didn't think I was being flippant, I just wanted to write it the way I'd tell it to someone. I always thought that was supposed to be good writing, but I'll look at it. They don't like it when I get too angry, so I'll tone that down a bit.

What techniques has this writer used to create this voice? There is an unflinching directness, a refusal to pull any punches—as well as an ironic viewpoint—from the first sentence. The portrayal of pain and emotional distress is consistent throughout the piece, as is a strong, vital descriptive ability.

> Well, good, they think I have something going for me. I'll just work at staying on point and keeping to the prompt.

What specific details, facts, etc., make this narrative real? There are several potent examples of strongly observed details, such as the wedding portrait, the hiding of the cigarettes, and the author's reaction to the Bette Davis film. The portrayal of the mother's unsuccessful efforts to quit smoking, especially the hiding of the packs of cigarettes that are later found by the author, also ring true and effectively ground the essay in a recognizable reality. But the author should go further, get under the surface of things, and give the reader a feeling of what made her mother a unique person, what made her important to the author.

> They like how I give details; I think I probably need to do more of that.

After the peer edit, it's time to write a second draft. In many cases, due to time limitations, this second draft may have to be your final draft. That's why it's so important to make the first draft really count.

Here is Chandra's revised draft. Read it and consider how it is stronger and more likely to make a positive impression on the admissions committee.

> Evaluate a significant experience, achievement, risk you have taken, or ethical dilemma you have faced and its impact on you.

The first paragraph has always been strong; she was right to leave it alone.

My mother's death was the most horrible thing I have ever had to witness; she was only forty-eight years old, which seems old to a sixteen-year-old, but it's pretty young to be dying. You always think of your parents as old, so much older than you—until one of them isn't there, and you realize that a person can be young and old all in the same moment, and the moment passes very quickly.

This paragraph was effective before, but now Chandra has added a detail that begins to give the reader a more thorough, more vivid picture of who her mother was, and why she was significant to the author. She has also artfully corrected the instance of awkward usage, with "our family" instead of "me and my family" being both grammatically and thematically an improvement.

It was cancer—pancreatic cancer, to be exact—that took her from our family. Not an easy death, by any means; she had intense, evil pain that almost never let up, she endured five hours of unbelievably invasive surgery that was supposed to extend her life and didn't, and I know that from the moment she was given her diagnosis, fear was a constant companion. That wasn't how she was used to living; she was used to laughter and joy and loving her family.

There were occasional mornings when she would declare that day to be a "mental health day," meaning we'd all play hooky and stay home from school, while she'd stay home from work. Sometimes we'd go shopping, sometimes we'd go to a movie, or sometimes on a rainy day, we'd stay in and watch old movies on television, which I think was her favorite thing to do. One of my Mom's favorites was a really old black-and-white film with Bette Davis, where she plays this woman who is dying from cancer. It's called Dark Victory. I used to love it because my mom did, but now it just makes me angry. I always thought of it as a sickly-sweet, romanticized portrayal of death, but after watching my mother, I now know the movie to be an outright lie. Bette Davis doesn't suffer the way my mother suffered; she suffers prettily, in furs and diamonds and satin. Then she gets to die prettily, in a gauzy fadeout, talking about meeting death "bravely and finely"; the whole thing actually looks glamorous. I can't remember anything brave or fine in how my mother died. I don't blame her for that; no one can be either brave or fine when they're being eaten alive by disease.

There is a silver-framed photo of my Mom on her Wedding Day, and she looks glamorous enough to make Bette pea-green with envy. She's in a beautiful lace dress, simple but elegant; her face is framed by a veil that might as well be a halo, and she holds a bouquet of gardenias. Her eyes shine and glow; the picture is so alive you feel she might start speaking to you from it. She would probably say how excited she is, how wonderful her wedding was, how she is looking forward to the life ahead of her. She doesn't know what's headed for her down the line. Every day, I wish she could have had some crystal ball; if she did, maybe she would have quit smoking.

The worst part is, I can barely remember her without a cigarette, from the time I was little. She did try to quit several times, and even once went for several months without a single cigarette, after my sister and I begged her relentlessly, but she always relapsed. She even smoked after the diagnosis, secretly; she would sneak them behind our backs when no one was in the room with her. She was strong about everything else; she never overate, she drank alcohol only in extreme moderation, and she had no interest in drugs of any sort. Which made

The improvement here is readily apparent; this paragraph is no longer just about the author, but about how special her mother was and why her loss is so significant.

A small change, but an important one: "Every day I wish she could have had some crystal ball…" helps show the author's love, defining her anger as being against the cancer, not against her mother.

Some very apt changes since the original draft. The focus, rather than being solely on the author's emotional response to the situation, now expresses empathy, as well as implicit frustration and anger. The reader is now more moved by the situation of the author.

A fine refocusing of this paragraph; now the author expresses her frustration at her sister's distance from the situation, without implying a resentment of her sister. Now the paragraph helps define the author's emotional state without implying that she is self-absorbed and unable to recognize anyone else's pain but her own.

The author, instead of being sidetracked by her emotional response, as in the previous draft, has illustrated effectively both her grief and loss, making the reader feel her emotions rather than simply hurling them in his or her face. There is no definitive conclusion, but there is no need for one. She has instead opened a poignant window on her present state and made the reader understand it.

me even more sad and angry that, after she died, I'd find packs of cigarettes stashed away in cupboards, in drawers, behind the computer. Why did this one thing have so much hold over her?

My sister tells me I need to accept what's happened and move on, that I shouldn't dwell on my grief and work on remembering happier times with Mom, and all the good things about her. I know this is true, but it's challenging; while Deirdre means well and loves me, she was away at college, taking finals, and never saw what I saw. She doesn't know how ugly and painful it became; it's not her fault, but she can't understand how it is for me. Maybe I'll be able to explain it to her down the line.

Now I have finals, and tests for college to study for, and Forensics and Drama Club, and basketball; Mom would tell me whenever I was having a tough time with anything to just "put your head down and barrel through." I'm trying to carry on as she would want me to. But every now and then, I catch a glimpse of Mom's wedding photo: the lace, the smile, and especially the eyes that can follow you wherever you are in the room. And I hope they are following me somehow; I have more questions than answers, and I hope that somehow she can give me just a hint or two somewhere along the line.

Analysis of Revised (or Final) Draft

What is this writer's point? The writer gives a genuine, moving account of her mother's death, the pain of witnessing that death, and how it has affected her personally.

What is her angle? The writer provides an honest, unstinting window into the emotional experience of her mother's illness and death, without descending into self-pity or allowing grief and anger to sidetrack the account.

What type or tone of voice has she created in her reader's mind? The author's voice is distinct and individual, with an undercurrent of irony that nicely balances the painful situation she is portraying.

What techniques has this writer used to create this voice? There is still the unflinching directness, but it is now balanced by a more humane and complete portrayal of what made the author's mother special to her. The strong, vital descriptive ability is still evident, but it is now tempered with a greater awareness of what the author's loss actually meant and why it mattered.

What specific details, facts, etc., make this experience real? Again, many fine descriptive elements are apparent, such as the wedding portrait, the hiding of the cigarettes, the author's reaction to the Bette Davis film, and the mother's unsuccessful efforts to quit smoking. However, there is now an evocative, fully rounded portrayal of the author's mother, which lends this essay a genuine feel for the meaning of loss and gives it a truly earned poignance.

POSSIBLE STEP 8: Rewrite Opportunity

MINI-LESSON 1:

Journal Writing

The simple truth is that journaling is an excellent habit to acquire. Writers' journals provide much more than just a record of the events of their lives, their observations and impressions, and their thoughts and feelings; journals serve as the medium by which writers can begin their creative process, experiment with multiple versions of the same project, even test completely new forms or approaches without fear of audience criticism.

And the fact always remains that regular journal writing provides the same benefits that an athlete's workouts or a performer's practices yield: Journaling helps the writer stay in shape.

Journal as Free-writing Exercise

"**Jeff**" attends the same magnet school as Chandra. He came to English class having read Arthur Miller's *The Crucible*, as assigned. Before there was any class discussion on the play, the teacher instructed the students to write in their journals a response to the following prompt:

What do you believe is the correct relationship between church and state?

Having done journal writing since at least fifth grade, Jeff knows that this does not have to be a "process writing" piece; it will not be graded. It is meant only for his eyes and can serve as a vehicle to start hashing out ideas and creating a bank to draw on for more developed essays. Knowing that he has only twenty minutes, he simply starts writing down his thoughts as they come to him, not worrying about structure or slant at this early point.

Here is Jeff's entry:

Jeff is off to a quick, and good start. He immediately relates the prompt to the play and begins to work out his opinion.

Jeff has the freedom here to debate with himself, without fear of judgment. This is what journal writing is for.

Unconcerned with organization, style, or slant, Jeff can take a critical look at the assigned text, forming his opinion of it and his response to the prompt.

Time has run out, and Jeff's teacher has begun to discuss Miller's play. Jeff has had a good opportunity to begin organizing his thoughts on the prompt.

> Arthur Miller certainly thought the church and state should be kept as far apart as possible. That's plain just from his choice of historical event he dramatizes in the play. The deck is a little bit stacked from the get-go. Of course, the play is really about McCarthyism, so his real point is zealotry, and how dangerous it is when it gets mixed up with politics and power. I think it's important to stand up for your beliefs and religion, but you shouldn't be stuffing them down anyone else's throats. Miller's a little bit preachy on the subject, so I'm not sure he isn't a little fanatical on the subject himself. He did have to testify at the hearings himself, so he maybe has an axe to grind. I think there are times when religious institutions should take moral stands on issues; when the Catholic Church said nothing about the Nazis or the Holocaust during World War II, that was an ethical lapse. I don't necessarily buy that religion should be totally removed from the public debate. But I have to agree that no one religion should hold complete political power over any country.

Analysis of Free-write Journal Entry

What is this writer's point? Responding to the question about the separation of church and state, Jeff comes to the conclusion that he believes they should be separate, but he has an interesting caveat.

What is this writer's angle? Jeff draws on the text of the play, the experience of the author, and other relevant historical facts to debate and finally define his opinion.

What type or tone of voice has he created in his reader's mind? This is a free-write, so there is no real intentional attempt at tone or voice.

What techniques has this writer used to create this voice? N/A

What specific details, facts, etc., help this writer establish his point? Jeff refers to the play, the personal history of the author, and the role of religion in history.

Journal as Light Practice

Chandra's school is only a few weeks away from its state-mandated writing assessment, so her teacher is having the class practice every day by assigning a journal entry prompt. The intent is to give the student plenty of practice writing in a timed, on-demand setting without creating additional hours of paper-grading for himself.

Chandra is a tennis player and appreciates the value of practicing daily in order to keep in shape, especially during the off seasons. She wants to do well on the assessment, so she does her best to make her journal entries more than free-writes; she wants them to be actual attempts at organized and coherent essays.

Here is one of the daily prompts Chandra's teacher assigned:

> Is it ever a mistake for a person to die for his or her principles? Why or why not?

Here is Chandra's response:

> There are a lot of things I would die for, I suppose. My country, my family, my freedom. Doesn't everybody feel that? It's what I grew up with. My family is very much a military family; dying for your principles was just an idea we all accepted. We live in a world where evil deeds—genocide, human trafficking, abuse of children and women—are daily events. Somebody has to be willing to put themselves on the line for what they believe in. Why even ask the question?

Chandra starts well; questioning the prompt itself is a good way to develop a personal slant or unique take on the subject.

- 21 -

My cousin went to Afghanistan and lost a leg; he didn't die for his country, but he was ready to. That certainly counts as dying for a principle. But when I think about it, the people who made 9/11 happen thought they were dying for a principle, too. Maybe dying for a principle really is a mistake if you're taking out innocent people with you. There was that Oklahoma City bomber, too, and the Unabomber; they all thought they had a principle at stake ,too. What kind of principle makes a person kill children? Maybe the question should be "Is it ever not a mistake to die for your principles?"

When Kevin came home from Afghanistan, he was withdrawn, angry, always snapping at people. He seemed so bitter and haunted and was like a stranger to all of us. You felt pain just to look at him, as if his pain was a cloud that followed him everywhere. Once someone came up to him on the street and thanked him for his service to the country, and Kevin actually cursed the guy out, screamed that the whole war was a scam, and he'd lost a leg for nothing. Looking at Kevin that day, I remember thinking no one should join the army, not ever. Does that mean I really wouldn't die for my principles after all?

I think about my other family members who have done military service, and none of them feel the way Kevin feels about it. They all believe in the principle, service to country and honor and the whole nine yards. Grandpa Jordan was in World War II, and Uncle Jim was in Vietnam; my cousin Lola is a Marine now, and probably deploying to Afghanistan in a month or two. They look at Kevin and shake their heads; his anger doesn't fit into their belief system. I respect them all, but I respect Kevin, too.

Chandra is structuring her entry as a debate, looking deeply at both sides of the question and making an interesting turnaround, ending with a provocative question.

Chandra is delving into the subject effectively. She may actually want to rethink ending every paragraph with a question; it becomes predictable and undercuts her effectiveness, and this third question seems a bit facile.

Slipping into vernacular is acceptable for a journal entry, but Chandra will want to be more polished on an actual test essay.

Chandra's use of personal experience is affecting, but she will have to work harder to relate this experience to the prompt.

So, perhaps it all comes down to the principle you're dying for—you have to choose your principles wisely. You have to make sure they're your own, and not something that's been imposed or indoctrinated into you.

> This is a strong conclusion, but it hasn't been entirely supported by what precedes it.

Analysis of Light Practice Journal Entry

What is this writer's point? Chandra begins to make an effective case that dying for one's principles can be a two-edged sword—sometimes admirable, sometimes tragically wrong-headed.

What is this writer's angle? Chandra references history, her family experience, and her own observations.

What type or tone of voice has she created in her reader's mind? The tone is direct but casual, possibly too casual for a more developed essay. Nevertheless, Chandra's openness to debate and probing mind make for an individual voice in the entry.

What techniques has this writer used to create this voice? Starting by debating the prompt itself, Chandra establishes a critical, intelligent, and nuanced tone; however, it needs to be more fully employed in the last two paragraphs.

What specific details, facts, etc., help this writer establish her point? Such details include: historical references to terrorist attacks, her family history, and most especially her uncle's experience in Afghanistan.

Journal as Heavy Training

Sometimes it's simply in your best interest as a writer to treat even a journal entry as if it were an important, high-stakes writing assignment. Remember that the marathon runner does not prepare for the Olympics by casually jogging a few times around the high school track.

"Eleanor" is in the same 11th-grade English class as Chandra. Their teacher, like Maya's last year, begins assigning issue-based journal prompts a few months before they are scheduled to begin their annual research project. This practice helps students think about possible topics and approaches.

Here is one of the daily prompts Eleanor's teacher assigned:

> **What do you believe is the best way for the United States to deal with its debt, while also trying to revive its economy?**

Eleanor knows that most questions like this one ask for both an opinion and factual support. As a person, she may feel that budget cutting and austerity measures are counterproductive and harm economic recovery, but she knows that without expert opinion, case studies, statistics, and so on, her opinion is just that—the opinion of an eleventh-grader. She also knows that she does not have time in the twenty minutes the class has been given to complete this exercise to perform real research and collect actual facts and expert opinions, but she wants to use this exercise as practice for her research project. She thinks a little harder and writes with a little more focus than she normally would on a journal exercise.

Here is Eleanor's response to the prompt:

Eleanor starts with a bold statement here, and it tips off the reader immediately to her opinion. This is fine in a journal entry, but she would probably want to modulate her tone in an actual essay.

Eleanor has effectively stated her thesis; now she needs to begin backing it up with supporting facts.

Eleanor is now beginning to cite concrete examples that support her thesis, but more specific facts would be needed in an actual essay.

Eleanor knows she has to back her thesis up with hard facts and careful research, or it will be dismissed as a political tract.

The current debate in this country over the national debt has been less of a serious conversation on economic policy and more of a political football being fumbled over by opposing teams. While there is little doubt that the nation's debt needs to be dealt with in the long term, in the short term, the fragile economic recovery could easily be toppled by some of the extreme budget cuts being proposed in the polarized political climate. There needs to be a more balanced approach to debt reduction, one that recognizes the need for growth. One needs only to look at history to see what kind of fiscal policy has helped the economy in the past, and what hasn't.

The history of the depression and the economic recession of the 1980s are two major examples of how the nation pulled itself out of economic downturn. It wasn't budget cutting that ended the depression and recessions of the past, but economic stimulus initiated by the government. (Here I would cite the actual facts and figures from my research.) John Maynard Keynes was a great noted economist who would have been opposed to budget cutting in the face of an economic crisis such as the nation finds itself in. He would have supported instead a broad-based stimulus that included infrastructure repair, supported public sector jobs such as teachers, firemen and police, and encouraged private sector hiring. (I need to actually read Keynes and quote his work to back this up.)

One can also look to the current economic crisis in Europe for an example of what doesn't work. The extreme austerity measures called for in Germany, France and proposed for Greece and much of the rest of Europe have not resulted in a reduction of debt or stabilization of the European economy, but instead have contributed to its crisis. The crumbling of the euro and the popular rejection of austerity measures in the recent French and Greek elections point to the need for a more balanced, holistic approach to solving the crisis.

Economic improvement, whether at home or abroad, cannot be achieved amidst partisan political extremists hurling sound bites and invective. It can't be achieved with a myopic view that values political turf over best practices. It can and must be achieved in an atmosphere of cooperation and collaboration, with both sides willing to compromise some points for the benefit of a higher goal. Debt can and must be reduced, but not at the expense of long-term financial improvement and stability.

She certainly will, but she has nevertheless built the structure of her thesis effectively here.

Eleanor is going out on a limb here; backing this statement up will be harder than in her previous paragraph.

Again, while Eleanor can get away with this in a journal entry, in an actual thesis, she would need to back this broad statement up with examples and facts.

In an actual research paper, Eleanor would need to have laid more groundwork for her rather grand and sweeping statements in this final paragraph.

Analysis of Heavy Training Journal Entry

What is this writer's point? Eleanor's thesis is that economic recovery cannot be achieved while initiating the major budget cuts being called for in the current political climate.

What is this writer's angle? Her angle is that a more balanced approach that includes economic stimulus and long-term debt reduction is the only viable approach.

What type or tone of voice has she created in her reader's mind? Eleanor is a fairly sophisticated writer, with a solid grasp of language and vocabulary, and she comes across as intelligent and informed. Sometimes, however, her voice becomes a bit grand and risks being perceived as pretentious.

What techniques has this writer used to create this voice? N/A

What specific details, facts, etc., help this writer establish her point? Eleanor begins with a bold statement, then moves on in her second paragraph to establish her thesis, then moves on to support that thesis. More research and facts would be needed to support her statements in an actual essay, but her structure is solid.

ASSIGNMENT 2:

Describe a Comic or Unfortunate Event

College and scholarship application writers tend not to be overly creative when they compose their personal essay prompts. After all, they really want to learn something about the person writing the essay, and they don't necessarily want to have to rely on inferences based on what the writer has to say about obscure or controversial topics. Last year, you wrote a fairly generic "Significant Experience" essay. One common version of this prompt instructs the student to write about a specific type of experience—humorous, inspiring, challenging, etc.

Eleanor's teacher assigns the class the following prompt. Here is a re-creation of Eleanor's work and process in response to it.

> Evaluate a personal experience that is possibly humorous or tragic *and its impact on you.*

STEP 1: Select a Topic

Eleanor looks at the topic with some trepidation; she knows that the most recent "comic or unfortunate" event to have impact on her is very personal and difficult to share, since she has been the target of school bullying. She considers other events that might be more workable:

When I got lost in the amusement park on my eighth birthday
When Grandma died
My first swimming lesson

But finally, Eleanor decides to go with her gut feeling that she should use the bullying incident, since it is the most compelling topic she can think of.

STEP 2: Develop a Slant/Angle/Hook

WHAT CAN MY ANGLE BE?

- How little you can do about being bullied in school—the teachers and administrators don't get it and aren't supportive, even behave as if it's your fault you're being bullied.
- How much it hurts to be called fat—how everyone is pressured to be thin, to adhere to some artificial standard, how anyone who doesn't is an outsider
- How it's changed me—how isolated I feel most or all of the time, how much I want to strike back.

STEP 3: Brainstorm, Discuss, Research

- Seeing the graffiti on my locker—the word "Fat," screaming in pink letters
- The ball hitting me in gym class—how the gym teacher made me feel, how she ignored the situation until the last possible moment, how she never really intervened
- The stuff even Mom says to me sometimes—well-intentioned, I suppose, but it feels like she's on the side of the bullies
- Thinking about my options—so little I can do, wanting to run away to Europe or anywhere, going to the principal, getting revenge, but how
- How bullying is kind of an institution in high school—it's an unwritten law, if you don't conform, if you're not one of the insiders, if you don't conform to their standards, if you join the wrong clubs and participate in the wrong activities and excel in the wrong subjects, you're going to get it

STEP 4: Outline

Opening: the whole pecking order of high school, the structure that dictates I must be bullied and humiliated

Complication/conflict: seeing the word "FAT" spray painted on my locker, how that made me feel; trying to figure out what to do or how to deal. Considering what my options might be and coming up empty.

Rising action: thinking of striking back, trying to figure out a word that could hurt Sondra the way "Fat" hurts me.

Climax: figuring out what that word can be, and thinking about spray-painting it on her locker. Wondering about how that would make her feel. Going to the garage at home and spraying that word over and over again, until the can is empty and I'm crying.

Falling action/denouement: Dad finding me in the garage and asking me what's going on. We finally talk about it.

STEP 5: First Draft

Humiliation in high school is a given; the only variable is the degree of humiliation that lies in store for you. When you're a girl who doesn't meet the current standard for style, coolness, or especially thinness, the odds that you will be continually humiliated go up exponentially. When you're a designated nerd, a brainiac with a 3.95 average, member of the math club and debating team and dance committee—well, you'd better develop a taste for living on the edge. You'd also better get used to a particular three-letter word—and it's not VIP.

> This is an effective opening, with a distinct voice, a well-defined point of view, and a fine summation of the problem the writer is confronted with. The use of the word "brainiac" may be risky, since it is not as yet officially recognized as a proper word. It may, however, be a calculated risk, as it does convey a contemporary attitude and helps define the author's voice.

The letters were spray-painted on my locker one Friday afternoon, right after my dreaded gym class, where one of my esteemed tormentors threw a basketball at my head and shouted the same three-letter word in full view of the rest of the sarcasm sorority. I wasn't given the Scarlet Letter, like Hester Prynne; my branding letters were fluorescent pink, stacked up on top of one another on the door of my hall locker, a calling card from a not-so-secret non-admirer. They glowed at me in dripping, still-wet enamel, sloppy and hostile and accusing.

> The descriptive power in this paragraph is palpable, effectively bringing the reader into the crux of the situation, as well as conveying suspense about what will happen next.

FAT.

The childish scrawl of the letters left little doubt in my mind as to their source. I peered through my taped-up eyeglasses (yes, they had broken when I'd been slammed by the bouncing ball) and tried to assess my options. Imminent flight seemed a very attractive choice, but unfortunately, I couldn't afford airfare to Buffalo, let alone any place I'd really want to go. Venice, Paris, San Francisco—all out of reach.

On to door number two: escalating to the higher authorities. A much less attractive option: ratting out anyone, even a sworn enemy, always has a way of coming back and biting you; besides, the higher authorities are more often than not, no brighter or empathetic than the troglodytes who are beating on you. The gym teacher, whose back had been conspicuously turned during the smack-down, suddenly decided to become cognizant and find out what was actually going on. Rushing over with great purpose, she shouted, "What exactly is going on here?" to me, with my broken glasses and bleeding nose. "I want an explanation now!" I gave her the news-flash, she directed a not-very-convincingly severe look at the usual suspects, then escorted me out of the gym to the school nurse. "Girl, you gotta find a way to make the others stop hating you so much." Then she went back toward the gym.

Oh, right. It's my fault.

On to option number three – wait, was there an option number three? Can't run, can't escalate, where does that leave me? Get even? Respond in kind? That's crazy, that's insane, I can't possibly—

What if I could? Miss Trash Talk wasn't the only one who could wield a can of spray-paint. Matter of fact, there's a can of an especially egregious lime green sitting in the garage at home, for some Halloween decorations my Mom was cribbing from Martha Stewart. I could just grab that and spell out—

What? SKINNY?

The author risks losing the empathy of the reader here; while the inherent unfairness of what is happening is plain, this paragraph brings an undercurrent of self-pity, a "poor me" attitude that is hard to identify with.

The author takes another risk here, considering this is meant to be an essay for a college entrance exam. While the use of colloquialism, contemporary slang, and a certain freedom with the restrictions of proper grammar lends color and affect, it may also result in demerits in the evaluation of the essay.

I racked my fevered brain to think of some equivalent insult. I couldn't. There didn't seem to be any word that stings a cool girl the way FAT stings someone like me. Maybe it has something to do with the way my Mom never says the word, yet somehow says it all the time. "Do you really think you should eat that, dear?" "Would you like to come with me to my aerobics class tonight?" Or my favorite: "I like you better in darker colors, sweetheart."

I'm not obese. I'm not unhealthy or sloppy or a glutton; I'm just not up to the current runway standard. I'm a little rounder, a little fuller, a little more human. That doesn't seem to be acceptable to very many people, though. Everyone seems determined to make me adhere to a standard I'm not sure I even buy into.

Walking home from school, all the voices seemed to meld in my head—my mother's, the haters at school, the gym teacher—a chorus of critics, relentless and unstoppable, chasing me back to my room, my bed, my head under the covers —

And then the word came to me. The word I could spray-paint on all of their lockers, the word that would strike back at them, the word that would sting.

SLAG.

I went into the garage and found the green paint. Some cardboard boxes, collapsed and leaning against the wall, were my practice canvases. I made the letters large and ugly, I let the spray-paint drip and pool into the cardboard, I sprayed the word again and again and again until the can ran dry, air hissing. Still I kept on spraying invisible letters in the air, not noticing the tears running down my face or my Dad standing in the garage entrance, watching me. He touched me on the shoulder to get my attention and I jumped away,

There is some very effective writing in this section, deepening the inner conflict of the narrator and bringing the reader further into her world. We might, however, benefit from getting to know the narrator's mother from something other than the implicitly negative comments to her daughter.

While this is on many levels a brave and admirable effort, the essay ultimately disappoints in that it continually dwells on the self-pity of the narrator, rather than showing her confronting the problem head-on, taking action in some way, or failing that, displaying a change in her attitude that holds some promise for more positive interaction going forward.

startled. He looked at me with his worried look, the look he always gets when I do something he can't process. I don't have the slightest idea of how to make him understand.

"Start from the beginning," he says. "We'll try to figure it out between us."

Analysis of First Draft

What is this writer's point? Essentially, the writer is confronting the issues of bullying, body image, and the problems of nonconformity in the social world of secondary schools. While at times we are drawn in by her account of the cruelty and pressure she is confronted with, the author frequently alienates the reader with a self-pitying tone and no genuine unique point or elevating conclusion.

What is her angle? One of the weaknesses of this particular essay is the lack of a truly defined slant on the subject. As potent as the topics of school bullying and body image are, there is no true individual point of view contributed by the author, no unique vision of the problem beyond the basics of "this is a bad thing and should not happen to anyone."

What type or tone of voice has she created in her reader's mind? The writer brings a frequently effective, sardonic, and unique voice to the essay, most especially in the opening paragraphs, which almost seem to satirize the attitudes and culture of contemporary high school. It is regrettable that this voice is not sustained throughout the essay.

What techniques has this writer used to create this voice? The first paragraph is very effective in establishing an ironic and humorous, if somewhat jaundiced, view of the superficial values and culture of modern high school, while conveying the problems confronting the nonconforming, marginalized student. The opening also benefits from a head-on, direct approach to the situation the narrator is facing.

What specific details, facts, etc., make this narrative real? The description of the spray-painted letters, the reaction of the gym teacher to the abuse in the gym, the quotes from the author's mother with veiled reference to weight are all well observed and well chosen. The essay would benefit overall from more of this kind of specificity in detail and characterization.

NOW plan your own essay, following the same process by which Eleanor arrived at her first draft.

STEP 1: Select a Topic

What experiences lend themselves to a successful evaluation?

What point would you want to make in evaluating each of these potential topics?

STEP 2: Develop a Slant/Angle/Hook

What will your angle be?

Where might you begin your evaluation?

What type or tone of voice do you want to create in your reader's mind?

STEP 3: Brainstorm, Discuss, Research

What specific details, facts, etc., will make this experience real and not merely hypothetical?

What specific details, facts, etc., will help you achieve your angle, tone, and mood (i.e., funny instead of somber, gentle instead of crude, etc.)?

STEP 4: Outline

STEP 5: First Draft

STEP 6: Peer Edit

What is this writer's point?

What is this writer's angle?

What type or tone of voice has the writer created in his or her reader's mind?

What techniques has this writer used to create this voice?

What specific details, facts, etc., make this experience real?

Here are her partner's comments and analysis and Eleanor's responses:

- This is an effective opening, with a distinct voice, well-defined point of view, and a fine summation of the problem the writer is confronted with. The use of the word "brainiac" may be risky, since it is not as yet officially recognized as a proper word. It may, however, be a calculated risk, as it does convey a contemporary attitude and helps define the author's voice.

- The descriptive power in this paragraph is palpable, effectively bringing the reader into the crux of the situation, as well as conveying suspense about what will happen next.

- The author risks losing the empathy of the reader here; while the inherent unfairness of what is happening is plain, this paragraph brings an undercurrent of self-pity, a "poor me" attitude that is hard to identify with.

- The author takes another risk here, considering this is meant to be an essay for a college entrance exam. While the use of colloquialism, contemporary slang, and a certain freedom with the restrictions of proper grammar lends color and effect, it may also result in demerits in the evaluation of the essay.

- There is some very effective writing in this section, deepening the inner conflict of the narrator and bringing the reader further into her world. We might, however, benefit from getting to know the narrator's mother from something other than the implicitly negative comments to her daughter.

- While this is on many levels a brave and admirable effort, the essay ultimately disappoints in that it continually dwells on the self-pity of the narrator, rather than showing her confronting the problem head-on, taking action in some way, or failing that, displaying a change in her attitude that holds some promise for more positive interaction going forward.

> These people are tough. Okay, so they like that I wrote about the bullying, but they thought I didn't have enough of a slant. I thought I had a definite slant, but maybe I'm confusing that with the voice I was using. I guess slant has more to do with a point of view on the subject. I'll have to do some brainstorming on what kind of slant I can use.
>
> They think I get self-pitying, which gets under my skin, since none of them has gone through it like I have. Or have they? I'll just have to watch for that, I guess.
>
> I'll have to think about structure, too, and making the thing more active. But how? I didn't ever confront anyone, I only talked to my Dad about it. Maybe I can write about the kind of confrontation I'd like to have?

Analysis of First Draft

What is this writer's point? Essentially, the writer is confronting the issues of bullying, body image, and the problems of non-conformity in the social world of secondary schools. While at times we are drawn in by her account of the cruelty and pressure she is confronted with, the author frequently alienates the reader with a self-pitying tone and no genuine unique point or elevating conclusion.

> My point, I thought, was how isolating it is to be the victim of bullying in school, how little recourse you have, how few options, how nobody seems to be on your side. I don't want to lose any of that, but I have to figure out a different point of view to keep it from sounding like a big whine session.

What is her slant? One of the weaknesses of this particular essay is the lack of a truly defined slant on the subject. As potent as the topics of school bullying and body image are, there is no true individual point of view contributed by the author, no unique vision of the problem beyond the basics of "this is a bad thing and should not happen to anyone."

> Looks like we're back to the slant problem. I have to figure that one out. Maybe I can turn it around so I come across as more of a determined survivor? As if the title were "How High School Tried to Kill Me, But Couldn't"?

What type or tone of voice has she created in her reader's mind? The writer brings a frequently effective, sardonic, and unique voice to the essay, most especially in the opening paragraphs, which almost seem to satirize the attitudes and culture of contemporary high school. It is regrettable that this voice is not sustained throughout the essay.

> This might be a clue—they like my humor. It's pretty dark humor; maybe I could rework the whole thing with a more humorous approach, a satirical attitude. That's beginning to sound like my slant.

What techniques has this writer used to create this voice? The first paragraph is very effective in establishing an ironic and humorous, if somewhat jaundiced, view of the superficial values and culture of modern high school, while conveying the problems confronting the nonconforming, marginalized student. The opening also benefits from a head-on, direct approach to the situation the narrator is facing.

> Right, they like it when I'm ironic and humorous. If I can keep a thread of that going through the whole essay, I won't come across as self-pitying, and it will definitely be a different slant on the subject than what they expect.

What specific details, facts, etc., make this narrative real? The description of the spray-painted letters, the reaction of the gym teacher to the abuse in the gym, the quotes from the author's mother with veiled reference to weight are all well observed and well chosen. The essay would benefit overall from more of this kind of specificity in detail and characterization.

> I guess I was kind of generic in the way I characterized everyone; I'll try to be more specific about who they are and maybe something about why they're the way they are.

STEP 7: Revised/Final Draft

After the peer edit, it's time to write a second draft. In many cases, due to time limitations, this second draft may have to be your final draft. That's why it's so important to make the first draft really count.

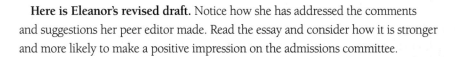

Here is Eleanor's revised draft. Notice how she has addressed the comments and suggestions her peer editor made. Read the essay and consider how it is stronger and more likely to make a positive impression on the admissions committee.

You wouldn't necessarily know it to look at me, but I'm a young woman with a taste for living on the edge. Sporting a 3.95 average, being head of the debating team and math club, and heading the dance committee all define me as a risk-taker. Factor in my fashion sense (Old Navy meets Salvation Army, I was once told), my not-ready-for-runway physique, and oh yes, eyeglasses and braces, and you have an absolute daredevil. Of course, some would say "target," especially when I'm traversing between my homeroom and my hall locker, a journey sometimes worthy of an episode on <u>Survivor</u>. But I prefer to stay positive.

> Eleanor has taken a completely different tack, one that makes her slant evident from the first sentence. Effective as her previous opening paragraph was, this is even stronger, effectively using irony and humor to slyly introduce the issue.

Staying positive—yes, that's the thing. Maintaining a positive attitude is key, especially when confronting a certain three-letter word that has been spray-painted on your locker. It was a Friday afternoon, right after gym class, where one of my esteemed classmates had given me some valuable coaching by pitching a basketball directly at my head. And as I regarded that three-letter word, admiring the finesse of the calligraphic hand that had executed it in dripping, hot-pink fluorescent glory, I took a step backward—as one does to evaluate any creative effort. Three letters, one under the other, spelling out—well, it wasn't VIP.

> Eleanor is continuing to use a darkly humorous and ironic voice and point of view, and building effectively to the event. Note that at no point does the previous underlying tone of self-pity emerge in this draft.

FAT.

Oh, well...how generous. First some coaching in gym, now some diet and exercise advice. Touching, how my classmate expressed her concern and care. The calligraphic quality I had stepped back to admire, which brought to mind the scrawl of a three-year-old, left little doubt in my mind as to the source. I peered through my taped-up eyeglasses

The twist Eleanor is putting on this draft continues to pay off, making her seem less like a self-pitying victim and more like an ironic, determined survivor. The "blunt instrument" reference may be a tad too dark, however.

(yes, they had broken, an unfortunate byproduct of the coaching session) and tried to assess the various ways I could express my thanks. A blunt instrument not being readily available, I thought perhaps I could commend her to the higher authorities, so that the thoughtfulness and caring she had shown me for so long could be properly rewarded.

Alas, however, the higher authorities at South Pacifica High are often less than empathetic to the concept of recognizing exceptional achievement. The gym teacher, for instance, barely noticed Sondra's extra effort on my behalf with the basketball. In fact, her back had been conspicuously turned through the whole coaching session, until it became evident that my nose was bleeding. At which point said gym teacher rushed over with great purpose, shouting something along the lines of "What exactly is going on here?" I have always admired her way with words. "I want an explanation now!" I gave her an update, and had no opportunity to express my thanks to Sondra before being escorted to the school nurse. "Girl, you gotta find a way to make the others stop hating you so much," I heard the teacher say on her way back to the gym.

Note how the ironic voice is gradually becoming less purely satirical and more pointed. This variation accomplishes two things: it keeps the tone from becoming monotonous, as well as developing suspense for the reader.

Hate me? My classmates? Seriously? I'm flabbergasted at the notion.

So, I would have to express my thanks to Sondra directly, perhaps show her some of the same kind of care and thoughtfulness she had been showing me. For the past two semesters.

But what? What would be creative enough, caring enough, <u>expressive</u> enough of my true gratitude? Ah, perhaps I could engage in some similar calligraphic expression on her locker. I remembered a spraycan of an especially egregious lime green that was conveniently sitting in the garage at home, for some Halloween decorations my Mom was cribbing from Martha Stewart. Perhaps I could give Sondra some nutritional advice of my own, as she seemed to have gone from a size 0 to something like a negative two. But since the word "anorexic" would have spilled onto the next locker, this seemed less workable.

I racked my fevered brain to think of some advice or words of wisdom to impart. My mother always has some choice <u>bon mots</u>:

"Do you really think you should eat that, dear?"

"Would you like to come with me to my aerobics class tonight?"

Or my favorite:

"I like you better in darker colors, sweetheart."

Everyone's so concerned for me. Oddly, I think about Sondra and my Mom, and they seem to have so much in common. They both try so hard to be perfect—dieting, exercising feverishly, working so hard to keep the surface up to standards. Sometimes, I think I see the same fear in their eyes. The fear they're not perfect. I never have that fear, I know I'll never be perfect. It makes me wish they'd relax all their efforts on my behalf.

Walking home from school, all the voices of concern seemed to meld in my head—my mother's, Sondra's, the gym teacher—a chorus of concern, concern that I'll never reach the perfection they want for me, never rise to their standard, never fit in.

And then the word came to me. The word that would be my gift to Sondra, and to all my other classmates who worked so hard to make me aware of my unworthiness, my lameness, my refusal to fit in or conform—

SLAG.

I went into the garage and found the green paint. Some cardboard boxes, collapsed and leaning against the wall, were my canvases. I practiced my

This section shows Eleanor is looking past her own issues and working to understand why her tormentors behave as they do. The comparison she makes between Sondra and her own mother is both disturbing and moving.

Eleanor has produced an unusually pointed, dark, and disturbing take on the subject of bullying. As opposed to the previous draft, she has developed a very strong, consistent, and individual slant on the topic and brought an unexpected level of irony that she not only sustains, but develops and modulates. The essay also builds much more effectively, is better structured, and while being true to the portrayal of cruelty that Eleanor has experienced, never lapses into self-pity but portrays instead a survivor's instinct and attitude.

calligraphy again and again, until the can ran dry, air hissing. Still I kept on spraying invisible letters in the air, until I suddenly noticed tears running down my face. I was wondering if I'd suddenly become allergic to Krylon paint when I noticed Dad standing in the garage entrance, watching me. He looked at me with some concern, and I thought perhaps he might have an idea of how I could properly express my thankfulness to Sondra and everyone else.

"Start from the beginning," he says. "We'll try to figure it out between us."

Analysis of Final Draft

What is this writer's point? The writer's point is obviously about the pain and humiliation of being bullied, but also about the price one pays in high school for being a nonconformist—and how the attitude of a nonconformist is perhaps the best coping tool for surviving.

What is her angle? She employs a satirical, falsely positive interpretation of the situation she is in, her tormentors, and her teachers.

What type or tone of voice has she created in her reader's mind? Her tone is a dark ironic take on the situation, pushed to the edge of extreme sarcasm. This effectively undercuts any element of self-pity, and makes the reader root for the narrator.

What techniques has this writer used to create this voice? She takes the reverse, almost perverse tactic, of portraying the bully as almost a friend trying to help, and the attacks she endures as "generous" and good "advice." Only very occasionally—and strategically—does she allow her anger to peek out from behind the satire.

What specific details, facts, etc., make this experience real? Such details include the following: the opening paragraph when the author portrays herself as "living on the edge"; the description of the spray-painted letters on her locker spelling "FAT"; the basketball attack; her mother's words about the writer's diet and body; the author reduced to tears while spray-painting in the garage.

Now write your revised draft.

ASSIGNMENT 3:

Fictional Narrative

Remember that a fiction or creative writing assignment is not a "throwaway" or a "freebie." Depending on the nature of the fiction you are assigned to write, you will apply, for the most part, the techniques and skills of good writing. The practice may be particularly beneficial since the exercise will allow you to organize and communicate facts, ideas, and details without having to read, research, or look beyond your own imagination for the material you will present.

Writing fiction might:

- allow you to be completely creative, unfettered by prescribed content,

- allow you to experiment with form and convention,

- liberate your language, especially the use of literary and rhetorical devices in even your nonfiction, academic writing,

- expose you to different ways to plan and draft all of your writing.

Thus, the assignment of a fictional narrative, or the permission to fictionalize in an essay, is much more than simply a "free-for-all," "extra-credit" throwaway. It has implications for a good deal of your future academic studies, possibly sharpening both your reading and your writing skills.

In fact, writing a series of fictional narratives can be excellent practice for the writing of your actual personal essays.

The development process of this narrative is, of course, essentially the same as the process for other, academic writing.

> Based on a real-life experience of your own or someone close to you, write a fictional narrative that illustrates a lead character meeting a challenge. While it is not necessary to be literal in your portrayal of the event that you're using to inspire you, you must nevertheless base your character and his or her situation in a recognizable, believable context.

"**Derek**" is interested in pursuing a career in screenwriting and film direction and wishes to go to a university with a strong, well-recognized film and writing program, such as NYU, The New School, or University of California, Los

Angeles. He has already tried his hand at writing a screenplay for a high-concept science fiction film that involved much more action than it did character and story. His writing teacher has challenged him to work more with character, theme, and structure, so he's hoping with the prompt he's been given to show that he can handle these elements.

Here is a re-creation of the process Derek used when he was given the prompt to write a fictional narrative based on a real-life experience of his own or someone close to him:

STEP 1: Select a Topic

Derek took his time considering what experience would make a good basis for his story. He wanted to make this narrative more *character driven*, as his writing teacher had suggested, so he first made a list of people he knew who were compelling characters and what it was that made them compelling. He also knew, however, that even the most interesting and believable character had to face some challenge, so he spent a good deal of time brainstorming a list of potential narrative conflicts.

> – Significant events: My best friend Clinton coming out of his coma after a week. Me breaking up with Cindy when I found out she was dating someone else. The day Mom and Dad told me they were divorcing.

Considering each event, Derek begins to narrow his choices, evaluating which might be too ordinary, too plot-centered, or too painful to write about.

> – Clinton being hit by the car—Well, it was pretty dramatic, and his recovery has been pretty challenging. But he'd have to be the lead character, and he was in a coma. How do I make that dramatic? I could maybe tell it from his point of view, and make him aware of what is going on, but unable to speak or move or do anything.
>
> – Me breaking up with Cindy—Not particularly unique. How would I make it different? It could end up sounding like some drippy chick flick.
>
> – Mom and Dad telling me they were breaking up—Well, who would be the lead character? Mom or Dad? Me? It might be interesting to do all three of our sides on it, but that's too much for a short story. I don't think I really want to go there, anyway.

> Derek may be limiting his choices too consciously here. The truth is that any of these events might be the basis for a good fictional narrative, if an interesting slant and compelling characterization are employed.

After his brainstorming session, Derek decides to base his short story on the experience of his friend who was hit by a car.

STEP 2: Develop a Slant/Angle/Hook

WHAT CAN MY ANGLE BE?

— I want to tell it from Clinton's point of view—he sees and hears everything going on around him, but is trapped inside of his injured body and can't say or do anything, can't even let people know that he hears them and sees them. I've heard that people in comas actually do have some awareness of their surroundings, so I'm pretty sure I can make this believable.

Note: At this point, Derek would be well advised to do some actual research on what the experience of people who have been in a coma actually is. While authors of fiction frequently take liberties with scientific, medical, or other kinds of facts, it is best to know what those facts are and have an idea of how far one may be exaggerating or distorting those facts. Readers are willing to take a leap of faith an author presents them with only if it feels like a reasonable leap and doesn't totally fly in the face of credibility.

STEP 3: Brainstorm, Discuss, Research

Having made his choice of event and slant, Derek lists possible elements that might be useful in creating the situation his lead character is in.

— Clinton was a jock, and it was hard for him to be immobilized and not know if he'd even walk again.

— He told me it hurt him just to look at his girlfriend while he was laid up in the hospital.

— How frustrating it was to him that he thought people weren't being straight with him, or were avoiding the subject of his injuries.

— How when I was in the room with him when he was comatose, it seemed like he was underwater, submerged.

— The doctor shining a light in his face was what made him finally wake up.

— He's better now, but he still doesn't know if he'll make a full recovery.

Derek is taking a fairly lazy approach in this step. Most notably, he's leaving out the critical area of research, not even bothering to go online and seek out information on coma patients and what their experiences are. He should also be taking the extra step of talking to his friend Clinton about his experiences and feelings and probably asking if he is comfortable with the idea of Derek basing a short story on his hospitalization.

STEP 4: Outline

Derek has decided to tell the story from the point when the character finds himself in the hospital:

- Opening/inciting incident: I'll open with Clinton being in the hospital. He "wakes up" and discovers he's trapped inside his body. He can't speak, can't move, but sees and hears everything around him. How torturous it is to him not to be able to communicate, how it feels like being submerged in water. Complication/conflict: Move on to how he doesn't know what his future is, how he thinks people are avoiding the issue while they're in the room with him. How hard it is to look at his girlfriend, how much she makes him want to cry out, move, do something.

- Plot exposition: Flashback then to when they met, how she made him feel.

- Rising action: Build his frustration until he HAS to do something.

- Climax: Finally manages to move a finger to let people know he's awake and aware.

- Falling action/denouement: I need to leave it open-ended; I don't want to show a complete recovery, just that he makes a first step. And I'll tell it all in present tense, first-person, to make it more immediate.

The choice of telling his story from a single character's point of view, especially when the journey that character takes is a largely internal one, is going to be a strong challenge for Derek. Likewise, electing to use present tense and telling the narrative in the first-person are strong choices. But the half-hearted outline above is not detailed or specific enough, and he is likely to be writing multiple drafts to compensate for his lack of preparation at this point.

In addition to describing his sequence of events, Derek has also opted to lay out his play in a graphic organizer. It is really no different from the many graphics he has filled out while studying literature. It is actually a good idea for him to apply what he has learned in one context to help him accomplish something in another.

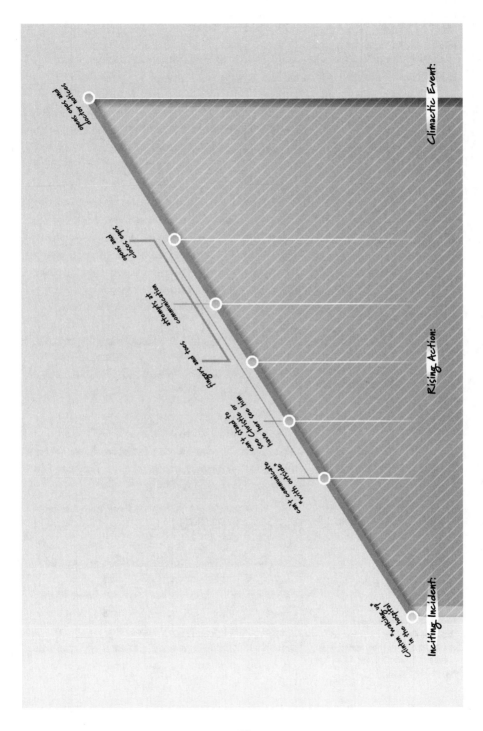

STEP 5: First Draft

Read Derek's first draft below and consider its strengths and weaknesses, and how successfully he has responded to his teacher's prompt.

Derek's opening paragraph is strong. He states what the event and challenge is, and we begin to hear the voice of the lead character.

At this point, Derek is missing an opportunity to start giving more specific information on the lead character's situation, his viewpoint, what his emotional state is within the moment he is telling the story. His first sentence is strong—"I don't know if I'm actually going to be able to move again"—but how does that make him feel? We're getting just facts, but not the voice of the character. There is also some cloudiness or inconsistency about the narrator's condition; if he's in a coma, can he really understand people? Who is "telling him" about the car accident if everyone believes him to be unconscious?

In this section, Derek is finally giving us some of the lead character's emotional response and his viewpoint, but this section would benefit from more specifics and descriptive power. His simile about the days disappearing like "raindrops on a windshield" is a good example of something he could do more of.

I don't remember the car hitting me. I only know it happened because people tell me it did. I'd say I'm having an out-of-body experience, but it's actually the opposite. I'm way inside my body. Trapped in my body, to be precise about it.

I don't know if I'm actually going to be able to move again. Or how much. No one's talking about that. I can remember I was coming from a swim meet, and that I'd placed third. I wasn't happy about that; I thought I'd win. I was grousing about it with my teammates when the Corvette charged out of nowhere and sent me thirty feet into the air and straight through a plate glass window. All of this is second-hand information; I only half remember talking to my friends. The 'Vette came up onto the sidewalk; drunk driver —or so I'm told.

I've been in critical care for most of a week—at least, I think. Could it be a month? I lose track of time here. Days seem to go on for years, but then again, they seem to disappear like raindrops on a windshield.

I'd ask someone to tell me how long I've been here, but I can't talk. I can't move my mouth. I don't know if that's because most of me is in some kind of cast, or if something else is wrong. Like I said, no one is talking, and I can't ask. I don't mean no one is talking to me; that happens all the time. My Mom, Dad, Christie—all of them come to me with brave put-on smiles. And they talk to me about stupid, irrelevant stuff, as if that will keep me from guessing how scared they all are.

Where it really gets weird is that I'm not sure they know I can hear them, or that I'm even present. Sometimes I'm not sure how present I really am. Sometimes it feels like I'm submerged, like I'm in the pool again, except I'm not moving, the water's turned to glue or Jell-O or something, and I'm just suspended there. Sometimes I wonder just how alive I really am.

It's hardest when Christie visits. Christie, with your streaked hair and impossible big, sad eyes. The way her eyes look at me now is nothing like the way they used to see me. I can remember the first time I actually felt her eyes on me; we weren't even talking to each other, she was talking to her friends and I was talking to my buds, and our eyes just kind of met by accident but held for just that moment. Awkward, so awkward, but I couldn't stop looking. I'd never felt anyone look at me that way before; Christie blushed redder than a rose, and I probably did, too.

At the time I thought, I'm not ready for this. Now I wonder if I'll ever be ready for it.

Her eyes are frightened now; concerned, sure, but what I really see is fear. Fear of how quickly things change, how quickly everything changes in the blink of an eye. She looks at me now like a broken thing, something that can't ever be fixed or mended. That look frightens me. I wonder what she's been told, what everyone but me has been told.

I try to move a finger, a toe, an eyebrow, anything—something to let them know I'm here inside. I concentrate; movement used to be so natural for me; now I only have thinking, only my mind caught inside this inert body. Concentrate, concentrate. I try to focus on my left index finger. Nothing. Christie isn't even paying attention. I concentrate harder, I close my eyes and I suddenly hear Christie shriek.

This section has Derek's strongest writing yet; he is now actually giving some real insight into his character's emotional state and developing a voice and tone that are specific and compelling. His description of feeling submerged, "the water's turned to glue or Jell-O or something," is affecting; however, it brings up the question for the reader of just how much Derek really knows about the mental state of patients who are comatose.

Here, Derek's narrative jumps too far forward, leaving the reader behind. He has pushed through to an ending without fully detailing his character's journey or challenges. The reader is left with the impression that Derek hasn't fully explored his topic, doesn't really know enough about the experiences of people who have been comatose or profoundly injured, and is only exploiting the emotional aspect of the situation to write a superficial, facile portrayal of it.

Wait, I just did that. I closed my eyes. I open them again and there's Christie, she's brought half the hospital staff with her, and she's on her cell phone. I know she's calling my Mom. A doctor shines a light in my eyes, getting into my face so close I feel her breath on my cheek.

"Well, Clinton," she says, cracking a smile. "It seems you've come back to us."

Analysis of First Draft

What is this writer's point? The point of the narrative is the difficulty of being unable to communicate or act to affect one's situation, especially for a young person.

What is his angle? The angle is the choice to tell his story from the point of view of a person who is comatose.

What type or tone of voice has he created in his reader's mind? There is the beginning of a distinct voice for the narrator, a young man who is used to being physically fit and active, but is suddenly immobilized. It needs, however, greater specificity and development.

What techniques has this writer used to create this voice? The writer employs a highly creative, imaginative portrayal of what it might feel like to be a comatose young man, but one who is aware of what is going on around him. He is, however, taking a big risk in asking the reader to make that leap of faith without more specific detail and a stronger rooting of his concept in a recognizable, believable reality.

What specific details, facts, etc., make this experience real? The narrative has several effective details and descriptions, such as the sense of being submerged, or the description of Christie, or the sense of fear and dread that the narrator feels. But much more exploration and detail are needed to make this an effective, believable narrative.

NOW plan your own fictional narrative, following the same process by which Derek arrived at his first draft. Remember that Derek thought about several possible topics and developed each of them to see which one would yield the best story.

STEP 1: Select a Topic

What experiences lend themselves to a successful evaluation?

What point would you want to make in evaluating each of these potential topics?

STEP 2: Develop a Slant/Angle/Hook

What will your angle be?

Where might you begin your evaluation?

What type or tone of voice do you want to create in your reader's mind?

STEP 3: Brainstorm, Discuss, Research

What specific details, facts, etc., will make this experience real and not merely hypothetical?

What specific details, facts, etc., will help you achieve your angle, tone, and mood (i.e., funny instead of somber, gentle instead of crude, etc.)?

STEP 4: Outline

STEP 5: First Draft

STEP 6: Peer Edit

What is this writer's point?

What is this writer's angle?

What type or tone of voice has the writer created in his or her reader's mind?

What techniques has this writer used to create this voice?

What specific details, facts, etc., make this experience real?

STEP 7: Revised/Final Draft

Derek, of course, initially believed his first draft to be a camera-ready selection of literature. Eventually, however, he remembered that this peer partner only wanted him to do well on this assignment, so he began to take the editor's comments seriously. **Here are his partner's comments and analysis and Derek's responses:**

- Derek's opening paragraph is strong. He states what the event and challenge is, and we begin to hear the voice of the lead character.

- At this point, Derek is missing an opportunity to start giving more specific information on the lead character's situation, his viewpoint, what his emotional state is within the moment he is telling the story. His first sentence is strong—"I don't know if I'm actually going to be able to move again"—but how does that make him feel? We're getting just facts, but not the voice of the character. There is also some cloudiness or inconsistency about the narrator's condition; if he's in a coma, can he really understand people? Who is "telling him" about the car accident if everyone believes him to be unconscious?

- In this section, Derek is finally giving us some of the lead character's emotional response and his viewpoint, but this section would benefit from more specifics and descriptive power. His simile about the days disappearing like "raindrops on a windshield" is a good example of something he could do more of.

- This section has Derek's strongest writing yet; he is now actually giving some real insight into his character's emotional state and developing a voice and tone that are specific and compelling. His description of feeling submerged, "the water's turned to glue or Jell-O or something," is affecting; however, it brings up the question for the reader of just how much Derek really knows about the mental state of patients who are comatose.

• Here, Derek's narrative jumps too far forward, leaving the reader behind. He has pushed through to an ending without fully detailing his character's journey or challenges. The reader is left with the impression that Derek hasn't fully explored his topic, doesn't really know enough about the experiences of people who have been comatose or profoundly injured, and is only exploiting the emotional aspect of the situation to write a superficial, facile portrayal of it.

> Okay, I guess I have to cop to the fact that I didn't do enough research on this. I'll start searching online to see what is actually known about the state of being comatose. Maybe somebody who experienced it has written about it.

Analysis of First Draft

What is this writer's point? The point of the narrative is the difficulty of being unable to communicate or act to affect one's situation, especially for a young person.

> It looks like at least I got that right. But somehow it should be more, maybe something more specific about the pain Clinton felt, how it's changed him, how uncertain his future is.

What is his angle? The angle is the choice to tell his story from the point of view of a person who is comatose.

> The good news is, my angle works. I just have to work harder to make the reader buy into it.

What type or tone of voice has he created in his reader's mind? There is the beginning of a distinct voice for the narrator, a young man who is used to being physically fit and active, but is suddenly immobilized. It needs, however, greater specificity and development.

> The note about talking to Clinton about this is a good one; that's something I should have done before even starting. I hope he's cool with me using his story. If he is, I'll probably learn a lot about what it felt like from his point of view.

What techniques has this writer used to create this voice? The writer employs a highly creative, imaginative portrayal of what it might feel like to be comatose, but aware of what is going on. He is, however, taking a big risk in asking the reader to make that leap of faith without more specific detail and a stronger rooting of his concept in a recognizable, believable reality.

> That means research, research, research. I hope I can find some info that supports my whole idea, or I'm in trouble on this one.

What specific details, facts, etc., make this experience real? The narrative has several effective details and descriptions such as the sense of being submerged, or the description of Christie, or the sense of fear and dread that the narrator feels. But much more exploration and detail are needed to make this an effective, believable narrative, and the ending feels forced, not sufficiently built toward.

> I think I have to look at the structure and see what I'm missing. I'll review the outline and figure out there how the narrative needs to build.

And here is Derek's final draft:

I don't remember the car hitting me. I only know it happened because I hear people talking about it. I'd say I'm having an out-of-body experience, but it's actually the opposite. I'm way inside my body. Trapped in my body, to be precise about it.

It's blurry inside here. I'm awake and yet I'm not; I can sense people and movement around me; I get vague outlines and muffled sounds. But I know I'm here, and something real is happening. I can feel the needle prick when a nurse gives me an injection or takes blood, but I can't flinch or moan or make any sign to show I'm not totally unconscious. Sometimes it feels like I'm submerged, like I'm in the pool again, except I'm not moving; the water's turned to glue or Jell-O or something, and I'm just suspended there. Sometimes I wonder just how alive I really am.

I don't know if I'm actually going to be able to move again, or how much. No one's talking about that, at least not that I can make out from the muffled sounds and garbled words I hear. I want to know. I need to know what's ahead for me, and at the same time I don't want to know. What if this is how it's going to be? Is this what it means to be a vegetable?

Memory is fuzzy too, but it's present, and it's not always a welcome visitor. I can remember I was coming from a swim meet, and that I'd placed third. I wasn't happy about that; I thought I'd win. I was grousing about it with my teammates when I heard a motor roaring behind me—that's the last thing I remember. Was it the noise of the engine of the car that hit me? Was it a truck, a sports car, a cement mixer? What did this to me? Who did this to me?

Derek has retained his strong opening paragraph, with a subtle but important change: "I only know it happened because I hear people talking about it" instead of "because people tell me it happened" reflects a stronger, more precise idea of the physical state the narrator is in.

Derek has expanded this paragraph in an important way, being much more descriptive and specific about his narrator's experience and sensations. It is apparent that he has done some research to find out what comatose patients can sometimes feel and that he has, perhaps, spoken to the friend he is basing this account on. He has also moved his effective description of being suspended from the later section in the first draft to this earlier part, a good choice to help create the sense of the narrator's isolation and frustration.

Here, Derek is making much stronger choices, being specific about the narrator's fears and giving the reader a true sense of what the narrator is experiencing.

Again, Derek is giving us a much deeper, nuanced window into the world of his narrator and the emotions and pain he is experiencing. He is also being much more consistent and believable in the portrayal of the experience of being comatose. He may want to rephrase the end of this paragraph, however, and steer away from the multiple questions, which become somewhat repetitive stylistically.

I must be in a hospital; I don't know if it's the emergency room or critical care or just what. How long have I been here, a week, a month? I have no idea, no sense of time. Days could go on for years, and I wouldn't know. I don't know if I'm still seventeen, or an old man. Days might disappear like raindrops on a windshield. The windshield of— what? A Corvette? Am I remembering that, or am I dreaming it?

I'd ask someone to tell me how long I've been here, but of course I can't talk. I can't move my mouth or anything else. I don't know if that's because most of me is in some kind of cast, or if something else is wrong. I do hear voices—Mom, Dad, Christie—all garbled, but I can make out who's speaking, and sometimes I can even make out a word or two. The voices all sound kind and calm and relaxed, like they're trying to reassure me somehow, which is one of the things that scares me the most. They don't know I can hear them, or that I'm even present. Sometimes I'm not sure how present I really am.

I can make out Christie's voice clearer than anyone's. Christie, with your streaked hair and impossible big, sad eyes. I can't see those eyes very well right now, but I can feel them, the way I always do. I can remember the first time I actually felt her eyes on me; we weren't even talking to each other; she was talking to her friends and I was talking to my buds, and our eyes just kind of met by accident but held for just that moment. Awkward, so awkward, but I couldn't stop looking. I'd never felt anyone look at me that way before; Christie blushed redder than a rose, and I probably did, too.

At the time I thought, I'm not ready for this. Now I wonder if I'll ever be ready for it.

This section benefits immensely from Derek's more detailed knowledge of his narrator's condition and experience, which has allowed him to be more consistent and believable in the portrayal of that condition.

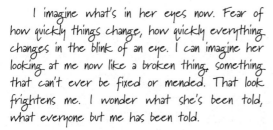

I imagine what's in her eyes now. Fear of how quickly things change, how quickly everything changes in the blink of an eye. I can imagine her looking at me now like a broken thing, something that can't ever be fixed or mended. That look frightens me. I wonder what she's been told, what everyone but me has been told.

I think I'd rather die than go on the way I am. But I don't want to die, I haven't lived enough. It's a cheat for me to die now, a rotten stinking lousy cheat. It sucks for me to check out now, I have to do something—

The addition of this paragraph is key; it escalates the narrator's emotional state and propels him toward action, laying the groundwork much more effectively for the ending that follows.

I try to move a finger, a toe, an eyebrow, anything—something to let them know I'm here inside. I concentrate; movement used to be so natural for me; now I only have thinking, only my mind caught inside this inert body. Concentrate, concentrate. I try to focus on my left index finger. Nothing. I concentrate harder, I close my eyes and I suddenly hear Christie shriek.

Wait, I just did that. I closed my eyes. I open them again and there's Christie, I can actually see her, she's not a shadow or a cloud or a mist anymore, she's Christie. Maybe I'm not a mist anymore.

Again, Derek shows much better understanding of what a comatose person would experience of the world around him, and how he or she would emerge from a coma. The result is much more believable and compelling.

Christie's brought half the hospital staff with her, and she's on her cell phone. I know she's calling my Mom. A doctor shines a light in my eyes, getting into my face so close I feel her breath on my cheek.

"Well, Clinton," she says, cracking a smile. "It seems you've come back to us."

Analysis of Final Draft

What is this writer's point? Derek's point is that the experience of being comatose is not a complete lack of consciousness, but rather a painful state of being trapped between two types of existence, of having an incomplete but real awareness of one's surroundings and situation.

What is his angle? The angle is the choice to tell his story from the point of view of a person who is comatose.

What type or tone of voice has he created in his reader's mind? He has created a believable and consistent voice for his narrator, a youthful voice that is acute, observant, and open.

What techniques has this writer used to create this voice? Derek tells his narrative in present tense and real time, making the reader feel his narrator's experience moment to moment. He has decided to make this essentially an internal narrative, effectively taking the reader through the inner conflicts and challenges going through the young man's mind as he emerges from a coma.

What specific details, facts, etc., make this experience real? The depiction of being in a coma as being trapped in a kind of half-world, the questions that haunt the narrator about his state and what his future might be, the flashback to when he met his girlfriend, and his projection of what she must be feeling all serve to make this an effective piece.

POSSIBLE STEP 8: Rewrite Opportunity

PART II:

Informative Writing

[showing what students know about a subject]

Up until now, we've treated informative writing as if it were a completely separate and independent mode of writing, and it is—in a very small sense. Most writing, however, regardless of its primary purpose, is also informative.

From now on, we're still going to work on perfecting the informative elements of your writing, but we're going to begin considering that information as a means to an end rather than the end in itself. Certainly throughout high school, college, graduate school—as far as you go with your formal education—you will be asked to "show what you know about a subject," but rarely will you be invited to provide a mind-dump of information.

Most of the "informative writing" you will be asked to do will actually be informative or entertaining or intended to fulfill some other purpose. The information you share will simply be necessary for you to meet that purpose.

Your actual purpose will also govern the amount and depth of information you share.

As was the case with personal writing, you will need always to remember that you need:

- **a point:** Why are you providing this information?

    and

- **an angle:** How do the information you provide and the techniques you use to provide it help to make your overall piece more powerful, interesting, memorable, etc.?

ASSIGNMENT 1:

Interview or Personal Profile

Here is a popular prompt that allows the writer to focus on information and presentation without the distraction of arguing a point or attempting to reveal a new insight.

> Interview a family member or friend who has had an extraordinary life experience, and explain how that experience affected your outlook or viewpoint.

The process is essentially the same:

STEP 1: Select a Topic

Having already written about his friend Clinton's experience coming out of a coma, **Derek** had to consider other family members and friends who had interesting experiences to relate.

> Mom training for the New York Marathon.
>
> Cindy going to Spain last summer as an exchange student.
>
> My grandfather Alistair's having been in a Japanese POW camp.

Derek began to list the positive and negative aspects of each of these topics, to narrow down his choice.

> – Mom training for the Marathon—not sure it's unique or important enough, a lot of people run marathons. Good on Mom for doing it, but I can't think of an angle that would make it unique.
>
> – Cindy going to Spain—she had a great time, learned a lot about Spain and the culture there, but not sure how that really affected me or my outlook.
>
> – Grandpa having been in a Japanese POW camp—it's an amazing story, and I think it's affected me in a lot of ways. Problem is, Grandpa Alistair died last year, so I can't interview him. I'd have to rely on memory, and his diaries and drawings. Plus whatever I can learn from research.

STEP 2: Develop a Slant/Angle/Hook

WHAT CAN MY ANGLE BE?

The way I learned about Grandpa having been in the POW camp was through his drawings. He used to say that drawing was what kept him alive then, through all the disease and mistreatment and all his buddies dying around him. I think that's what affected me the most; it made me want to be an artist too. So I think that will be my angle right there.

STEP 3: Brainstorm, Discuss, Research

After deciding on his angle, Derek proceeded to brainstorm and research. He began this process by writing down everything he could from his memories of his grandfather's stories about the camp:

- Him showing me the drawings of his friends, telling me their names, and their stories. Whether they had survived or not.
- The way his art changed while he was in the camp—how it became darker, sadder, sometimes violent but still beautiful.
- How he nearly died in the camp from malaria, looked like a skeleton or scarecrow, but still kept drawing.
- The abuse he got from the guards; how one of them almost killed him.
- The morning he woke up next to his best buddy, and found out he had died.
- How he always said The Bridge on the River Kwai was pale next to what he'd been through.

Derek continued writing down many memories, but after a while, he decided it was time to do a little historical research. He began by going online and searching under "The Death Railway," the infamous railroad between Burma and Thailand that had been built by forced labor—including his grandfather. Here are some facts Derek found:

- About 330,000 forced laborers worked on the railway, 61,000 of whom were Allied POWs. About 16,000 died during the construction; about 90,000 other conscripted workers from other parts of Asia died as well.
- The bridge was built because Japan needed a route between Burma and Thailand to bring supplies. Japan had seized Burma from Britain in 1942; they needed the supplies to maintain control, but sending them by sea meant being vulnerable to Allied attacks.

– Hellfire Pass was one of the hardest sections of the line to build, since it was the largest rock cutting of the entire railway; the location was remote, and the workers lacked the proper tools for the job. Sixty-nine men were beaten to death by the guards while it was built, and many more died from disease.

STEP 4: Outline

Derek has decided to open the profile with his earliest memory of his grandfather and the first time he heard about the camp and the railway, constructing the essay much the way he might structure a screenplay:

I. My love of Grandfather's drawings when I was little
  A. fun...colorful
  B. looped and curved lines
  C. weird points of view
    1. van Gogh or Picasso
    2. like that guy who has the never-ending staircase or the hand drawing itself

II. The different one frightened me
  A. straight lines, sharp angles
  B. no color—very dark red
    1. almost brown
    2. thick ink...flaky and crusted
  C. not normal artist paper
    1. poor and yellowed
  D. the image itself

III. Grandfather's story
  A. artist in London
  B. drafted

C. Singapore...1942
D. Same as The Bridge on the River Kwai
E. Worked on the famous bridge
  1. Death Railway
  2. 61,000 Allied POWs
  3. 16,000 died
F. Grandfather drew this painting as a self record
  1. ink was really blood

IV. Other pictures
  A. Jack Spofford
  B. Harry Ackland

V. What I realized
  A. attracted to art...film
  B. promised to make a better The Bridge on the River Kwai.
    1. not glamorize but show horror

STEP 5: First Draft

I always loved my Grandfather's drawings, from the time I was little. I didn't understand them, but I liked them. They were fun and colorful, amusing pictures of people and animals with puzzled expressions in odd positions. The viewpoints were always "off," as if you were under them and beside them at the same time. They were almost like the weird perspectives of a Picasso or even that artist who drew the never-ending staircase or the hand that is drawing itself. (Find name). The world my grandfather drew was different from mine, and I often thought I'd like to visit there. Like Alice visiting Wonderland or falling down the rabbit hole. I was not the only one who liked my grandfather's work. Many people did. For a very long time, Grandpa Alistair was a very successful artist, showing his drawings in galleries all over the world, and having them published in major magazines.

But this was a different kind of drawing, not like anything I'd seen before. It frightened me, yet I couldn't look away from it. The lines seemed jagged, violent, and there was no color to soften the image. The only color on the paper was a very dark red, almost brown, dried and encrusted looking. The paper itself was not the usual fine rag paper of his other drawings. This was yellowed and crumpling and seemed to be disintegrating. Most of all, the image was nothing that could have come from my grandfather's brain. It was a man, gaunt to the point of being almost a skeleton. The clothes hung from him in tatters like a scarecrow or a Halloween mummy, and the man's face was the most pained, haunted expression I had ever seen. Somehow, even at the young age of twelve, I knew this was not the picture of a costume or a ghost-story monster. The expression on the face was too real.

Derek's opening paragraph is not bad. Some readers may be put off by his stylistic sentence fragments, so he will have to pay attention to them. One factual error, though, is that *Alice in Wonderland* is the novel in which she falls through the rabbit hole. If Derek wants to name both books, he should place Alice either in Looking Glass Land or have her slip through the looking glass.

This is not a bad introduction. Derek has introduced his topic (his grandfather) but not yet the point or the angle, the "extraordinary life experience, and...how that experience affected [Derek's] outlook or viewpoint."

This abrupt transition is a stylistic and structural risk. It may pay off in suspense and reader interest, or it may cause the reader to give up. After all, we don't yet have a sense of why Derek wants us to know about his grandfather.

Although Derek is taking some risks here, it still is not stylistically logical to say there is "no color" in one sentence and then describe the "only color" in the next.

It's still not certain whether Derek's stylistic and structural choice is going to pay off. We are still uncertain of much of the point of this essay.

Word choice and sentence structure are a little repetitive, but it does seem as if Derek is beginning something of a narrative that might reveal his point and angle.

This is an excellent example of how an essay can build to a "payoff," or a "reveal." We do suddenly have a sense of the grandfather's "extraordinary life experience," and Derek has apparently chosen to frame his profile as a narrative, possibly even telling it in his grandfather's own words.

It made me almost sick to my stomach, but I couldn't look away.

I had found this drawing in my grandfather's studio, where I wasn't supposed to go unless he invited me. I heard him come up behind me and tried to slip the drawing back under the pile of work on top of his drafting table, where I'd found it. But he caught me red-handed when he came in. What surprised me, though, was that he wasn't angry with me. Instead of grabbing the picture from my hand, he simply took it and laid it on the drawing table. Then, instead of scolding me, he simply took my hand and led to me to the small sofa he had in his studio.

"You wonder who he was, don't you?" Grandpa Alistair said, softly. I was surprised and relieved he wasn't angry, but I wasn't prepared for what he said next. "It's a self-portrait, Derek. That's your Grandfather, many years ago." I knew he'd been in the war, but he never talked about it. No one in the family ever brought it up, and I was about to learn why.

He told me that the brown stuff, the crusted, flaking ink was blood. His blood. He said that that was all he had available, and he felt he had to record what he was going through at that moment. I looked up at him, not knowing what to say. He said he had taken the picture from the locked cabinet where he stored it because he had decided it was time to show it to me. He hadn't intended for me to trespass and discover it, but he wasn't upset that I had found it.

Then he told me his story.

My Grandfather Alistair was a young artist in London when he was conscripted into the British Army; he was stationed in Singapore when Malaya fell to the Japanese in 1942. He was then sent to the Kwai jungle, and forced into labor on what would be called the "Death Railway," a railroad the Japanese were building. The movie, <u>The Bridge on the River Kwai</u> supposedly tells the story of the building of a bridge for that railway. My grandfather hated that movie, though. He called it "watered down tripe." He said the forced labor, the harsh conditions, and the brutal treatment by the Japanese guards seemed almost glamorous in the movie compared to how bad it really was.

That's why he drew this painting, he told me, to make a record of what it was like at that place and time. He said it was the drawing that kept him alive. The guards tried to make him stop, but he wouldn't. They'd confiscated some of his drawing, but he hid the rest. He said he did it to stay alive. And to keep an accurate historic record.

My grandfather told me that some 330,000 forced laborers worked on the Death Railway. Of those, possibly 61,000 were Allied POWs, 16,000 of whom died. Aside from the maltreatment, the prisoners endured starvation, horrendous living conditions, and diseases like malaria and beriberi. He said he was down to 40 kilos at one point, which is less than 90 pounds. That's when he drew the picture I had seen. A guard had beaten him badly, he was starved almost to death, and he knew he needed to record this event, make sure no one ever forgot or tried to make it seem less horrible than it was.

He unlocked a drawer in the file where he kept most of his drawings and took some out to show me. They were other prisoners, friends he made in the camp. He told me their names and talked about them as if he still knew them, was still in contact with them.

It was hard for my twelve-year-old mind to absorb what my grandfather was telling me. I didn't know what I was supposed to do or say.

It is a little disappointing that Derek has chosen to summarize and paraphrase his grandfather's story when he started out in the grandfather's own voice.

Derek is slowly losing much of the punch with which he started. His grandfather is now far removed from the situation, and the fact that the POWs merely "died" severely lessens the impact of the brutality the grandfather hoped to record in his drawing.

Derek does bring his grandfather back into the narrative, but the details in this paragraph are dry in comparison to Derek's vivid style in his introduction. Phrases like "he said," and "he told me" are getting repetitive and tedious.

If Derek remembers the names and any of the details, he must tell his reader; this is some of the information we need to fully appreciate this piece. If he chooses, even though he is writing a piece of nonfiction, he can fictionalize the names to protect the men's and their families' privacy.

Suddenly, without meaning to, Derek has turned this into his story. This certainly is a requirement of the prompt, but he has not done as much with his grandfather's story as he could have.

Finally, I asked, "How did you make it out of there?"

His answer was that a part of him didn't make it out of there. The part that didn't die, that he had kept alive by drawing, was freed when the Allies liberated the camp. He said that the day he drew that first picture, he was nearly killed. The Japanese had already lost the war, but the POWs in his camp didn't know that. The guard, though, probably did because they'd grown even more brutal than normal. Searching the prisoners' huts, he'd found my grandfather's drawings. He was going to destroy them, destroy the only proof there was of their inhumanity. My grandfather said, at that moment, he didn't really care whether he lived or died, but he refused to see his efforts destroyed. With surprising strength for a man in his condition, he fought tooth and nail. He said the guard was about to draw his sword when there was a great shout from the other prisoners. The Allies had arrived.

This is potentially a powerful climax, but it is severely weakened by Derek's stylistic choices. He needs to revisit the risks he took at the beginning of the essay.

Once he was back in London, my grandfather picked up his career as an artist and illustrator, and his drawings caught the attention of my grandmother, who was at that point a junior editor at the New Yorker. She got a few of his drawings published, then managed to get him an offer to do the cover art for the magazine. He came to New York, they met, and he never went back to England.

It was my grandmother who made him show the war drawings to the galleries. He'd always been too afraid to show them, thinking they were too graphic and disturbing. But it was my grandmother who echoed my grandfather's original intent of keeping an accurate record. Why keep the record if no one was going to see it? They would then still forget and glamorize.

Here, Derek gives himself a good opportunity to remind his reader of the connection between his grandfather's story and the fictionalized film account.

Some of those drawings are now in the Imperial War Museum in London.

After Grandpa showed me his drawings and told me his story, I began to draw myself, and he encouraged me to either attend an art school after high school or major in art in college. When I gravitated toward film rather than art, I think he was a little disappointed; I think he still bears a grudge against <u>The Bridge on the River Kwai</u>. But the last visit I had with him, a week before he died, I told him that some day I wanted to do a film based on his experiences at the camp, one that would tell the truth of what he had been through.

"That would be excellent, Derek," he said, smiling. "If you need a point of reference, there's always the drawings. They're yours now."

> For some reason, Derek returns to his grandfather's voice at the end, when he should maintain that voice throughout. He also needs to do more to strengthen his reader's appreciation of the "truth" of his grandfather's drawings and the "falsehood" of the film.

Analysis of First Draft

What is this writer's point? The writer shows how his grandfather used art to survive the most horrible period of his life. There is also the suggestion that art can lie, as well as tell the truth.

What is his angle? The author's angle is the human need for creativity, especially in the most dire of circumstances. There is also the potential of posing this narrative as a first-person account, through the grandfather's point of view.

What type or tone of voice has he created in his reader's mind? Derek begins quite strongly with an authoritative, graphic, almost visual tone. He loses this quickly, however, and falls into a comparatively flat academic/narrative voice.

What techniques has this writer used to create this voice? Vivid descriptions and bits of dialogue reveal the potential strengths of this essay.

What specific details, facts, etc., make this essay informative and powerful? The self-portrait of the grandfather from the camp, the story of the deaths of his friends, the need for creativity whether drawing or playing music or performing, and the historical facts presented all contribute to the power of the essay.

NOW plan your own essay, following the same process by which Derek arrived at his first draft.

STEP 1: Select a Topic

What experiences lend themselves to a successful evaluation?

What point would you want to make in evaluating each of these potential topics?

STEP 2: Develop a Slant/Angle/Hook

What will your angle be?

Where might you begin your evaluation?

What type or tone of voice do you want to create in your reader's mind?

STEP 3: Brainstorm, Discuss, Research

What specific details, facts, etc., make this essay informative and powerful?

What specific details, facts, etc., will help you achieve your angle, tone, and mood (i.e., funny instead of somber, gentle instead of crude, etc.)?

STEP 4: Outline

STEP 5: First Draft

STEP 6: Peer Edit

What is this writer's point?

What is this writer's angle?

What type or tone of voice has the writer created in his or her reader's mind?

What techniques has this writer used to create this voice?

What specific details, facts, etc., make this essay informative and powerful?

STEP 7: Revised/Final Draft

Here are the editor's comments and analysis and Derek's responses:

- Derek's opening paragraph is effective and gives the reader a good deal of information without making it feel overly expositional. His descriptive abilities are also in good form here.

- The descriptive nature of this paragraph is very powerful and grabs the reader's attention thoroughly. The sense of suspense is built nicely, with the mystery of the origin and meaning of the drawing, and young Derek's being discovered by his grandfather in a forbidden intrusion motivating the reader to see what happens next.

- This is an excellent example of how an essay can build to a "payoff," or a "reveal," that surprises and illuminates the readers, keeping them invested in the story.

- Here, Derek effectively integrates researched historical fact with his grandfather's personal experience. He also moves his grandfather's narrative forward and develops his slant on the story he's telling.

- This paragraph feels a bit fact-heavy at the opening, and is not quite as fluidly integrated as the previous paragraph. Nevertheless, Derek still manages to make those facts relate immediately to the personal story of his grandfather's experience and, again, moves the narrative forward.

- Derek's storytelling here betrays his cinematic aspirations, which is both a plus and, in some ways, a minus. Effectively as he is telling this narrative, the reader has the feeling of being pulled along, and that possibly some steps or details have been skipped over in favor of moving the story forward. It is also apparent that the Japanese guards are only vague, faceless villains; no effort to give them dimension or depict their viewpoint is being made.

- These paragraphs, while nicely written, seem unnecessary in an essay of this length, and not especially germane to the main point or slant of the story. Since the essay is a little lengthy at this point, they could probably be cut.

- The denouement here is efficiently handled, but perhaps a bit too hastily and neatly wrapped up. Overall, the reader has been given a satisfying essay in this draft. But a fine effort could probably be made better if Derek expands his historical research to give the reader more fully characterized renderings of the Japanese guards and what may have motivated their brutality, and perhaps allow himself to step outside the realm of his memory and ask questions that he couldn't have known to ask at age twelve.

I think the one thing they seem to focus on the most is the point of view and narrative voice. I think I can do this from Grandfather's point of view, but I don't think I can re-create his accent.

I suppose I can do a little more research on the Japanese experience during all this; I'll see what I can find out. I think I understand what they mean about my facts being dry and removing Grandfather from the narrative. He was one of those 61,000 Allied POWs.

I do remember a lot of the details of the men in the pictures. But I think I will make up names. It's not my right to tell their stories, just as it was no one's right in my family to tell Grandfather's until he wanted to tell it.

I'll look at paragraph 8 and see if there's anything I've skipped over there. I don't think so, but I'll look it over. And I'll look at the ending, too. Maybe there's something I can add there to make it feel more complete.

Analysis of First Draft

What is this writer's point? The writer shows how his grandfather used art to survive the most horrible period of his life. There is also the suggestion that art can lie, as well as tell the truth.

> Yes. And I know what I can say about <u>The Bridge on the River Kwai</u> to strengthen that part.

What is his angle? The author's angle is the human need for creativity, especially in the most dire of circumstances. There is also the potential of posing this narrative as a first-person account, through the grandfather's point of view.

> I think I can work this from Grandfather's POV and ramp up some of the details of the brutality of the guards, the forced labor, and so on.

What type or tone of voice has he created in his reader's mind? Derek begins quite strongly with an authoritative, graphic, almost visual tone. He loses this quickly, however, and falls into a comparatively flat academic/narrative voice.

> I was actually worried that the details at the beginning would turn off the reader. I can certainly maintain that tone throughout the essay.

What techniques has this writer used to create this voice? Vivid descriptions and bits of dialogue reveal the potential strengths of this essay.

> More dialogue and more vivid details.

What specific details, facts, etc., make this essay informative and powerful? The self-portrait of the grandfather from the camp, the story of the deaths of his friends, the need for creativity whether drawing or playing music or performing, and the historical facts presented all contribute to the power of the essay.

> More dialogue and more vivid details; more facts about the Japanese guards and their motivations; more details about the men in the pictures.

Here is Derek's revised draft. Notice how he has addressed the comments and suggestions his peer editor made. Read the essay and consider how it is stronger and more likely to make a positive impression on the admissions committee.

Derek has essentially retained his opening paragraph, correcting the one factual error and eliminating the potentially problematic sentence fragments.

I always loved my Grandfather's drawings, from the time I was little. I didn't understand them, but I liked them. They were fun and colorful, amusing pictures of people and animals with puzzled expressions in odd positions. The viewpoints were always "off," as if you were under them and beside them at the same time. They were almost like the weird perspectives of a Picasso or M.C. Escher, who drew the never-ending staircase and the hand that is drawing itself. The world my grandfather drew was different from mine, and I often thought I'd like to visit there, like Alice visiting Wonderland or slipping through the Looking Glass. I was not the only one who liked my grandfather's work. For a very long time, Grandfather Alistair was a very successful artist, showing his drawings in galleries all over the world, and having them published in major magazines.

The picture I was looking at now was nothing that could have come from my grandfather's imagination. It was a man, gaunt to the point of being almost a skeleton. The clothes hung from him in tatters like a scarecrow or a Halloween mummy, and the man's face was the most pained, haunted expression I had ever seen. Somehow, even at the young age of twelve, I knew this was not the picture of a costume or a ghost-story monster. The expression on the face was too real.

It made me almost sick to my stomach, but I couldn't look away.

I had found this drawing in my grandfather's studio, where I wasn't supposed to go unless he invited me. I heard him come up behind me and tried to slip the drawing back under the pile of work on top of his drafting table, where I'd found

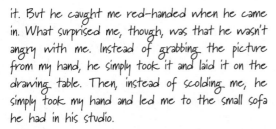

it. But he caught me red-handed when he came in. What surprised me, though, was that he wasn't angry with me. Instead of grabbing the picture from my hand, he simply took it and laid it on the drawing table. Then, instead of scolding me, he simply took my hand and led me to the small sofa he had in his studio.

"You wonder who he was, don't you?" Grandfather Alistair said, softly. I was surprised and relieved he wasn't angry, but I wasn't prepared for what he said next. "It's a self portrait, Derek. That's your Grandfather, many years ago."

I knew he'd been in the war, but we'd never spoken about it. No one in the family ever brought it up. "The red-brown stuff there, you see?" he continued. "There was no more ink and no paint. I used my blood. That's why it's caking like that." I looked up at him, not knowing what to say. His eyes looked down at me and softened, then hardened. "I think it's time. Time for you to hear the story. I spent most of the war in a prison camp, you see. That picture tells only a tiny story about what they did to us there. They beat us, starved us, even murdered some of us. All to build a railway."

My Grandfather Alistair was a young artist in London when he was conscripted into the British Army; he was stationed in Singapore when Malaya fell to the Japanese in 1942. He was then sent to the Kwai jungle and forced into labor on what would come to be called the Death Railway, a railroad the Japanese were constructing between Burma and Thailand. "That movie, <u>The Bridge on the River Kwai</u>, was watered-down tripe," he said, looking angry. "Hollywood. They wanted adventure and suspense, not horror. They didn't even begin to show how bad it was." He picked up the drawing carefully. "This is what kept me alive,

The best case would be for Derek to be able to quote his grandfather verbatim. If that is not possible, there is nothing unethical with Derek's re-creating what he remembers of the grandfather's words, tone, and intent. He cannot, however, intentionally create details that he knows do not reflect reality.

Hopefully, the grandfather really did say something like this. Otherwise, Derek is creating fiction for the sake of his own point at the end about art and the truth.

Derek. The drawings. I never stopped making them. The guards tried to make me, they tried to take them away, but I kept them hidden. If I hadn't been able to draw, I wouldn't have survived. I had to set it down, make a record. I had to express what was being done to us."

"I was down to 40 kilos at one point," Grandfather said, indicating the drawing. "Less than 90 pounds in your terms. We were lucky to get some rice and scraps to eat, and I'd had dysentery to boot. That's when I made this. The guard had beaten me about the head so badly I was bleeding. I used the blood in the drawing. I had to do something with it, there wasn't any doctor or medical treatment, Lord knows."

These are precisely the types of details that Derek needed to keep his account vivid and emotional.

"How could they be so mean to you?" I asked. He looked a bit surprised at the question; after a moment, he looked at me. "They didn't respect us because we had surrendered. Japanese soldiers never surrendered; they were trained as soldiers to die first. So we were less than human to them, I suppose. I think maybe we frightened them on some level, too; we represented failure in some way and they couldn't conceive of that."

Again, this is important and interesting new information. It rounds out the grandfather's profile and shows him to have been a thoughtful man, not a victim filled with regret.

He opened a drawer in the file where he kept most of his drawings, and took some out to show me. They were other prisoners, friends he made in the camp. "That's Jack Spofford, a Lieutenant," he said, showing a sketch of a very tall man with a wry smile. "We called him Spratt because he was always lean, even before he got to the camp. Funny chap. I woke one morning to find him dead in the cot next to mine. I wasn't even sure if it was the malaria or just starvation."

"This is Harry Ackland, he used to make drawings too, good ones. Many of us did. Or the musicians would play when no one was looking. Sometimes we even sang and performed. It was all we had, you see. All that kept us going." He put the drawing down. "Harry didn't make it. Beaten to death. Same guard who nearly killed me." I looked at the drawing. "Was he afraid?" I asked. "Harry was never afraid," he replied. "No, the guard. Was he afraid?" Grandfather thought for a moment, his brow furrowed. "Yes," he replied, "I suppose he must have been terrified. They all must have been terrified."

My Grandfather's sudden revelation of his wartime history was a lot for my twelve-year-old mind to absorb. "How did you make it out of there?" was all I could think of to say.

Again, providing names and brief descriptions is exactly what Derek needed to do.

"There was no real way out, except dying," he replied. "Those of us that managed to stay alive were there until the war ended and the Allies came to liberate the camp." He sat down, suddenly tired. "That day, I was nearly killed. We didn't know the Japanese had lost the war, but the last couple of weeks the guards had been more than usually brutal. The one who'd beaten me before found my stash of drawings under my bed, and was going to take them and destroy them. I don't know where I found the strength, I could barely stand, but something in me just made me rise up and fight him. I didn't care if I died or lived, I only cared that the drawings somehow survived. I threw myself at him, tried to gouge his eyes, rip at his face, anything. I startled him; there was fear in his eyes, which amazed me. He was about to draw his sword, and there was this huge commotion. It was the Allied troops. That was when we knew the war was over."

Notice that Derek really is not straying from his outline or his original account. All he is doing is providing more vivid detail and giving his grandfather a voice.

After Grandfather showed me his drawings and told me his story, I began to draw myself. He liked my sketches and paintings, and he encouraged me to find my own perspective. I've since decided to study film instead of drawing, and I think this disappointed him a little. I think he was just a little bitter about the way Hollywood glamorized what had been the most horrible part of his life.

Still, the last time I saw him before he died last year, I promised that I would one day do a film based on his experiences at the camp, one that would be truer than <u>The Bridge on the River Kwai</u>.

"That would be excellent, Derek," he said, smiling. "If you need a point of reference, there's always the drawings. They're yours, and they will remind you the truth of the story."

Derek has successfully returned to the Hollywood theme and a strong hint of the truth of art versus the falsehood of art he seemed to want to explore in his earlier draft.

Analysis of Final Draft

What is this writer's point? Derek's point hasn't changed. He still explores the power of art and the responsibility of the artist to tell the truth.

What is his angle? The author's angle is clearer in this draft—to tell the grandfather's story in the grandfather's own voice and to juxtapose his own film aspirations with his grandfather's dislike of film to illustrate the two sides of the artistic narrative.

What type or tone of voice has he created in his reader's mind? The essay reads like a memoir, both the grandfather's and the author's. There is an interesting blend of sorrow and reflection.

What techniques has this writer used to create this voice? Giving the grandfather his own voice is an important choice. Derek is also quite skillful at contrasting his twelve-year-old self as he is hearing the story for the first time with his seventeen-year-old self looking back on this experience and looking ahead to his own career as a film artist.

What specific details, facts, etc., make this essay informative and powerful? Derek has eliminated the dry statistics and replaced them with people's names and descriptions of their personalities. He mentions the "food" on which the prisoners subsisted, and he provides a much more graphic view of the grandfather's brutal beating at the hands of a guard.

POSSIBLE STEP 8: Rewrite Opportunity

ASSIGNMENT 2:

Book or Article Report

As you should expect, the structure of a book (or article) report is not very different from any other academic essay you will write. It is fairly important to follow a consistent pattern in the reports you write so that the person(s) for whom you are writing the reports can predict what information they are going to find and where they will be able to find it.

Essentially, in a basic book or article report, the introductory paragraph(s) will reveal the basic information about the piece being reviewed and make some statement about what the piece is about and how it goes about exploring its subject.

The body paragraphs follow through and expand on the topic and approach of the piece. The exploration of the approach might include some evaluation of the writing style, the overall readability of the piece, and a discussion of the author's bias or objectivity or fairness or whatever might color a reader's appreciation of the piece.

Finally, the concluding paragraph(s) wrap up the review, give a critique of the book or article, and give supporting information for that opinion, as well as who the intended or best audience would be, and how they might react to the piece.

In addition to her eleventh-grade English class, **Eleanor** is taking journalism. This teacher has a weekly "outside article review" requirement for all of his journalism students. Here is the assignment template he distributed early in the school year and Eleanor's work for one of her article reports.

Notice how the teacher's assignment template follows the typical process for writing an academic essay.

STEP 1: Select a Topic

Title: "The Falling Man"

Author: Tom Junod

Source Information (publication, publishing company, copyright date, etc.):
published in Esquire, 8 September 2003

Genre: nonfiction

STEP 2: Develop a Slant/Angle/Hook

– **What is the general subject or topic of this piece?** the history of a news photograph from the September 11 attacks that was initially syndicated worldwide, then almost banned from public view.

– **What is the author's angle, theme, or thesis?** Junod is tackling the emotional and political circumstances that surround 9/11, comparing this event to other historical tragedies and questioning what distinguishes this particular photograph from other photos of other tragedies, what made it taboo for people to see.

– **Who is the author? What are his or her qualifications to write on this subject?** Tom Junod has worked for Esquire since 1997, after working for Life, Gentlemen's Quarterly, and Sports Illustrated, among others. He has won two National Magazine Awards, recognized as the most prestigious award in magazine writing.

STEP 3: Brainstorm, Discuss, Research

Is there an obvious slant or bias? What evidence from the text can you provide to support your claim?

– There is some inherent bias in favor of viewing the photograph as a piece of journalistic record, understandable since Junod is a well-known, experienced reporter.

"The photographer [Richard Drew] is no stranger to history; he knows it is something that happens later. In the actual moment history is made, it is usually made in terror and confusion, and so it is up to people like him—paid witnesses—to have the presence of mind to attend to its manufacture. The photographer has that presence of mind and has had it since he was a young man. When he was twenty-one years old, he was standing right behind Bobby Kennedy when Bobby Kennedy was shot in the head. His jacket was spattered with Kennedy's blood, but he jumped on a table and shot pictures of Kennedy's open and ebbing eyes, and then of Ethel Kennedy crouching over her husband and begging photographers—begging him—not to take pictures..."

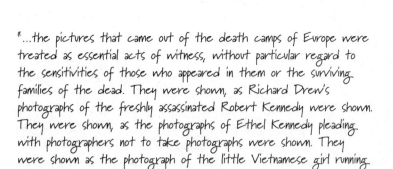

"...the pictures that came out of the death camps of Europe were treated as essential acts of witness, without particular regard to the sensitivities of those who appeared in them or the surviving families of the dead. They were shown, as Richard Drew's photographs of the freshly assassinated Robert Kennedy were shown. They were shown, as the photographs of Ethel Kennedy pleading with photographers not to take photographs were shown. They were shown as the photograph of the little Vietnamese girl running naked after a napalm attack was shown..."

"...The picture went all around the world, and then disappeared, as if we willed it away. One of the most famous photographs in human history became an unmarked grave, and the man buried inside its frame—the Falling Man—became the Unknown Soldier in a war whose end we have not yet seen..."

Is it well written? What is the writing style? Is there a notable tone? Generally, is the writing effective, powerful, difficult, beautiful?

Extremely well written, it is obviously the work of an expert and gifted journalist. The voice is unsparing and unsentimental, but also poetic, ironic, and emotionally rich.

- "In the picture, he departs from this earth like an arrow. Although he has not chosen his fate, he appears to have, in his last instants of life, embraced it. If he were not falling, he might very well be flying. He appears relaxed, hurtling through the air. He appears comfortable in the grip of unimaginable motion..."

- "...There was no terror or confusion at the Associated Press. There was, instead, that feeling of history being manufactured; although the office was as crowded as he'd ever seen it, there was, instead, 'the wonderful calm that comes into play when people are really doing their jobs...'"

- "...From the beginning, the spectacle of doomed people jumping from the upper floors of the World Trade Center resisted redemption. They were called 'jumpers' or 'the jumpers,' as though they represented a new lemminglike class. The trial that hundreds endured in the building and then in the air became its own kind of trial for the thousands watching them from the ground..."

He's respectful of people who have a different view of the photo, but his bias toward journalistic freedom is inherent:

– "In most American newspapers, the photograph that Richard Drew took of the Falling Man ran once and never again. Papers all over the country, from the Fort Worth Star-Telegram to the Memphis Commercial Appeal to The Denver Post, were forced to defend themselves against charges that they exploited a man's death, stripped him of his dignity, invaded his privacy, turned tragedy into leering pornography. Most letters of complaint stated the obvious: that someone seeing the picture had to know who it was. Still, even as Drew's photograph became at once iconic and impermissible, its subject remained unnamed…"

– "…The resistance to the image—to the images—started early, started immediately, started on the ground. A mother whispering to her distraught child a consoling lie: 'Maybe they're just birds, honey…'"

– "…But now the Falling Man is falling through more than the blank blue sky. He is falling through the vast spaces of memory and picking up speed…"

If there is a distinct mood or tone, discuss that as well. Junod's voice is very distinct; reportorial but with a storyteller's sense, employing a poetic descriptive quality balanced with an unflinching, hard-nosed approach to the facts of the story.

Generally, does the author achieve his or her purpose? I would say definitely yes; he makes a strong case for reconsidering our attitude toward this photo and much of the photographic and film records of 9/11 that have been suppressed by the media in the name of sensitivity to the victims and survivors.

What are the strengths and weaknesses of the piece?

Strengths: Junod's voice, the structure of the article, the language and descriptive quality, the way Junod makes his case for a reassessment of the photo and what it means.

Weaknesses: As strong and beautifully written as the article is, there is one thing lacking in Junod's assessment: he doesn't explore enough of what may separate the experience of 9/11 from historical tragedies such as the Holocaust, or what it possibly has in common with the media coverage of the Vietnam War and the Kennedy assassinations. He doesn't take into account the immediacy of modern-day media, and the different experience the WTC attacks were, as events occurring in real time, before a live audience, covered on national and international television.

Do you agree with the author's arguments and conclusions? I'm undecided; I believe in a free media, and I believe in the importance of documenting history as it happens, but I do think there is a place for some discretion in what the public is shown when tragic events are being covered.

Was the ending/conclusion satisfying? Why or why not? In a storytelling and/or reporting sense, I would say yes. Again blending his journalistic style with his poetic descriptive powers and a sense of irony, he makes both the photograph and the man an effective metaphor for our response to an unfathomable tragedy and the need for remembrance.

What is your overall response to the book or article? Did you find it interesting, moving, dull? It's a really fine piece of work, even if I do have a major reservation. It is the kind of article that prompts the best kind of discussion and debate.

Ultimately, was the thesis supported by sufficient evidence? Largely, yes, I think he makes his case very effectively. Again, there is in my opinion a major point he fails to address, but the article is still very affecting, intelligent, and well supported.

Would you recommend this book or article? (To whom? Under what circumstances?) I would recommend this article to just about anyone—unless that person had too close of an experience of 9/11, and might be upset, as people were with the photograph and the sculpture by Eric Fischl.

STEP 4: Outline

Eleanor approaches this step by dividing it into two sub-steps. First, she examines the questions and organizes them into categories, ordering them in a way that she thinks will help her communicate her ideas to her reader in an organized and meaningful manner.

I. Main idea:
   A. What is thesis?
   B. What is conclusion?
   C. Slant or angle?
      Intended audience?

II. Description of Article
   A. Quality of writing
   B. Notable language use
   C. Is article successful?/
      Does author achieve
      purpose?

III. Article's strengths:
   A. Qualifications of writer
   B. Quality of evidence
   C. Quantity of evidence

IV. Article's weaknesses:
   A. Bias
   B. Quality of evidence
   C. Quantity of evidence

V. Recommendation

Then, she draws from the answers she provided on the assignment template to draft an outline specific to the article on which she is reporting.

I. Main idea:
There is something to be learned from all news photos, even disturbing ones.

   A. What is thesis?
   Censoring disturbing images from the 9/11 attacks actually is a disservice to victims and survivors, since it helps to erode the memory of the event and the victims.

   B. What is conclusion? We need to reevaluate our attitude toward images like the photo of the Falling Man, and Eric Fischl's sculpture of the falling woman.

   C. Slant or angle?
   Intended audience?
   Intended audience is both the general public and those who work in media, especially those who control what is covered, what is shown, and what is not.

II. Description of Article:
Nonfiction, with an editorial slant; meant to persuade.

   A. Quality of writing:
   Writing is expert, reportorial narrative with a storytelling feel.

1. Use of metaphor, irony, characterization.

2. Language is descriptive, frequently poetic, compelling.

B. Notable language use: Third-person narrative.

C. Is article successful? Does author achieve purpose Successful if a bit one-sided.

　1. Thesis is strong and well supported, but misses one key point.

　2. Author makes his point well, but it could be debated.

III. Article's strengths:

A. Qualifications of writer: Author is a veteran, well-recognized journalist.

　1. Winner of two National Magazine Awards.

　2. Has written for Esquire, Life, Sports Illustrated and GQ, among others.

B. Quality of evidence: Evidence is in-person interviews and research.

　1. Interviews of photographer,

families of victims, media executives

2. Author has examined historical records of the day, personal accounts, media coverage.

C. Quantity of evidence: Numerous examples of how media made decisions on what to show and what not to show regarding the event coverage.

IV. Article's weaknesses:

A. Bias: Author disregards argument against showing all images of the tragedy, and does not engage in any in-depth discussion of why 9/11 might be a different event from any other.

B. Quality of evidence: The author only uses facts and stories that support his point of view.

　1. What might separate 9/11 from other historical tragedies?

　2. What might the impact of its being a "real-time" tragedy, covered on television

worldwide as
it was actually
happening?

3. Weren't similar
decisions made
about coverage
of WWII and
Vietnam?

C. Quantity of evidence:
What is Junod not
reporting that might
contradict his point?

V. Recommendation:
Recommended because
of the skill and beauty of
the writing, the compelling
points it makes, and the
unique voice of the author,
as well as the intelligence
and persuasiveness of its
point. Also recommended,
as it is the level of
article that will inspire
debate on that point. Not
recommended for anyone
who had too painful or close
an experience of 9/11.

STEP 5: First Draft

Tom Junod's "The Falling Man" is plainly the work of a deeply talented and highly skilled journalist, tackling one of the key issues of our modern world: how and why we react the way we do to images and media coverage of the events of September 11, 2001. Citing Richard Drew's photograph of a man falling from the North Tower, Junod effectively illustrates the reaction to coverage of an event that felt completely unprecedented. A picture that would appear in the New York Times and newspapers all over the world the day after the tragedy, only to be immediately suppressed after criticism that it was exploitive and in poor taste, it represents something very opposite from media insensitivity to Junod, it represents the need to remember. Junod comes to this assessment with a calm, distanced and journalistic approach that is arguably only possible nearly a decade after the event. He also brings a storyteller's skill set, with poetic descriptive power, a compelling structure any screenwriter

This opening sentence is a bit plodding and not especially inspired, but Eleanor can rework it in the next draft. It does state the author's thesis competently, so it will do as a start.

This last sentence, while good, is a bit long, and would probably benefit from being broken down into two sentences in the next draft.

- 82 -

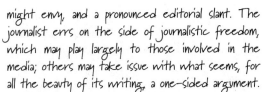

might envy, and a pronounced editorial slant. The journalist errs on the side of journalistic freedom, which may play largely to those involved in the media; others may take issue with what seems, for all the beauty of its writing, a one-sided argument.

Eleanor is tipping her hand a bit too early here; she should save her critical evaluation for the later part of the essay.

Junod's talent is evident from the first paragraph of the article, describing the photo itself and the emotions and thoughts it inspires. "In the picture, he departs from this earth like an arrow. Although he has not chosen his fate, he appears to have, in his last instants of life, embraced it. If he were not falling, he might very well be flying. He appears relaxed, hurtling through the air. He appears comfortable in the grip of unimaginable motion. He does not appear intimidated by gravity's divine suction or by what awaits him..." From this elegiac description of the photo, Junod delves into the background of the photographer, Richard Drew—who as a young man was present at the assassination of Robert Kennedy, an event he also photographed, while Ethel Kennedy pleaded that no pictures be taken. Working for the Associated Press, Drew was propelled not by a paparazzo's exploitive agenda but by a journalist's vocation to document history—an ethic Junod plainly shares and champions. When Drew returns to the AP office from Ground Zero with his photos, the office is neither in chaos or confusion, but filled with news professionals immersed in their work, "the wonderful calm that comes into play when people are really doing their jobs," as the photographer describes it. That calm would not be shared by the world outside, most especially when Drew's photograph of the falling man was published in the New York Times the next day, and around the world. That morning, newspapers all over the country found themselves on the defensive for having published the photograph, and it was never printed again. The emotional reaction seemed to

Eleanor is sticking to her outline, and it is serving her well here.

spill into a subliminal popular judgment of those who had jumped to escape the inferno; they were sometimes referred to as "jumpers," which seemed somehow to translate into "cowards." When a reporter tried to track down the identity of the man in the photograph, victim's families were nearly universal in rejecting the idea that their loved one might have been the falling man; he found himself forcefully ejected from the funeral of one victim when he tried to show the picture to the family, who were outraged at the very suggestion that the falling man might have been their relative.

Television networks also began to edit out film of the "jumpers," and anything else that might have been deemed too disturbing to show the general public: "...At CNN, the footage was shown live, before people working in the newsroom knew what was happening; then, after what Walter Isaacson, who was then chairman of the network's news bureau, calls 'agonized discussions' with the 'standards guy,' it was shown only if people in it were blurred and unidentifiable; then it was not shown at all..." This attitude toward the images of the falling bodies from the towers would linger for years, and even to the present day; Eric Fischl's sculpture Tumbling Woman, meant as a tribute to the jumping victims, was placed on display at Rockefeller Center for a mere week before it was removed amidst the same kind of outcry that had greeted Drew's photograph, even prompting a bomb threat. Junod makes an effective case for this being perhaps the wrong kind of sensitivity; if photographs of the worst horrors of the Holocaust could be made public soon after the liberation of the internment camps, why do we look away from the Falling Man? If we can look at the photos of Robert Kennedy dying, of the My Lai massacre, if we can bear witness to the history of all these

Eleanor needs to take care that she is reviewing the article here and not merely summarizing it.

horrific events, doesn't the Falling Man deserve a similar act of witness from us? It's a powerful and persuasive argument—but Junod fails to engage in any discussion of what separates the events of 9/11 from everything else we have experienced of history through the media.

Tom Junod has qualifications in abundance to make his argument persuasive; he is an award-winning journalist with two National Magazine Awards to his credit, and has worked not only for Esquire, but for Life, Sports Illustrated, Gentlemen's Quarterly, and several other noted publications. His writing is inspired and compelling, and he does his homework in the manner of a first-rate journalist, interviewing sources as divergent as Drew, Eric Fischl, Jerry Speyer (trustee of the Museum of Modern Art, who withdrew Fischl's sculpture from view), reporter Peter Cheney (who tried ceaselessly to identify the falling man), and family members of the victims. He creates a picture of the world after 9/11 that is poignant, ironic, and clear-eyed all at once. He lays out his case for a re-evaluation of the Falling Man photograph, Fischl's sculpture, and all the other horrific images of that day, and he makes his case strongly—but he hasn't totally convinced me.

Why do we treat September 11, 2001, differently from other horrific events of the last century? What separates it in our minds and emotions? Why can we look at photographs and films of Auschwitz and Bergen-Belsen, at the My Lai or Kent State photographs, or the Zapruder film, but the Falling Man is still somehow taboo? I believe this is the single question Junod fails to engage with, and it is the only weak link in his thesis. To my mind, what separates the memory of 9/11 is the fact that it was the first event of its magnitude to play out in real time, as it was happening, to a global audience that stopped dead in

> The essay is now back on track, taking an analytical approach to the article and not merely rehashing its content. Eleanor does need some of the summary to set this section up, but in the next draft, she can probably condense that section and get to reviewing the article sooner.

> This is a bit of a laundry list and should be edited down in the next draft.

Really fine analysis from Eleanor here. She can make it stronger with a little backup, possibly citing some other opinions from other media experts on the impact of 9/11 and what separates it in the public mind.

its tracks to watch, knowing people were dying and the world was changing. It became a shared media experience unlike any before it, without the distancing and buffering of any time lapse or editing.

"The Falling Man" is nevertheless an article to be read, discussed and analyzed seriously. Certainly anyone involved in media or journalism needs to read this and evaluate their attitude toward photographs such as Richard Drew's, and what its significance is. Those who had a more personal experience of September 11, those who lost loved ones or were in-person witnesses to the horror of that day, may feel Junod doesn't quite get it, doesn't understand what separates that day from all others. It's a debate that most likely will never be resolved, but Junod works hard nevertheless to give the falling man, and all the falling men and women, their due.

Eleanor wraps this up well, expressing both her admiration of the article and her reservation about it.

Analysis of First Draft

What is this writer's point? Eleanor is making the point that "The Falling Man," while an expertly written and, in many ways, a beautiful article, nevertheless misses a key point about the media coverage of 9/11 and what made that event different from all others.

What is this writer's angle? While admiring and appreciating the article and the author's thesis, she points out what may be a serious flaw in his argument.

What type or tone of voice has the writer created in her reader's mind? Eleanor shows a mature, reportorial tone, objectively evaluating the work while appreciating how well-researched, creatively written and compellingly presented the author's argument is. As was noted earlier, she does present herself as intelligent and informed, but her voice is often too grand, bordering on the pretentious.

What techniques has this writer used to create this voice? Eleanor keeps her voice cool, considered, and objective in a journalistic, reviewer's tone. She expresses admiration for the author's talent, while maintaining a critical distance from both the article and the larger subject matter.

What specific details, facts, etc., make this report a valid and valuable assessment of the book or article? Eleanor refers only to the factual elements within Junod's article; she would be well advised to strengthen her own thesis about the article and its flaws by backing her opinion up with some other expert opinion on the media coverage of the September 11 attacks.

NOW plan your own article review, following a process similar to the one Eleanor followed.

STEP 1: Select a Topic

Choose a book or article and jot down the following information:

Title:

Author:

Source Information (publication, publishing company, copyright date, etc.):

Genre:

STEP 2: Develop a Slant/Angle/Hook

You may find it helpful to use the same template Eleanor used. If there is additional information or insight you think would be important to share with your reader, by all means, include it here and in Step 3.

What is the general subject or topic of this piece?

What is the author's angle, theme, or thesis?

Who is the author? What are his or her qualifications to write on this subject?

STEP 3: Brainstorm, Discuss, Research

Is there an obvious slant or bias? What evidence from the text can you provide to support your claim?

Is it well written? What is the writing style? Is there a notable tone? Generally, is the writing effective, powerful, difficult, beautiful?

If there is a distinct mood or tone, discuss that as well.

Generally, does the author achieve his or her purpose?

What are the strengths and weaknesses of the piece?

Do you agree with the author's arguments and conclusions?

Was the ending/conclusion satisfying? Why or why not?

What is your overall response to the book or article? Did you find it interesting, moving, dull? Ultimately, was the thesis supported by sufficient evidence?

Would you recommend this book or article? (To whom? Under what circumstances?)

STEP 4: Outline

STEP 5: First Draft

STEP 6: Peer Edit

You and your partner might find it helpful to use the same questions Eleanor and her partner used:

What is this writer's point?

What is this writer's angle?

What type or tone of voice has the writer created in his or her reader's mind?

What techniques has this writer used to create this voice?

What specific details, facts, etc., make this report a valid and valuable assessment of the book or article?

Here are Eleanor's editor's comments and analysis as well as her responses:

- This opening sentence is a bit plodding and not especially inspired, but Eleanor can rework it in the next draft. It does state the author's thesis competently, so it will do as a start.

- This last sentence, while good, is a bit long, and would probably benefit from being broken down into two sentences in the next draft.

- Eleanor is tipping her hand a bit too early here; she should save her critical evaluation for the later part of the essay.

- Eleanor is sticking to her outline, and it is serving her well here.

- Eleanor needs to take care that she is reviewing the article here and not merely summarizing it.

- The essay is now back on track, taking an analytical approach to the article and not merely rehashing its content. Eleanor does need some of the summary to set this section up, but in the next draft, she can probably condense that section and get to reviewing the article sooner.

- This is a bit of a laundry list and should be edited down in the next draft.

- Really fine analysis from Eleanor here. She can make it stronger with a little backup, possibly citing some other opinions from other media experts on the impact of 9/11 and what separates it in the public mind.

- Eleanor wraps this up well, expressing both her admiration of the article and her reservation about it.

And here is Eleanor's reaction:

I figured I'd fix that opening sentence anyway. It was just a way to get the essay going.

That's an easy fix; I'll rework it into two sentences.

I'll take that part out; editor's probably right—I should save it for later in the essay, when I really address it.

Good to know, I'll definitely keep sticking to the outline.

Maybe I need to put some more editorial commentary into that section.

Again, an easy fix. Maybe I don't have to give all the names.

Okay, good. Maybe I can get away with just editing the stuff down, but I probably should still get more of my own slant on the article in.

I'll see what research I can find to back up my opinion here.

Looks like I made my point pretty well. Good!

Analysis of First Draft

What is this writer's point? Eleanor is making the point that "The Falling Man," while an expertly written and, in many ways, a beautiful article, nevertheless misses a key point about the media coverage of 9/11 and what made that event different from all others.

> Yes! My point is clear, and the editor understands it on the first try.

What is this writer's angle? While admiring and appreciating the article and the author's thesis, she points out what may be a serious flaw in his argument.

> Still clear on what I'm up to. All good news.

What type or tone of voice has the writer created in her reader's mind? Eleanor shows a mature, reportorial tone, objectively evaluating the work while appreciating how well-researched, creatively written and compellingly presented the author's argument is. As was noted earlier, she does present herself as intelligent and informed, but her voice is often too grand, bordering on the pretentious.

> I'm glad he gets that I do admire the article, it's really well written, and Tom Junod is the kind of journalist I'd like to be. I'm glad I could make my critical point while still stating how fine the work is. I don't think it's pretentious to use language that shows intelligence and a firm grasp of language.

What techniques has this writer used to create this voice? Eleanor keeps her voice cool, considered and objective in a journalistic, reviewer's tone. She expresses admiration for the author's talent, while maintaining a critical distance from both the article and the larger subject matter.

> All good news. The second draft on this should be fairly easy.

What specific details, facts, etc., make this report a valid and valuable assessment of the book or article? Eleanor refers only to the factual elements within Junod's article; she would be well advised to strengthen her own thesis about the article and its flaws by backing her opinion up with some other expert opinion on the media coverage of the September 11 attacks.

> Okay, time for some research. I'm on it.

Here is Eleanor's revised draft.

Why do we react to the portrayal of the events of September 11, 2001, as we do? Tom Junod's "The Falling Man" considers this question in the context of an image that was both immediately iconic and instantly reviled. Richard Drew's photograph of a man falling from the North Tower became a lightning rod for criticism of the media in the immediate wake of the tragedy, and Junod effectively portrays the reaction to coverage of an event that felt completely unprecedented. The photograph was published in the New York Times and newspapers all over the world the day after the attacks, only to be immediately suppressed after criticism that it was exploitive and in poor taste. It nevertheless represents something very opposite from media insensitivity to Junod; it represents the need to remember. Junod is a skilled storyteller, as well as a journalist, with poetic descriptive power, a compelling sense of structure any screenwriter might envy, and a pronounced editorial slant that he does not shrink from.

Junod's talent is evident from the first paragraph of the article, describing the photo itself and the emotions and thoughts it inspires: "In the picture, he departs from this earth like an arrow. Although he has not chosen his fate, he appears to have, in his last instants of life, embraced it. If he were not falling, he might very well be flying..." From this elegiac description of the photo, Junod delves into the background of the photographer, Richard Drew—

Note how Eleanor has reworked the previously overlong and plodding sentence into two sentences. Although the rhetorical question can be a clichéd and overused opening device, there are still times it can be used to challenge and involve the reader immediately.

This section benefits greatly from Eleanor's reworking of it; no longer are there any run-on sentences, and the paragraph builds much more effectively.

Eleanor has removed the sentence that tipped off her critical attitude toward the article, saving that for the section where she delves deeper on that issue. Good choice.

Eleanor has chosen to cut down the quotation, which was more than a bit long. Again, appropriate choice.

who as a young man was present at the assassination of Robert Kennedy, an event he also photographed, while Ethel Kennedy pleaded that no pictures be taken. Working for the Associated Press, Drew was propelled not by a paparazzo's exploitive agenda but by a journalist's vocation to document history— an ethic Junod plainly shares and champions. When Drew returns to the AP office from Ground Zero with his photos, the office is neither in chaos or confusion, but filled with news professionals immersed in their work, "the wonderful calm that comes into play when people are really doing their jobs," as the photographer describes it. There was no calm the following morning; newspapers all over the country found themselves on the defensive for having published the photograph, and it was never printed again. When a reporter tried to track down the identity of the man in the photograph, victims' families were nearly universal in rejecting the idea that their loved one might have been the falling man. He found himself forcefully ejected from the funeral of one victim when he tried to show the picture to the family, who were outraged at the very suggestion that their relative might have been one of the "jumpers."

Eleanor has effectively edited her summary of the article, giving the reader only the most necessary information to build her critique.

Television networks also began to edit out film of people falling from the towers, and anything else that might have been deemed too disturbing to show the general public: "...At CNN, the footage was shown live, before people working in the newsroom knew what was happening; then, after what Walter Isaacson, who was then chairman of the network's news bureau, calls "agonized discussions" with the "standards guy," it was shown only if people in it were blurred and unidentifiable; then it was not shown at all..." This attitude toward the images of the falling bodies from the towers would linger for years, and even to the present day; Eric Fischl's sculpture "Tumbling Woman," meant as a tribute to the jumping victims, was placed on display at Rockefeller Center for a mere week before it was removed amidst the same kind of outcry that had greeted Drew's photograph, even prompting a bomb threat. Junod makes an effective case for this being perhaps the wrong kind of sensitivity; if photographs of the worst horrors of the Holocaust could be made public soon after the liberation of the internment camps, why do we look away from the Falling Man? If we can look at the photos of Robert Kennedy dying, of the My Lai massacre, if we can bear witness to the history of all these horrific events, doesn't the Falling Man deserve a similar act of witness from us? It's a powerful and persuasive argument—but Junod fails to engage in any discussion of what separates the events of 9/11 from everything else we have experienced of history through the media.

Eleanor has left this section as it was, and with good reason; she builds to her central critique of the article very effectively here.

Tom Junod has qualifications in abundance to make his argument persuasive; he is an award-winning journalist with two National Magazine Awards to his credit, and has worked not only for Esquire, but for Life, Sports Illustrated, Gentlemen's Quarterly and several other noted publications. His writing is inspired and compelling, and he does his homework in the manner of a first rate journalist, interviewing diverse sources and giving plenty of anecdotal background. He creates a picture of the post 9/11 world that is poignant, ironic, and clear-eyed all at once. He lays out his case for a re-evaluation of the Falling Man photograph, Fischl's sculpture, and all the other horrific images of that day, and he makes his case strongly—but he hasn't totally convinced me.

Eliminating the laundry list of sources is a better choice here.

Why do we treat September 11, 2001, differently from other horrific events of the last century? What separates it in our minds and emotions? Why can we look at photographs and films of Auschwitz and Bergen-Belsen, at the My Lai photograph, or Kent State, or the Zapruder film, but the Falling Man is still somehow taboo? I believe this is the single question Junod fails to engage with, and it is the only weak link in his thesis. To my mind, what separates the memory of 9/11 is the fact that it was the first event of its magnitude to play out in real time, as it was happening, to a global audience that stopped dead in its tracks to watch, knowing people were dying and the world was changing. It became a shared media experience unlike any before it, without the distancing and buffering of any time lapse or editing. <u>Time Magazine</u> cites a survey that showed, in the months following the attacks, 4% of all Americans, and fully 11.2% of all New Yorkers, were suffering from post-traumatic stress disorder. <u>Science News</u> conducted a study, on the brink of the tenth anniversary of the event in which images of the attack, mixed with other images, were shown to individuals unconnected to the attacks—nevertheless, the images produced high levels of anxiety in the subjects. Plainly, the images from that day affect people in a unique and disturbing way, and Junod does little in the article to address that.

"The Falling Man" is nevertheless an article to be read, discussed, and analyzed seriously. Certainly, anyone involved in media or journalism needs to read this and evaluate their attitude toward photographs such as Richard Drew's, and what its significance is. Those who had a more personal experience of September 11, those who lost loved ones or were in-person witnesses to the horror of that day, may feel Junod doesn't quite get it, doesn't understand what separates that day from all others. It's a debate that most likely will never be resolved, but Junod works hard to give the falling man, and all the falling men and women, their due.

Eleanor's research seems a bit dropped in here; nevertheless, she manages to strengthen her analysis of the article.

Eleanor overall has done a fine job of polishing her work; she may want to rework the last section to integrate her supportive research from *Time* and *Science News* a bit more.

Analysis of Final Draft

Has the writer's new draft strengthened her point in the rewrite?

She has reworked several grammatical problems that were getting in the way, such as run-on sentences and awkward usage, and has done some judicious editing. The result is an overall stronger, more concise piece of writing.

Has the rewrite helped the writer to define her slant?

She has removed a sentence early on that tipped off the reader to her critical take on the article and reserved it for further down, where she delves into her point in more depth and detail. This is a good choice and strengthens the definition of her point of view.

How has the tone or voice been clarified, altered, or strengthened in the rewrite?

The tone was strong in the first draft, but has been clarified by her edits, grammatical fixes, and more restrained use of quotations.

What new details, facts, etc., have been included to make this a more potent assessment of the book or article?

She has included data from a *Time Magazine* survey on the public's reaction to images of the September 11 attack that support her thesis.

NOW write your final draft.

POSSIBLE STEP 8: Rewrite Opportunity

MINI-LESSON 1:

The Reading Check Essay: Summary

Sometimes your teacher will make a reading assignment and then ask you to write something simply to verify that you did, in fact, do the reading and got something out of what you read. These quick, informal writing opportunities do not need to be as tightly focused or strictly disciplined as other, more formal writing assignments, but they do need to communicate clearly to whomever is going to read them what you read and what you learned from it.

When **Chandra** began her first semester of her junior year, she was promoted to a more challenging English class. Her English teacher gave her the following form to make a record of the catch-up reading she wanted Chandra to do. It will serve as a workable template whenever you need to verify completion of an independent reading assignment.

Title: Is It a Crime for a Citizen of the United States to Vote?

Author: Susan B. Anthony

Source Information (publication, publishing company, copyright date, etc.): University of Missouri, Kansas City http://law2.umkc.edu/faculty/ projects/ftrials/anthony/anthonyaddress.html

Genre: nonfiction

What is the general subject or topic of this piece?

Susan B. Anthony, after being arrested for attempting to vote in the presidential election, lays out her argument for women's suffrage.

What is the author's approach to that topic?:

Anthony makes her case on several fronts: the government does not have the power to confer or deny rights to any of its citizens— those rights are intrinsic and inalienable; none of the documents of the founders, including the Preamble to the Constitution, specifies that only males are entitled to the rights it states; to tax women while denying them the vote amounts to taxation without representation.

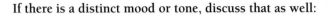

If there is a distinct mood or tone, discuss that as well:

While scholarly and legalistic in its approach, the tone of the piece is very political, employing impassioned oratory and rhetoric.

Does the author achieve his or her purpose?

Yes, Anthony achieves her purpose in laying out a clear, legalistically solid, constitutional argument for women's suffrage, while making an inspirational, politically charged speech.

How?:

Point by point, citing the Preamble, the Constitution, the very basis for the founding of the country itself, and then quoting sources from James Madison to Thaddeus Stevens, and the New York State Constitution, Anthony lays out her case very much as a lawyer would, but also brings her passion and sense of mission to the piece, personalizing it from the opening by telling how she herself had been arrested for attempting to vote.

Brief summary of reading:

Anthony begins by addressing her audience as "friends" and "fellow-citizens." She then lays out the thesis that she violated no law in appearing to vote in the previous presidential election. Anthony's line of reasoning is essentially that the Constitution grants all citizens of the United States the right to vote. As she is a citizen, she was merely exercising her constitutional right. As the federal Constitution protects this right, no individual state has the right to deny or restrict it.

One premise on which she bases her thesis is the observation that the Constitution does not grant rights but secures them. It is not within the power of a government to grant a right that is, according to the documents of the United States, inalienable. Submitting to a government

A summary or synopsis does not ordinarily invite direct quotations from the text, but in a case like this, Chandra wants to use Anthony's precise words because no other words can convey Anthony's meaning as succinctly as these.

Notice that Chandra is not trying to re-create the speech. Her goal is simply to tell her reader essentially what the speech says.

involves surrendering brutality and unjust means, not the abdication of one's God-given rights.

She quotes the Declaration of Independence to support her interpretation of the relationship between governments and rights. All men are created equal; they are endowed by their Creator with their inalienable rights; governments are instituted to secure those rights. She emphasizes that the quoted passage neither grants rights, nor excludes anyone from enjoying them. Anthony also points to the "consent of the governed," by which just governments govern. How, she asks, can the governed provide or withhold their consent if they are denied access to the ballot?

Similarly, Anthony relies on the stated rights of "life, liberty, and the pursuit of happiness." Denying one the right to vote, she asserts, cannot be considered a means toward securing these rights for the persons who are disenfranchised. In fact, to deny the right to vote would be to deny the citizen these inalienable rights. And governments, according to Anthony's interpretation of the Declaration of Independence, neither grant nor deny—they secure.

- - -

To further support the logic of her thesis—that women already enjoy the lawful right to vote and she, therefore, committed no crime in appearing to cast a ballot—Anthony cites that women constitute some half of the United States population. Denying this half of the population the right to vote denies them the ability to oppose unjust laws or to support just ones. It is taxation without representation. Contrary to the ideals of the Declaration of Independence, they are indeed governed without their consent.

Anthony then refers to the Constitution to support her argument.

. . .

Anthony also cites the Constitution of the State of New York, as this is the state in which she was arrested for appearing to vote and the state in which the convention at which she delivered this address was held. FACT CHECK. JUST MAKE SURE THAT HER ARREST WAS NEW YORK STATE. AND SPEECH WAS ALSO SENECA NEW YORK. The New York State Constitution, like the federal Constitution, begins with the phrase, "We the people..."; this same sentence recognizes the role of the Constitution to "secure [the] blessings [of] liberty." Again, the constituted government does not grant a liberty but secures it. She cites specific articles of the New York Constitution that address the issue of rights and equal rights, especially those that prohibit disenfranchising any citizen unless the prohibition from voting has been imposed by a jury.

. . .

She counters the argument that only masculine pronouns are used in the federal and various states' constitutions as proof that the rights protected by documents apply only to men by telling the story of a group of singing sisters who were required to pay taxes from their wages but were not afforded the right to vote like any other tax-paying citizen. It doesn't seem to bother Anthony that, by her own account, the oldest sister was "scarce eighteen," so she would not have been old enough to vote anyway.

This type of commentary is really not appropriate for summary. The summary is a report of what the reading says, not what you thought of it.

- - -

States are threatened with loss of representation in the House of Representatives if they do not extend to all citizens, who were previously denied rights—like the right to vote— yet states do not seem to include women among the ranks of disenfranchised citizens. She quotes the fourteenth amendment, which was written to establish the rights of immigrants and former slaves: "The citizen's right to vote shall not be denied by the United States, nor any state thereof; on account of race, color, or previous condition of servitude." Anthony presents the fact that the Amendment prohibits denying or abridging the right as proof that the right already exists. The Constitution and its Amendments do not grant these rights, they merely secure or protect them.

It is a little unclear here whether this is a summary of what Anthony said or commentary on Chandra's part.

- - -

Anthony closes her speech with a series of appeals: to the juries who might judge the cases of women like her who try to vote and are arrested, to the judges who hear those cases and might be in a position to "legislate from the bench" (those who criticize "activist judges" should note that this is not a new thing), and to women in general not to give up the fight, but to keep it a peaceable battle, a battle for equality under the law for all citizens.

Here is more, ultimately inappropriate commentary.

ASSIGNMENT 3:

Literary Analysis—Fiction

As we began to explore last year, the process of analysis is very different from other types of literary study. Analysis is not the process of figuring out what a text means—that's interpretation. Analysis is more the process of figuring out how and why a text works—or doesn't work. Think about the movie, play, album, or book critic. The reviewer does not offer only a summary of the main ideas and a declaration of what it's supposed to mean; the critic evaluates the work as successful or not and then explains to his or her audience what makes the piece successful (or *not*).

It involves examining organizational patterns, structures, word choice, and the other tools available to the writer. It is an examination of the writer's craft.

The development process of a literary analysis is, of course, essentially the same as the process for other academic writing.

Derek is in the same English class as Chandra, but he is a recent transfer from another state. He has found the transition to his new school difficult because in his old school, the students did all of their reading in class, and then they discussed what they read. Before he transferred, he'd written only one essay all year, a speculative essay on what life must have been like for the early European settlers of New England.

STEP 1: Select a Topic

Derek's class is reaching the conclusion of a long unit in which they studied three plays, largely from a feminist perspective: William Shakespeare's *Macbeth*, Henrik Ibsen's *A Doll's House*, and Tennessee Williams's *The Glass Menagerie*.

The teacher has said that she wants the students to "write something about the roles of women in these three plays."

STEP 2: Brainstorm, Discuss, Research

For "research," Derek may want to consult a few outside sources, but it is more important that he read the plays specifically to mine them for insight into how the female characters operate and what roles they play in the overall plots. Even if he presents ideas he learned in other research, he is going to have to provide evidence from the plays themselves for any point he wants to make.

He begins his research by asking himself a number of questions.

What women are there to write about?

Lady Macbeth, Lady Macduff, the Witches (?)

Nora

Amanda, Laura

What roles do these women play in their plays?

Lady Macbeth really plays only a supporting role. She is not the main character and really doesn't do any of the dirty work.

Lady Macduff does not add enough to the play to worry about, and I'm not sure we can even talk about the witches as women from a feminist perspective.

Nora is the main character, but when you think about it, really the trouble she gets into is because she wants to help her husband. She plays a supporting role.

Laura is quiet and dependent. She almost doesn't play a role, except to be weird.

Amanda is strong...but nasty. She's selfish, and kind of dependent like Laura. She drives out Tom because she is afraid Tom will leave, and she uses Jim as a tool to escape their lives.

What do all of these women have in common?

Lady M and Nora both play supporting roles and get in trouble trying to help their husbands.

Amanda and Laura aren't really supportive, but they're not really in charge of their situation. They give Tom and the missing father too much power.

They are all destroyed...L.M. commits suicide, Nora is banished (?)...Amanda and Laura are left kind of destitute and homeless.

> To be fair, most of these insights came out of classroom discussion. Still, if Derek understands them and can defend them with support from the plays, there is no reason he cannot use them in his essay. It is **important to note**, however, that Derek is inaccurate in his understanding of the conclusion of *A Doll's House*. Nora's leaving is a show of strength, not a punishment for her wrongdoing.

How do I put a feminist spin on these plays?

Playwrights are all men. Is this how they view women, or are they trying to show something?

"Patriarchal" society hates strong women? Only allows women to be shown as weak or outranked by men? If they exert any kind of power, they are destroyed?

> Derek is on the right track, but he does not have nearly enough material to support a thesis, especially given the fact that his understanding of one of the plays is flawed.

STEP 3: Draft a Thesis

Because of his previous school background, Derek has only an elementary understanding of what a thesis is. This will be a step he will have to keep revisiting—along with the previous step—in order to produce a passable essay.

Macbeth, A Doll's House, and The Glass Menagerie can all be regarded as feminist plays because the main characters are women who are weaker than men and are ultimately destroyed for their strength, proving that the patriarchal society of today hates strong women.

> This is a seriously flawed thesis. It is factually incorrect, wordy, and the sentence structure is awkward.

Women who try to help their men in a patriarchal society are destroyed.
　— Laura and Amanda do not try to help their men.

　— I should probably make sure it's clear that this is a literature essay and not something for social studies.

In some plays, women are depicted as inferior to men so that they play only supporting roles in the plot, and they are destroyed in the end for showing strength.

- Laura and Amanda still do not play supportive roles.

- They are dependent but not "supporting."

- Is Lady Macbeth destroyed because of her strength, or does her suicide prove she is really weak?

This is a good sign. Derek is re-evaluating some of his understanding of the plays.

- Laura and Amanda are completely dependent

- Neither can do anything to help their situation: business school, selling magazine subscriptions.

- Must have a man support them: Tom and Jim.

- Lady Macbeth cannot kill Duncan herself because he looked like her father(?) Freudian? Oedipal(?)

- Nora must have adult male signature, so she forges her father's.

Technically, by thinking of these ideas and noting them, Derek has returned to Step 2.

In some plays, women are depicted as inferior to men so that they...cannot support themselves or even take direct action to help themselves or their families.

In our patriarchal society, there is no room for the strong and independent woman who can support herself. And this is true of drama as well.

What a playwright makes happen to his characters often shows his society's view of things. In patriarchal societies, women must be inferior to men or they are punished.

- These are all famous plays by famous authors and very well-known characters.

- Are they the most famous female characters?

- Maybe the most interesting?

Some of drama's most famous female characters reflect either their time period's or their playwright's attitudes toward women.

> The problem with many of these is that they are not arguable; they are essentially statements of broad, general fact.

According to feminist literary theory, the way playwrights like Shakespeare, Ibsen, and Williams treat their female characters shows that society's attitudes towards women have not changed all that much since the sixteenth century.

> Derek is struggling with the idea of an arguable point that can be supported with evidence from the plays. Perhaps he needs to think more in terms of what the author has done in creating these characters than on what the characters mean or reflect.

STEP 2: Brainstorm, Discuss, Research Revisted

> Writing can be a cyclic and recursive process, so it is not necessarily a hardship for Derek to revisit an earlier step.

How would each play be different if it weren't for this female character?
 – Would Macbeth have killed Duncan if LM hadn't taunted him into it?

 – In the background of the play, Torvald would have died if Nora had not borrowed the money, but he would have been safe from blackmail, scandal, and from being ruined if Nora had not forged her father's signature.

 – If Laura weren't so weird and Amanda so clingy and desperate, Tom probably would not have left. Or he wouldn't have left so quickly without making sure they were taken care of. It's easy to see how they help to make his life unbearable, and they cause their own downfall.

Return to STEP 3: Draft a Thesis

The women in some plays might seem like the victims of a patriarchal society, but if you really analyze their role in the play, you can see how the playwright is using them as the main cause of the unhappy ending.

> This is very poorly worded, but a good, solid intent is there. Now Derek has something to argue.

STEP 4: Outline

Derek is uncertain how to structure this essay, so he decides to follow a traditional, academic outline format. This is always a safe choice if the topic, time allowance, or some other factor makes the planning and writing of the essay more challenging.

Thesis: The women in some plays might seem like the victims of a patriarchal society, but if you really analyze their role in the play, you can see how the playwright is using them as the main cause of the unhappy ending.

I. Lady Macbeth

    A. Immediately thinks of murder

    B. Mentions it to MB without his ever bringing up the subject

    C. Psychologically abuses Macbeth

        1. questions his manhood

        2. questions his love for her

    D. Berates him afterward

    E. He admits the best part of his life is over, and it is her fault.

II. Nora

    A. Nora's desire to spend vs. Torvald's dislike of debt

    B. She confesses that she borrowed money and has been lying about it.

        1. We're probably supposed to forgive her for her deceit because she did it for a "good cause"?

        2. Why did she borrow from someone like Krogstad?

    C. She lies

        1. about where she got the money

        2. criminally forging her father's signature

        3. even something as trivial as where the cookies came from

    D. Considers suicide rather than face the consequences of what she has done

    E. Torvald faces scandal and ruin through no fault of his own.

III. Amanda

At some point, Derek has decided that discussing Laura does not support his thesis. While a factor in Tom's "downfall," she does not really do anything to contribute to it.

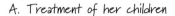

A. Treatment of her children

   1. Means of support

      (a) Laura's business school

      (b) the gentleman caller

      (c) Tom's job

      (d) reaction to Merchant Marine letter

   2. Nagging and annoying

      (a) stories about her past

      (b) instructions about how to eat

      (c) nag about movies and zoo (how they spend their time)

B. General attitude

   1. Bitter

   2. Frightened

   3. Resentful (Go back and find places where Tom reminds Amanda of his father/her husband...and she takes a lot of her anger toward her husband out on Tom.)

Although the "process" is usually presented as a sequence, it can be very recursive. There is nothing wrong with Derek's realizing at the outline phase that he needs to return to the reading and brainstorming phase.

STEP 5: First Draft

Although he has not yet located all of his support, and some of the sub-topics on his outline seem underdeveloped, Derek believes he is ready to write his first draft. Since he will take this essay through at least two drafts, it won't necessarily hurt anything for him to write that draft now.

In feminist literary theory, they like to read every work as if the female characters are victims of a man-dominated, patriarchal society in which they are oppressed and treated as inferior. Characters like Lady Macbeth, Nora Helmer (from Henrik Ibsen's A Doll's House), and Amanda from The Glass Menagerie are usually considered as women who have been forced into subordinate roles because, as women, they can have no power of their own. These feminists see these women as victims, destroyed in their attempts to exert their strength and act like men's equals. The women in these plays, however, might seem like the victims of a patriarchal society, but if you

There is nothing wrong with a "contrary-to-common-belief" argument, but this sentence is inaccurate and a little dismissive sounding; it also includes an incorrect pronoun reference.

Derek has made a few word changes in his thesis to fit the context of the introductory paragraph. Ultimately, this introductory paragraph does not work. It does state the thesis, and it does introduce the three characters to be discussed, but it does not point to how Derek is going to analyze the women's roles and support his thesis.

Second-person is never appropriate in purely academic writing. This phrasing also tends to make the tone of this paragraph too conversational.

Derek might be correct in supposing his reader is not familiar with the term "vehicle," but the wording and sentence structure of this explanation are awkward and intrusive. He needs to explore the use of subordinate clauses so as not to draw too much attention from his main ideas.

really analyze their roles in the play, you can see how the playwright is using them as the main cause of the unhappy ending.

Lady Macbeth is not the tragic hero, but she is the reason the play is a tragedy. As you know, a tragedy is a play that has a tragic hero, and a tragic hero is a character who experiences a rise and then a huge fall to destruction as a result of his tragic flaw. You could almost say that Lady Macbeth is Macbeth's tragic flaw because she encourages his rise to the top, but she also lays the groundwork for Macbeth's destruction and death. The literary name for what Lady Macbeth is, is "vehicle." A "vehicle" is the specific thing a writer uses to accomplish a specific need in his story. If the writer needs his characters isolated in a dark and lonely house that they can't get out of, he might write a heavy rainstorm, and the roads get flooded. Or he might make it winter, and there's a blizzard. William Shakespeare, the author of <u>Macbeth</u>, uses Lady Macbeth as the vehicle that introduces and encourages the murder of Duncan. Without this murder, there would be no need of a tragic downfall or Macbeth.

It is Lady Macbeth who immediately thinks of murdering Duncan when she gets Macbeth's letter in Act I scene 5. It is Lady Macbeth who suggests the murder to Macbeth. He does not suggest it to her. And it is Lady Macbeth who psychologically and emotionally abuses Macbeth so that he'll do the murder when he almost backs out of it. Then she berates him for feeling guilty, and she tells him he will go mad if he keeps thinking about it. Well, she doesn't think about it or express any guilt and she is the one who goes insane and kills herself. So she's no victim of a patriarchal society's oppression. She is in full control of the situation, and when the people decide to attack Scotland and kill Macbeth, it is because

- 108 -

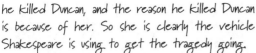

he killed Duncan, and the reason he killed Duncan is because of her. So she is clearly the vehicle Shakespeare is using to get the tragedy going.

Nora, in Henrik Ibsen's <u>A Doll's House</u>, is another example. All the feminists want to see her as a strong, independent woman who does what she does out of love and because she has no legitimate way to help her husband. Well, first of all, we know that she likes to spend money and is extravagant while he is thrifty and very afraid of debt. All the while he is talking about how worried he was that if he died and they were in debt, how would she repay it, she knows that they are in debt. So, she is keeping secrets from her husband and making him out to be a fool and a hypocrite. We're probably supposed to forgive Nora for her deceit because she did it for a "good cause," But Krogstad also did what he did for a good cause, and he's supposed to be the villain of the play. So, why should Nora be let off the hook? Not only did she borrow money without her husband's knowledge, she forged a dead man's signature in order to borrow it. She has opened the door to let scandal into the respectable and hardworking Torvald's home. She's a liar, even lying about something as trivial as where she got the cookies she's eating. And when she's caught and about to be exposed, she doesn't own up to her actions like a man, she considers killing herself. The end of the play, when Torvald is spared disgrace, is not because of her—it is because of her that he faced disgrace to begin with—it is because Krogstad gives in and gives them the papers. When she announces that she is leaving Torvald because <u>he</u> is not the man she thought he was, she again opens him up to scandal. The banker whose wife left him. She's not a heroine. She's selfish and evil. If she killed herself, he'd be the banker whose wife killed herself. Either way, he's stuck with a scandal.

This paragraph does address the topic, and it does follow the outline, but it has several fairly severe problems. For support, all Derek does is allude to the play. He needs to point out to the reader exactly where in the text the ideas he's claiming are present can be found. His sentence structure is also immature and makes the paragraph sound rushed. It reads almost like a rant more than it does an explanation of a valid viewpoint.

Derek needs to exercise much more control over his material and his tone. This paragraph reads like an excellent free write, but it is far too underdeveloped, unfocused, and rushed to satisfy as a strong draft of an essay.

At this point, Derek seems to be losing sight of his topic. This essay is not supposed to be an analysis or evaluation of the characters, but an analysis of their roles in their plays. It is clear that Derek disagrees with the predominant feminist readings of these plays, but he is not providing the necessary textual support in the balanced, academic language that his reader expects.

At this point, the reader must ask, "Example of what?" In the previous paragraph, the essay lost its focus. Derek needs to return to his thesis that these characters are dramatic vehicles to produce their plays' tragic ends.

This paragraph does not seem likely to restore this essay to its thesis.

Derek's assertions might be valid, but he must support them with evidence from the text. How else can he hope to clarify his thesis for the reader who doesn't understand or convince the reader who doesn't agree?

This specific reference is better than the vague generalities Derek has provided so far, but to fully drive his point home, he still needs to quote from the text.

Amanda in The Glass Menagerie is the final example. You might be tempted to say that Amanda is the victim of her husband's alcoholism and the fact that he abandoned her and her two children. But I say she probably drove him away the same way she drove away Tom. In all of her stories about her past, she says she had plenty of gentleman callers, so why did she choose a man who was not a wealthy Southern gentleman? She's either lying about her past, or she was a silly girl who then could not deal with the consequences of her foolish decision. In The Glass Menagerie, Amanda is not the victim, she is the victimizer. She is bitter, desperate, and she treats her children poorly. Rather than being human beings in their own rights, Tom and Laura are nothing to Amanda but means of support. The only reason Amanda sends Laura to business school and is so desperate for Tom to bring home a gentleman caller is so that she (Amanda) will be taken care of if Tom leaves. As for Tom, it's the same thing. She doesn't care whether he gets fired or not, she only cares that she and Laura are taken care of. That's exactly what she tells Tom when she says she knows he's going to join the Merchant Marine. She doesn't care at all about Tom's happiness, only her own well-being. She's also a nagging and annoying person. Her endless stories about her past are annoying. Tom and Laura even say so. Tom can't even eat his dinner without her nagging him how to chew. And whenever either of them leaves the apartment, all she can do is nag at them about where they've been and how they've spent their time.

Her general attitude is bitter. Her husband left her, and she's had a hard life. Well, why did she marry him in the first place? I think most of the time when she's nagging at Tom, she's really nagging at her husband, and Tom simply reminds her of him. That isn't fair to Tom who has his own dreams and desires. It's no wonder he left.

The women in these plays, then, are not what feminist critics make them out to be: victims of a patriarchal plot to keep them submissive. They are simply vehicles for the playwright to move along the plot and bring about the sad ending of the play. Most of these women suffer nothing but the consequences of their own actions.

Well, Derek does return to his thesis, but he has not provided any evidence or examples to show the validity of that thesis.

Analysis of First Draft

What is this writer's purpose? The writer says his purpose is to challenge the allegedly predominant feminist view that, in the male-dominated worlds of their plays, characters like Lady Macbeth, Nora Helmer, and Amanda Wingfield cannot exert power directly and must operate subtly or indirectly.

What is this writer's thesis? The thesis is that, rather than reflecting an oppressed womanhood, these characters are merely dramatic vehicles to motivate the plays' outcomes.

What key points has the writer identified to *clarify* his thesis? The writer defines "vehicle" to make it clear to his reader what he is talking about.

What key points has the writer identified to support his thesis?

The key points he has identified are:

- Lady Macbeth is essentially responsible for Macbeth's actions and, thus, his downfall.

- Nora acts without her husband's knowledge or consent, and whatever course of action she pursues at the end will result in scandal for him; thus, she is the cause of his downfall.

- Amanda's attitude and actions drive Tom away, and she is, therefore, the cause of his grief and her own downfall.

One key problem is that, after his unsupported discussion of Lady Macbeth, this writer loses sight of these points and of his thesis in general.

What verifiable facts does the writer provide to illustrate and support his key points? This is a severe problem. This writer makes many claims, and offers many assertions, but he does not provide a single verifiable fact (either direct quotation or close paraphrase).

NOW plan your literary analysis, following the same process by which Derek arrived at his first draft.

STEP 1: Select a Topic

STEP 2: Brainstorm, Discuss, Research

What specific details, facts, etc., will provide sufficient background, definitions, and evidence to support an argument?

What specific details, facts, etc., will help you achieve your purpose (i.e., inform, persuade)?

What specific details, facts, etc., will help you achieve a desired tone (i.e., academic, authoritative, humorous, etc.)?

STEP 3: Draft a Thesis

Make sure your thesis is arguable—neither simple fact nor pure opinion.

Make certain you have or know you can find sufficient evidence and examples to explain and support your key points.

STEP 4: Outline

STEP 5: First Draft

STEP 6: Peer Edit

What is this writer's purpose?

What is this writer's thesis?

What key points has the writer identified to *clarify* the thesis?

What key points has the writer identified to support the thesis?

What verifiable facts does the writer provide to illustrate and support the key points?

STEP 7: Revised/Final Draft

Here are Derek's editor's comments and analysis, as well as his responses:

- There is nothing wrong with a "contrary-to-common-belief" argument, but this sentence is inaccurate and a little dismissive sounding; it also includes an incorrect colon reference.

- Derek has made a few word changes in his thesis to fit the context of the introductory paragraph. Ultimately, this introductory paragraph does not work. It does state the thesis, and it does introduce the three characters to be discussed, but it does not point to how Derek is going to analyze the women's roles and support his thesis.

- Second-person is never appropriate in purely academic writing. This phrasing also tends to make the tone of this paragraph too conversational.

- Derek might be correct in supposing his reader is not familiar with the term "vehicle," but the wording and sentence structure of this explanation are awkward and intrusive. He needs to explore the use of subordinate clauses so as not to draw too much attention from his main ideas.

- This paragraph does address the topic, and it does follow the outline, but it has several fairly severe problems. For support, all Derek does is allude to the play. He needs to point out to the reader exactly where in the text the ideas he's claiming are present. His sentence structure is also immature and makes the paragraph sound rushed. It reads almost like a rant more than it does an explanation of a valid viewpoint.

- Derek needs to exercise much more control over his material and his tone. This paragraph reads like an excellent free write, but it is far too underdeveloped, unfocused, and rushed to satisfy as a strong draft of an essay.

- At this point, Derek seems to be losing sight of his topic. This essay is not supposed to be an analysis or evaluation of the characters, but an analysis of their roles in their plays. It is clear that Derek disagrees with the predominant feminist readings of these plays, but he is not providing the necessary textual support in the balanced, academic language that his reader expects.

- At this point, the reader must ask, "example of what?" In the previous paragraph, the essay lost its focus. Derek needs to return to his thesis that these characters are dramatic vehicles to produce their plays' tragic ends.

- This paragraph does not seem likely to restore this essay to its thesis.

- Derek's assertions might be valid, but he must support them with evidence from the text. How else can he hope to clarify his thesis for the reader who doesn't understand or convince the reader who doesn't agree?

- This specific reference is better than the vague generalities Derek has provided so far, but to fully drive his point home, he still needs to quote the text.

- Well, Derek does return to his thesis, but he has not provided any evidence or examples to show the validity of that thesis.

And here are Derek's responses:

> I can mention that Lady Macbeth causes Macbeth's downfall. Nora causes Torvald's scandal, and Amanda is responsible for her own downfall.
>
> Cut out all second-person.
>
> Here's how I can fix those sentences:
>
> Basically, more than a character in her own right, Shakespeare uses Lady Macbeth as a "vehicle" to bring about Macbeth's tragic down-fall. A vehicle is when the author creates a situation or character only because he needs some way to make something happen.
>
> Basically, more than a character in her own right, Shakespeare uses Lady Macbeth as the "vehicle" to bring about the tragic hero's downfall. Vehicles like this are often used by the writer to make important parts of the plot happen.
>
> Basically, not really a character in her own right, Lady Macbeth is the "vehicle" Shakespeare uses to bring about the tragic hero, Macbeth's, downfall. Such vehicles are necessary when the author needs some way to make important plot developments happen.
>
> Direct quotations? Okay, I can do direct quotations.
>
> I'll make sure I develop my points okay. I'll repeat the statements from the introduction to keep my body paragraphs focused.
>
> Evidence from the text. I will give evidence from the text.

Analysis of First Draft

What is this writer's purpose? The writer says his purpose is to challenge the allegedly predominant feminist view that, in the male-dominated worlds of their plays, characters like Lady Macbeth, Nora Helmer, and Amanda Wingfield cannot exert power directly and must operate subtly or indirectly.

What is this writer's thesis? The thesis is that, rather than reflecting an oppressed womanhood, these characters are merely dramatic vehicles to motivate the plays' outcomes.

What key points has the writer identified to *clarify* his thesis? The writer defines "vehicle" to make it clear to his reader what he is talking about.

What key points has the writer identified to support his thesis?

The key points he has identified are:

- Lady Macbeth is essentially responsible for Macbeth's actions and, thus, his downfall.

- Nora acts without her husband's knowledge or consent, and whatever course of action she pursues at the end will result in scandal for him; thus, she is the cause of his downfall.

- Amanda's attitude and actions drive Tom away, and she is, therefore, the cause of his grief and her own downfall.

One key problem is that, after his unsupported discussion of Lady Macbeth, this writer loses sight of these points and of his thesis in general.

> I'll make sure I mention these key points in my body paragraphs and then quote from the plays to support them.

What verifiable facts does the writer provide to illustrate and support his key points? This is a severe problem. This writer makes many claims, and offers many assertions, but he does not provide a single verifiable fact (either direct quotation or close paraphrase).

> That's the direct quotations again.

Here is Derek's second draft:

In feminist literary theory, female characters are usually seen as victims of a male-dominated, patriarchal society in which they are oppressed and treated as inferior. Characters like Lady Macbeth, Nora Helmer (from Henrik Ibsen's A Doll's House), and Amanda from The Glass Menagerie are usually considered as women who have been forced into subordinate roles because, as women, they can have no power of their own. These feminists see these women as victims, destroyed in their attempts to exert their strength and act like men's equals. The women in these plays, however, might seem like the victims of a patriarchal society, but if you really analyze their roles in the play, you can see how the playwright is using them as the main cause of the

Derek still has not removed the "you" he claimed he would.

unhappy ending. Lady Macbeth is essentially responsible for Macbeth's actions and, thus, his downfall. Nora acts without her husband's knowledge or consent, and whatever course of action she pursues at the end will result in scandal for him; thus, she is the cause of his downfall. Amanda's attitude and actions drive Tom away, and she is therefore the cause of his grief and her own downfall.

Lady Macbeth is the reason The Tragedy of Macbeth is a tragedy. A tragedy is a play that has a tragic hero, and a tragic hero is a character who experiences a rise and then a huge fall to destruction as a result of his tragic flaw. You could almost say that Lady Macbeth is Macbeth's tragic flaw because she encourages his rise to the top, but she also lays the groundwork for Macbeth's destruction and death. Lady Macbeth is basically not really a character in her own right; Lady Macbeth is the "vehicle" Shakespeare uses to bring about the tragic hero, Macbeth's, downfall. Such vehicles are necessary when the author needs some way to make important plot developments happen. She introduces the idea and encourages the murder of Duncan. Without this murder, there would be no need of a tragic downfall for Macbeth.

It is Lady Macbeth who immediately thinks of murdering Duncan when she gets Macbeth's letter in Act I, scene 5. When she says, "Yet do I fear thy nature; It is too full o' the milk of human kindness to catch the nearest way," that "nearest way" is killing Duncan, and she says that it would go against Macbeth's nature to do that. The entire rest of the scene is Lady Macbeth's going on about how she needs to be prepared to convince him that this is what they have to do:

...Hie thee hither, That I may pour my spirits in thine ear; And chastise with the valour of my tongue

Technically, Derek does what his peer editor has suggested by stating his sub-points, but it is a clumsy fix.

Again, Derek performs a technical fix. He cuts out the second-person, but this is still a repetitious, intrusive sentence defining tragedy and tragic hero.

This is good. Derek is finally not only making an assertion and then tossing in a quotation, he is now *discussing* his point and *showing* his reader how the text supports that point.

She says this only seconds after learning that Macbeth is destined to be king. Her first thought is that Duncan must be murdered, and she knows that Macbeth will not want to do it. She will have to convince him.

It is Lady Macbeth, therefore, who suggests the murder to Macbeth. He does not suggest it to her. They have this conversation when he arrives home:

MACBETH—Duncan comes here to-night.

LADY MACBETH—And when goes hence?

MACBETH—To-morrow, as he purposes.

LADY MACBETH—O, never shall sun that morrow see!

He innocently assumes Duncan is going to spend the night and then leave, which is his plan. But she assumes that, by the next day, Duncan will not be alive to leave as he plans.

It is Lady Macbeth who psychologically and emotionally abuses Macbeth so that he'll do the murder when he almost backs out of it. He says he won't do it, and she tells him, ""Wouldst thou have that Which thou esteem'st the ornament of life, And live a coward in thine own esteem, Letting 'I dare not' wait upon 'I would.'" He says he won't do it because it's wrong. She says he's afraid and will live his whole life not having what he wants because he's afraid to reach out and grab it.

His sentence structure still feels rushed, and his tone is too casual, but Derek's case is much stronger by his providing specific, textual evidence.

Then, she berates him for feeling guilty, and she tells him he will go mad if he keeps thinking about it. Well, she doesn't think about it or express any guilt, and she is the one who goes insane and kills herself. So she's no victim of a patriarchal society's oppression. She is in full control of the situation, and when the people decide to attack Scotland and kill Macbeth, it is because he killed Duncan, and the reason he killed Duncan is because of her. So, she is clearly the vehicle Shakespeare is using to get the tragedy going.

Nora, in Henrik Ibsen's <u>A Doll's House</u> is another example of a character who is a vehicle for the plot more than an actual character. Feminist critics want to see her as a strong, independent woman who does what she does out of love and because she has no legitimate way to help her husband. The first thing we learn about her and Torvald is that she likes to spend money, while he is thrifty and very afraid of debt.

Our first introduction to her is her coming in from Christmas shopping and over-tipping the porter who has helped her carry her packages:

> Nora. (To the Porter, taking out her purse.) How much?
>
> Porter. Sixpence.
>
> Nora. There is a shilling. No, keep the change.

Then, she defends her spending to Torvald:

> Nora. Come in here, Torvald, and see what I have bought.
>
> Helmer. Bought, did you say? All these things? Has my little spendthrift been wasting money again?
>
> Nora. Yes but, Torvald, this year we really can let ourselves go a little. This is the first Christmas that we have not needed to economise.
>
> Helmer. Still, you know, we can't spend money recklessly.
>
> Nora. Yes, Torvald, we may be a wee bit more reckless now, mayn't we? Just a tiny wee bit! You are going to have a big salary and earn lots and lots of money.
>
> Helmer. Yes, after the New Year; but then it will be a whole quarter before the salary is due.
>
> Nora. Pooh! we can borrow until then.

Sentence structure and the resultant voice are still problems.

You may disagree with Derek's point, but he does state it a lot more clearly in this draft.

- 119 -

Derek might be getting a little carried away with his quotations. A close paraphrase or direct reference and summary would also serve as textual support.

And he explains why he is afraid of going into debt:

> Helmer. Suppose, now, that I borrowed fifty pounds today, and you spent it all in the Christmas week, and then on New Year's Eve a slate fell on my head and killed me...No debt, no borrowing. There can be no freedom or beauty about a home life that depends on borrowing and debt.

There is nothing wrong with what Torvald is saying here. He is not being cruel to Nora. He is not depriving her of necessities or even of some luxuries like the Christmas tree and the presents.

All during this conversation, she knows that they are, actually, in debt. So, she is keeping secrets from her husband and making him out to be a fool and a hypocrite. We're probably supposed to forgive Nora for her deceit because she did it for a "good cause," but Krogstad also did what he did for a good cause, and he's supposed to be the villain of the play. So, why should Nora be let off the hook? Not only did she borrow money without her husband's knowledge, she forged a dead man's signature in order to borrow it. She has opened the door to let scandal into the respectable and hardworking Torvalds home. She's a liar, even lying about something as trivial as where she got the cookies she's eating. And when she's caught and about to be exposed, she doesn't own up to her actions like a man; she considers killing herself. This is how she is the cause of her husband's downfall, not a character who changes or grows, but the vehicle to create an unhappy ending. Nora acts without her husband's knowledge or consent, and whatever course of action she pursues at the end, whether it be suicide or leaving him, will result in scandal for him; thus, she is the cause of his downfall.

The end of the play, when Torvald is spared disgrace, is not because of her—it is because of her that he faced disgrace to begin with—it is

This paragraph is still largely a digression from Derek's point about Nora's role in the play.

Derek remembered he had said that he would restate his key points, but this is not enough to bring his essay back on track.

because Krogstad gives in and gives them the papers. When she announces that she is leaving Torvald because he is not the man she thought he was, she again opens him up to scandal. He will be the banker whose wife left him. If she killed herself, he'd be the banker whose wife killed herself. Whatever she does, he's stuck with a scandal. It's pretty apparent that Ibsen is using Nora, not as a character who inspires us with her growth or downfall, but merely as the vehicle by which the honest man of integrity is brought to ruin.

Amanda in The Glass Menagerie is also a character who is more vehicle of destruction than full character. Feminist critics say that Amanda is the victim of her husband's alcoholism and the fact that he abandoned her and her two children. But I say that, looking at how she treats her children, especially Tom, in the play, she probably drove him away the same way she drives Tom away. In all of her stories about her past, she says she had plenty of gentleman callers, so why did she choose a man who was not a wealthy Southern gentleman? She's either lying about her past, or she was a silly girl who then could not deal with the consequences of her foolish decision.

Amanda's attitude and actions drive Tom away, and she is therefore the cause of his grief and her own downfall. Amanda is bitter, desperate, and she treats her children poorly. Rather than being human beings in their own rights, Tom and Laura are nothing to Amanda but means of support. The only reason Amanda sends Laura to business school and is so desperate for Tom to bring home a gentleman caller is so that she (Amanda) will be taken care of if Tom leaves. In Scene Two, after she learns that Laura has dropped out of business school, Amanda says, "I've seen such pitiful cases in the South—barely tolerated spinsters living upon the grudging patronage of a sister's

These last few sentences do help. The reader has not lost track of Derek's thesis. Sentence structure and word choice, however, still severely deprive Derek's unconventional thesis much of its power.

"Vehicle of destruction" might be an overstatement, but this sentence serves its purpose much better than the one in Derek's first draft does.

The reference is fine. It is easily verifiable that Amanda tells many stories about her past, and she does indeed boast of the number of gentleman callers she had. Still, Derek is not supporting a valid argument by speculating why the father left. His use of rhetorical questions is not effective either. He relies too heavily on his readers to make his argument for him.

Likewise, this sentence adds nothing to his argument. Speculating on her character rather than analyzing her role does not address his thesis.

As in his previous discussions, Derek repeats a sentence given to him by his peer editor. It does remind the reader of Derek's thesis, but it seems out of context in this appraisal of Amanda's character.

husband or a brother's wife!—stuck away in some little mousetrap of a room—encouraged by one in-law to visit another—little birdlike women without any nest—eating the crust of humility all their life! Is that the future that we've mapped out for ourselves?"

As for Tom, it's the same thing. She doesn't care whether he gets fired or not; she only cares that she and Laura are taken care of. That's exactly what she tells Tom when she says she knows he's going to join the Merchant Marine. In Scene Four, during one of their few sincere conversations, Amanda tells him, "I saw that letter you got from the Merchant Marine. I know what you're dreaming of. I'm not standing here blindfolded....Very well, then. Then do it! But not till there's somebody to take your place." On the surface, it might seem as if she understands Tom, but ultimately, she doesn't care at all about his happiness, only her own well-being. He can pursue his dream after she and Laura are taken care of. Amanda is also a nagging and annoying person. Her endless stories about her past are annoying. In Scene One, Tom and Laura even say so:

> Tom: I know what's coming.
>
> Laura: Yes. But let her tell it.
>
> Tom: Again?
>
> Laura: She loves to tell it.

Tom can't even eat his dinner without Amanda nagging him about how to chew: "Honey, don't push with your fingers. If you have to push with something, the thing to push with is a crust of bread. And chew — chew!"

And whenever either of them leaves the apartment, all she can do is nag at them about where they've been and how they've spent their time. It is, in fact, an argument about Tom going

---

While it is a good thing that Derek is providing specific textual support, he seems to be falling into a structure of introducing a point and then providing a quotation without then discussing how that quotation supports the point he has brought up.

out and where he's going that finally drives him away. After Jim leaves, Tom says he is going to the movies. He and Amanda fight, and she yells at him, "Go to the moon—you selfish dreamer." Tom replies that he went "much farther [than the moon]." He is now haunted by what may have happened to Laura, whom he did love, after he left. The unhappy ending, the point of the play, is his grief. Amanda, rather than serving as a fully developed character, is the vehicle by which Tom is driven to leave his sister, and his life is reduced to a guilty, grief-filled existence.

Regardless of how feminist critics view these women, it is clear that the playwrights did not intend for them to represent female oppression. All of these women do wrong and cause the destruction of the important men in their lives. The women in these plays, then, are not what feminist critics make them out to be: victims of a patriarchal plot to keep them submissive. They are simply vehicles for the playwright to move along the plot and bring about the sad ending of the play. Most of these women suffer nothing but the consequences of their own actions.

> This discussion is more successful than in the first draft, but the concluding sentence is, perhaps, a little heavy-handed.

Analysis of Revised (Second) Draft:

What is this writer's purpose? The writer's purpose is to challenge the predominant feminist view that, in the male-dominated worlds of their plays, characters like Lady Macbeth, Nora Helmer, and Amanda Wingfield cannot exert power directly and must operate subtly or indirectly. He contends that the women are merely narrative vehicles used to bring about the unhappy conclusions of the plays.

What is this writer's thesis? The women in these plays are not characters in their own right. Each woman is merely a vehicle to bring about the downfall of the male character in the play.

What key points has the writer identified to *clarify* the thesis?

The most important point of clarification is the information this writer provides on the narrative vehicle and how it functions.

What key points has the writer identified to support the thesis?

- Lady Macbeth is essentially responsible for Macbeth's actions and, thus, his downfall.

- Nora acts without her husband's knowledge or consent, and whatever course of action she pursues at the end will result in scandal for him; thus, she is the cause of his downfall.

- Amanda's attitude and actions drive Tom away, and she is, therefore, the cause of his grief and her own downfall.

What verifiable facts does the writer provide to illustrate and support his key points? In this draft, the writer provides many more direct quotations, especially from *Macbeth* and *A Doll's House*.

POSSIBLE STEP 8: Rewrite Opportunity

Derek's second draft was quite a bit better than his first draft, but his word choice and sentence structure still create a voice that is too casual and at times almost enraged. His essay would, therefore, profit from a second revision.

Look at the notes that accompany Derek's essay, as well as his editor's analysis. Then, consider how the following third draft addresses the scorers' comments and improves the overall quality of Derek's essay:

Here are the comments and analysis of the revised draft as well as Derek's responses:

- Derek has still not removed the "you" he claimed he would.

- Technically, Derek does what his peer editor has suggested by stating his sub-points, but it is a clumsy fix.

- Again, Derek performs a technical fix. He cuts out the second-person, but this is still an intrusive sentence defining tragedy and tragic hero.

- This is good. Derek is finally not only making an assertion and then tossing in a quotation, he is now *discussing* his point and *showing* his reader how the text supports that point.

- His sentence structure still feels rushed, and his tone is too casual, but Derek's case is much stronger by his providing specific, textual evidence.

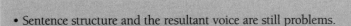

- Sentence structure and the resultant voice are still problems.

- You may disagree with Derek's point, but he does state it a lot more clearly in this draft.

- Derek might be getting a little carried away with his quotations. A close paraphrase or direct reference and summary would also serve as textual support.

- This paragraph is still largely a digression from Derek's point about Nora's role in the play.

- Derek remembered he had said that he would restate his key points, but this is not enough to bring his essay back on track.

- These last few sentences do help. The reader has not lost track of Derek's thesis. Sentence structure and word choice, however, still severely deprive Derek's unconventional thesis much of its power.

- "Vehicle of destruction" might be an overstatement, but this sentence serves its purpose much better than the one in Derek's first draft does.

- The reference is fine. It is easily verifiable that Amanda tells many stories about her past, and she does indeed boast of the number of gentleman callers she had. Still, Derek is not supporting a valid argument by speculating why the father left. His use of rhetorical questions is not effective either. He relies too heavily on his readers to make his argument for him.

- Likewise, this sentence adds nothing to his argument. Speculating on her character rather than analyzing her role does not address his thesis.

- As in his previous discussions, Derek repeats a sentence given to him by his peer editor. It does remind the reader of Derek's thesis, but it seems out of context in this appraisal of Amanda's character.

- While it is a good thing that Derek is providing specific textual support, he seems to be falling into a structure of introducing a point and then providing a quotation without then discussing how that quotation supports the point he has brought up.

- This discussion is more successful than in the first draft, but the concluding sentence is, perhaps, a little heavy-handed.

Here is Derek's third (and final) draft:

In feminist literary theory, female characters are usually seen as victims of a male-dominated, patriarchal society in which women are oppressed and treated as inferior. Characters like Shakespeare's Lady Macbeth, Henrik Ibsen's Nora Helmer, and Tennessee Williams's Amanda Wingfield are usually considered to be women who have been forced into subordinate roles because, as women, they can have no power of their own. Feminist critics see these women as victims, destroyed in their attempts to exert their strength and act like men's equals. A close examination of the roles these characters play in their plays reveals how the playwright is using them as the main cause of the play's unhappy ending. Lady Macbeth plans a scheme Macbeth would never have done without her. Since his downfall is the consequence of this scheme, she is the cause of his downfall. Before A Doll's House begins, Nora acted without her husband's knowledge, making both of them vulnerable to scandal. By the end of the play, whatever course of action she decides to pursue will result in scandal for him. Tom does not leave Amanda and Laura as much as Amanda drives him away, thus causing his grief and her own downfall.

Lady Macbeth is the reason The Tragedy of Macbeth is a tragedy. The key to tragedy is the fact that the hero somehow brings about his own fall through his tragic flaw. It is fair to say that Lady Macbeth is Macbeth's tragic flaw. She encourages his rise to the top, but she also lays the foundation for his destruction. Lady Macbeth is not really a character in her own right, but the "vehicle" Shakespeare uses to bring about the tragic hero's downfall. Such vehicles are necessary when the author needs some way to make important plot developments happen. Lady

This is a much more academic and less hostile-sounding reference than the previous draft's "these feminists."

Another good fix that eliminates the second-person.

Derek is not toying with content that has been working, but he is working hard to tighten up his sentence structure and word choice.

Macbeth introduces the idea and encourages the murder of Duncan. It is this murder that leads directly to Macbeth's downfall.

It is Lady Macbeth who first thinks of murdering Duncan when she gets Macbeth's letter in Act I, scene 5. When she says, "Yet do I fear thy nature; It is too full o' the milk of human kindness to catch the nearest way," that "nearest way" is killing Duncan, and she says that it would go against Macbeth's nature to do that. The entire scene focuses on Lady Macbeth's acknowledgment that she needs to be prepared to convince him that this is what they have to do:

> ...Hie thee hither, That I may pour my spirits in thine ear; And chastise with the valour of my tongue

Another good fix. Derek has taken the editor's comments seriously about his tone.

She says this only seconds after learning that Macbeth is destined to be king. Her <u>first thought</u> is that Duncan must be murdered, and she knows that Macbeth will not want to do it. She will have to convince him.

It is Lady Macbeth, therefore, who suggests the murder to Macbeth. He does not suggest it to her. They have this conversation when he arrives home:

> MACBETH—Duncan comes here to-night.
>
> LADY MACBETH—And when goes hence?
>
> MACBETH—To-morrow, as he purposes.
>
> LADY MACBETH—O, never shall sun that morrow see!

He innocently assumes Duncan is going to spend the night and then leave, which is his plan. But she assumes that, by the next day, Duncan will not be alive to leave as he plans.

It is Lady Macbeth who psychologically and emotionally abuses Macbeth so that he'll do the murder when he almost backs out of it. He says he won't do it, and she asks him, "Wouldst thou have that Which thou esteem'st the ornament of life, And <u>live a coward</u> in thine own esteem, Letting <u>'I dare not'</u> wait upon 'I would?'" He insists that he is no murderer, that he is brave enough to do what a man must do, but murder is beyond a man's obligation. However, she retorts that he's afraid. He will live his whole life not having what he wants because he's afraid to reach out and grab it.

Simply eliminating some of the conjunctions slows the pace of these sentences.

Then, she berates him for feeling guilty, and she tells him he will go mad if he keeps thinking about it. Ironically, she is the one who does not express any guilt, and she is the one who goes insane and kills herself. So, she's no victim of a patriarchal society's oppression. She is in full control of the situation. The only limitation she blames on being a woman is the fact that she cannot kill Duncan herself. When Malcolm raises an army in England, and they attack Scotland, Macduff kills Macbeth because he killed Duncan, and the reason he killed Duncan is because of his wife. She is clearly the vehicle Shakespeare uses to initiate the tragic plot.

This is not completely accurate, and needs textual support, but it is well stated. Derek has done an admirable job toning down the fervor of his previous drafts.

Much better than his previous "When they attack Scotland."

Again, Derek's statement is not 100% factually accurate, but he has managed to maintain an even and academic tone.

Much better word choice.

Nora, in Henrik Ibsen's <u>A Doll's House</u> is another example of a character who is a vehicle for the plot more than an actual character. Feminist critics like to read her as a strong, independent woman who does what she does out of love and because she has no legitimate way to help her husband. Unfortunately, her situation and actions are not so cut and dried. The first thing we learn about Nora and Torvald is that she likes to spend money, while he is thrifty and afraid of debt.

Derek adds a nice statement of insight, but he slips back into conversational or colloquial word choice.

The audience's first introduction to Nora is the opening of the play as she enters from Christmas shopping. Her first action in the play is to overtip the porter who has helped her carry her packages:

It is always a good choice to avoid first-person, as well as second-person.

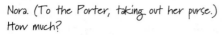

Nora. (To the Porter, taking out her purse.) How much?

Porter. Sixpence.

Nora. There is a shilling. No, keep the change.

He jokes about her spending, but you can tell there's an element of truth when he calls her his "little spendthrift," and accuses her of "wasting money again."

Her defense of her spending and his response both show how different their approaches to money are. Still, the fact remains that Torvald is the sole "bread-winner" of the family, it is his responsibility to make certain that everyone in the family has the necessities, and he wants more than anything to avoid debt:

Nora. Yes but, Torvald, this year we really can let ourselves go a little. This is the first Christmas that we have not needed to economise.

Helmer. Still, you know, we can't spend money recklessly.

Nora. Yes, Torvald, we may be a wee bit more reckless now, mayn't we? Just a tiny wee bit! You are going to have a big salary and earn lots and lots of money.

Helmer. Yes, after the New Year; but then it will be a whole quarter before the salary is due.

Nora. Pooh! we can borrow until then.

In response, Torvald explains why he is afraid of going into debt:

Helmer. Suppose, now, that I borrowed fifty pounds today, and you spent it all in the Christmas week, and then on New Year's Eve a slate fell on my head and killed me...No debt, no borrowing. There can be no freedom or beauty about a home life that depends on borrowing and debt.

This is still a problematic section for Derek. He is perilously close to losing his point about Nora's wastefulness in blow-by-blow plot summary and illustrative quotation.

There is nothing wrong with what Torvald is saying here. He is not being cruel to Nora. He is not depriving her of necessities or even of some luxuries like the Christmas tree and the presents.

The point is that, all during this conversation, Nora knows that they really are in debt. She is not only keeping secrets from her husband, but turning him into a fool and a hypocrite. While feminist critics argue that Nora is the sympathetic character here because, as a woman, she had no other means to help her husband than to borrow money without his knowledge, the fact remains that she is deceitful. And it is this trait that will bring about her own and her innocent husband's downfall. Another illustration of Nora's deceitfulness, to establish for the audience that this is a character trait and not unique to the money issue, is the business with the macaroons. Throughout the first act, Nora is eating macaroons from a bag that she hides in her pocket. The way she wipes her mouth just as Torvald enters for the first time establishes that she is hiding the cookies from him. Later in the act, when she offers Dr. Rank one of her macaroons, he comments that he thought Torvald had banned the cookies from his house. She lies and tells the doctor, "these are some Christine gave me." When Mrs. Linde protests that she did not bring the cookies, Nora interrupts her and complicates her lie: "Don't be alarmed! You couldn't know that Torvald had forbidden them."

Feminist critics point to Torvald's banning the cookies as evidence of his condescending and authoritarian attitude toward his wife. They also dismiss his reason as condescending as well, that the sugar in the cookies will ruin Nora's teeth. What is more important, however, is Nora's deception in disobeying her husband, but disobeying only in secret and lying when she seems to be

Derek might be successfully bringing this portion around to its point.

caught. There is something unethical about Nora's bringing Mrs. Linde into a matter that should be between her and her husband.

Nora, then, is deceitful by nature. Already the audience has caught her in lies and additional lies to cover the first ones. By the time we learn that, not only did Nora borrow the money, she committed fraud by forging her father's signature, we should recognize Nora as a deceitful woman— not a heroine, and certainly not a victim.

A feminist critic would encourage the reader to forgive Nora for her deceit. She did it for a "good cause." The fact remains, however, that Krogstad committed a similar crime, and for a similar reason. If a feminist reading requires the reader to forgive Nora, then Krogstad must be forgiven as well. He cannot be the villain of the play just because he is a man.

It is Nora who has opened the door to let scandal into the respectable and hardworking Torvald home. And when she's caught and about to be exposed, she still doesn't own up to her actions. Like a coward, she considers killing herself. This is how she is the cause of her husband's downfall, not a character who changes or grows, but the vehicle to create an unhappy ending. Nora acts without her husband's knowledge or consent, and whatever course of action she pursues at the end, whether it be suicide or leaving him, will result in scandal for him. Thus, she is the cause of his downfall.

The end of the play, when Torvald is spared disgrace, is not because of her—it is because of her that he faced disgrace to begin with—it is because Krogstad gives in and gives them the papers. When she announces that she is leaving Torvald because <u>he</u> is not the man she thought he was, she again opens him up to scandal. He will be the banker whose wife left him. If she killed herself, he'd be the banker

This is a good bit better, more pointed, and less reliant on random quotations than previous iterations of this portion of the essay are.

Derek senses that he is once again losing his focus and tries to restore it with this sentence.

whose wife killed herself. Whatever she does, he's in the middle of a scandal. It's pretty apparent that Ibsen is using Nora, not as a character who inspires the audience with her growth or downfall, but merely as the vehicle by which the honest man of integrity is brought to ruin.

Amanda in Tennessee Williams's <u>The Glass Menagerie</u> is also a character who is more vehicle of devastation than full character. Feminist critics say that Amanda is the victim of the culture of the "Old South" that turned strong-willed women into men's playthings and her husband's alcoholism and abandonment of her and her two children. One only needs to look at how she treats her children, especially Tom, to suspect that she drove her husband away the same way she drives Tom away. If her stories about her numerous gentleman callers on Blue Mountain are true, the reader can't help but wonder why she ended up marrying a northern commoner who worked for the phone company. Why didn't she marry one of the wealthy Southern landowners she claims courted her? Amanda must be either lying about her past, or she was a silly girl who is now facing the consequences of her foolish decision. Since there is no other evidence in the play to support the idea that Amanda is a liar, the most likely conclusion is that Amanda chose poorly. Her choice, then, led to her current situation, not the lack of options as feminist critics would claim.

Amanda's attitude and actions drive Tom away, and she is therefore the cause of his grief and her own downfall. Amanda is bitter and desperate, and she treats her children poorly. Rather than being human beings in their own rights, Tom and Laura are nothing to Amanda but means of support. The only reason Amanda sends Laura to business school and is so desperate for Tom to bring home a gentleman caller is so that she, Amanda,

> "Vehicle of devastation" is not really an improvement over Derek's word choice in his previous draft.

> Although he is caught with some repetitive word choice, Derek has succeeded in defusing this statement of its sentiment, making it more academic—about the play rather than his reaction.

> Interestingly, this is not a rhetorical question. Derek is bringing up an actual question Williams raises for his audience.

> These sentences serve two important purposes for Derek. First, they return the essay to its actual topic, a disagreement with a feminist reading of the play. They also anchor Derek's rejection of the notion that Amanda is lying in the play.

will be taken care of if Tom leaves. In Scene Two, after she learns that Laura has dropped out of business school, Amanda says, "I've seen such pitiful cases in the South—barely tolerated spinsters living upon the grudging patronage of a sister's husband or a brother's wife!—stuck away in some little mousetrap of a room—encouraged by one in-law to visit another—little birdlike women without any nest—eating the crust of humility all their life! Is that the future that we've mapped out for ourselves?"

The "we" is Laura, and she has "mapped out" that future for her mother and her by dropping out of school. If Amanda were really worried about Laura's future, she would have said, "Is that the future you've mapped out for yourself?" But she includes herself in it as well. Her concern is for her own future at least as much as it is about Laura's.

Similarly, Amanda doesn't care whether Tom gets fired or not; she only cares that she and Laura are taken care of. That's exactly what she tells Tom when she says she knows he's going to join the Merchant Marine. In Scene Four, during one of their few sincere conversations, Amanda tells him, "I saw that letter you got from the Merchant Marine. I know what you're dreaming of. I'm not standing here blindfolded....Very well, then. Then do it!" At first, it might seem as if she understands Tom, but ultimately, she doesn't care at all about his happiness, only her own well-being. After seemingly giving Tom "permission" to go with the Merchant Marine, she places a condition on that permission: "But not till there's somebody to take your place."

Tom can pursue his dream *after* she and Laura are taken care of.

Another fact that supports the idea that Amanda is not a powerless or innocent victim is

This little bit of discussion that Derek has added is excellent. Rather than simply tossing out a quotation and allowing his readers to come to their own conclusion, Derek specifies the significance of the quotation. Notice also that Derek takes his analysis to the level of individual words and their impact on a reader's understanding.

This is not worded as well as it might have been, but it is a good attempt on Derek's part to remind his reader—and himself—that he is analyzing Amanda's character only as a part of a larger analysis to show that the feminist view of these characters is not necessarily accurate.

that she is just a nagging and annoying person. Her endless stories about her past are annoying. In Scene One, Tom and Laura even say so:

> Tom: I know what's coming
>
> Laura: Yes. But let her tell it.
>
> Tom: Again?
>
> Laura: She loves to tell it.

You can almost hear the exasperation in Tom's voice and Laura's pleading as they are both about to be subjected to another one of Amanda's stories about her gentleman callers.

The discussion of the quotation is good, but Derek has allowed himself to slip into second-person again.

Tom can't even eat his dinner without Amanda nagging him about how to eat it: "Honey, don't push with your fingers. If you have to push with something, the thing to push with is a crust of bread. And chew — chew!" Her conversation is genuinely disgusting: "Animals have sections in their stomachs which enable them to digest food without mastication, but human beings are supposed to chew their food before they swallow it down." Her talk drives Tom away from the table, just as it will eventually drive him away from home: "I haven't enjoyed one bite of this dinner because of your constant directions on how to eat it. It's you that makes me rush through meals with your hawk-like attention to every bite I take. Sickening — spoils my appetite — all this discussion of — animals' secretion — salivary glands — mastication!"

Derek still has a tendency to overuse the statement-quotation structure, but this expanded discussion of Amanda's treatment of Tom is considerably better than in previous drafts.

And whenever either of them leaves the apartment, all she can do is nag at them about where they've been and how they've spent their time. It is, in fact, an argument about Tom going out and where he's going that finally drives him away. After Jim leaves, Tom says he is going to the movies. He and Amanda fight, and she yells at him, "Go to the moon—you selfish dreamer."

Tom replies that he went "much farther [than the moon]." He is now haunted by what may have happened to his mother and sister after he left. The unhappy ending, the point of the play, is his grief. It begins with Tom's memory, and it ends where it began.

For Tennessee Williams, Amanda is the vehicle by which Tom is driven to leave his sister, and his life is reduced to a guilty, grief-filled existence.

Regardless of how feminist critics view these women, it is clear that the playwrights did not intend for them to represent female oppression. All of these women do wrong and cause the downfall of the important men in their lives. The women in these plays, then, are not what feminist critics make them out to be: victims of a patriarchal plot to keep them submissive. They are simply vehicles for the playwright to move the plot along and bring about the sad ending of the play. Lady Macbeth, Nora Helmer, and Amanda Wingfield suffer nothing but the consequences of their own actions.

> This is a significant change in word choice: "downfall" instead of "destruction."

> Repeating the characters' names rather than simply referring to them as "these women" makes for a much stronger ending.

Analysis of Third (Final) Draft:

What is this writer's purpose? The writer's purpose is to challenge the predominant feminist view that, in the male-dominated worlds of their plays, characters like Lady Macbeth, Nora Helmer, and Amanda Wingfield cannot exert power directly and must operate subtly or indirectly. He contends that the women are merely narrative vehicles used to bring about the unhappy conclusions of the plays.

What is this writer's thesis? The women in these plays are not characters in their own right. They are merely vehicles to bring about the downfalls of the male characters in the plays.

What key points has the writer identified to clarify the thesis? The most important point of clarification is the information this writer provides on the narrative vehicle and how it functions.

What key points has the writer identified to support the thesis?

- Lady Macbeth is essentially responsible for Macbeth's actions and, thus, his downfall.

- Nora acts without her husband's knowledge or consent, and whatever course of action she pursues at the end will result in scandal for him; thus, she is the cause of his downfall.

- Amanda's attitude and actions drive Tom away, and she is, therefore, the cause of his grief and her own downfall.

What verifiable facts does the writer provide to illustrate and support his key points? In this draft, the writer provides many more direct quotations from all three of the plays in question.

ASSIGNMENT 4:

Literary Analysis—Nonfiction

In addition to AP English Language and Composition, **Jeff** is taking AP U.S. History. The teacher has assigned the class to examine the structure and language of Abraham Lincoln's Gettysburg Address and suggest why it is considered one of the United States' most memorable speeches. Here is Jeff's work as he composed his essay.

STEP 1: Select a Topic

This is an easy step for Jeff since the topic is assigned. Typically, however, analysis of nonfiction involves close examinations of the language, structure, and other tools or techniques of the writer. Analysis is not the process of determining what the text means but how it is constructed.

STEP 2: Brainstorm, Discuss, Research

The "research," of course, includes reading the speech and mapping out the sequence of ideas and noting significant features of the language.

HOW DOES LINCOLN BEGIN HIS SPEECH? WHAT IDEA? WHAT APPEAL?

There are three main parts of the speech:

- The first part is the past..."Fourscore and seven years ago..."

- The first part recalls The American Dream... "our fathers brought forth on this continent a new nation..."

- And the glittering ideal of what America was supposed to be... "conceived in liberty and dedicated to the proposition..."

It is an appeal to memory...an appeal to emotion? Reminding his listeners of the ideals of the nation? Maybe in 18—(CHECK YEAR)... people were sick of the war... Lincoln makes an idealistic appeal to help them transcend their current discontent.

WHAT'S IN THE MIDDLE? WHAT'S THE TRANSITION?

- Second part is the present..."Now we are engaged..." "We are met..."

- Transition is in "now" and in the reference to "that nation [the one mentioned in the first paragraph] or any nation so conceived..."

The appeal is still general and idealistic. He never mentions United States specifically...he does not cite any specific causes of the war, just the idealistic "to test whether...can long endure."

HOW DOES HE END? WHAT IDEA OR SENTIMENT?

- Third part looks to the future..."shall not perish..."

- Most idealistic of the three parts...they are [literally] dedicating a cemetery , but he idealizes it that the men who died there already dedicated it with their lives... not death in a war a lot of people thought was stupid but sacrifices, consecrating hallowed ground to the idealistic nation. Still general and idealistic terms... "Of the people, by the people, for the people..."

SENTENCE LENGTH? STRUCTURE? REPETITION OF WORDS OR STRUCTURES?

- I don't see much about the sentences. But there are some important word choices:

- civil war: a civil war is when one faction in a nation fights against another faction in the same nation. Lincoln is saying that America was a single nation with two factions fighting each other. The South called it "the War Between the States" because they strongly believed in the sovereignty of each individual state.

    dedicate/dedicated—6 times out of 262 words:

    first paragraph—dedicated to the proposition...

    second paragraph—"so dedicated" refers to first paragraph, but adds cohesion...idea of first paragraph into second paragraph...

    —"dedicate" also to hallow the ground of the battlefield for a cemetery

    third paragraph—dedicate = consecrate = hallow...the dead soldiers already "dedicated" the land...

    —we must dedicate ourselves.

    consecrate/hallow—twice each

    words that mean the same thing as <u>dedicate</u>, <u>consecrate</u>, and <u>hallow</u>:

    first paragraph—

    second paragraph—

third paragraph—"brave" (?), "nobly," "great task," "honored dead," "increased devotion," "last full measure of devotion" (DEVOTION IS USED AT LEAST TWICE IN THE SPEECH), "highly resolve."

final sentence—repeated structure—prepositional phrases "of...by... for." Repetition of "the people..."

> In order to address the requirements of the assignment, Jeff has done a fine job mining the short address for specific and verifiable examples of structure and language use that would support a thesis about the effectiveness of the speech.

STEP 3: Draft a Thesis

Jeff's essay will not be strictly a persuasive essay, but his essay must develop and support a thesis. Here are several of his attempts and some of his thoughts about what works, what doesn't, and why.

Abraham Lincoln's 18 — (CHECK DATE) Gettysburg Address is such a powerful speech because, in it, he spans the past, present, and future and appeals to his audience's emotions, especially their patriotism and idealism.
  – This seems too narrow. It almost says everything I'd say in the essay itself. It's not really arguable, almost just a statement of fact.

The famous speech today known as the Gettysburg Address is so memorable because, really, with Lincoln's masterful manipulation of language and his appeals to emotion, it is almost propaganda.
  – Maybe calling it propaganda is too strong. The speech is meant to be inspiring, to encourage the people not to lose heart in the long and difficult war.

Abraham Lincoln's famous Gettysburg Address is such a memorable speech in American History because it is so inspirational, and it is the structure of the speech and Lincoln's masterful manipulation of language that helps to make it so inspirational.
  – I think this says what I want to say, but it's an awful long and clumsy sentence.

Because he wanted to deliver an inspirational address,

Knowing that he wanted to deliver an inspirational address,

- 139 -

Knowing that he needed to deliver an inspirational address,

Knowing that he needed to inspire his audience in only a few words,

Knowing that he needed to inspire his audience...

Knowing that he only had a few words to inspire his audience...

Knowing that he had only a few words to inspire his audience, Abraham Lincoln chose his words and structured his speech to remind them of what America was intended to be and to tap into their idealism so they would not give up the fight they were growing tired of.

— This is a lot better, but it is still a very clumsy sentence.

Knowing he had only a few words to inspire his war-weary audience, Abraham Lincoln carefully chose his words and structured his speech to appeal to the listeners idealism, reminding them of what America was originally supposed to do, and what it was that they were still fighting for.

> Jeff has done a nice job brainstorming several possibilities, diagnosing their problems, and working toward fixing them. His final attempt is not yet perfect, but he will still have opportunities to refine it.

STEP 4: Outline

This is an academic essay, essentially a thesis-proof piece. Jeff decides, therefore, to follow a traditional, academic outline format.

Thesis: Knowing he had only a few words to inspire his war-weary audience, Abraham Lincoln carefully chose his words and structured his speech to appeal to the listeners' idealism, reminding them of what America was originally supposed to do, and what it was that they were still fighting for.

I. Structure

   A. Past to future of America

      1. First paragraph

         a. Fourscore and seven years ago...

      2. Second paragraph

         a. Now we are engaged...

         b. [Today] we are met...

      3. Third paragraph

         a. "world will little note, nor long remember..."

         b. "it can never forget..."

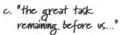

c. "the great task remaining before us..."

d. "shall have a new birth..."

e. "shall not perish..."

B. Traces "American Dream"

  1. First paragraph (past)

    a. a new nation

      (1) conceived in liberty

      (2) dedicated to the proposition

  2. Second paragraph (present)

    a. Civil war

    b. Test whether a nation so conceived and so dedicated...

  3. Third paragraph (future)

    a. unfinished work

    b. of the people, by the people, for the people

C. Unified by language

  1. dedicate/dedicated

    a. six times out of 262 words

      (1) second paragraph

        [a]"so dedicated" refers to first paragraph, but adds cohesion...idea of first paragraph into second paragraph...

        [b] "dedicate" also to hallow the ground of the battlefield for a cemetery

      (2) third paragraph

[a]dedicate = consecrate = hallow...the dead soldiers already "dedicated" the land...we must dedicate ourselves.

II. Idealistic Language

A. References to United States

  1. "a new nation, conceived in liberty, and dedicated to the proposition that all men are created equal"

  2. "this nation, under God" (third paragraph)

  3. "that Government of the people, by the people and for the people"

B. Names and Causes of war

  1. Civil War not "War Between the States"

  2. "test whether...can long endure"

  3. "the great task remaining before us"

  4. "that cause for which they here gave the last full measure of devotion"

C. Words that express holiness of the Union's Cause

  1. "brave men living and dead"

  2. "nobly"

  3. "great task"

  4. "honored dead"

  5. "increased devotion"

  6. "last full measure of devotion"

The idea that what he had been calling simply "idealistic" language actually gave the cause a "holy" aspect occurred to Jeff while he was writing his outline, and he decided to incorporate it.

By their very nature, formal outlines tend to make a topic appear rigid and linear. Still, Jeff seems to be off to a good start, knowing that he wants to develop his thesis by categorizing his evidence, not by merely summarizing or paraphrasing the speech.

STEP 5: First Draft

Jeff is definitely ready to write his first draft.

Twice, Jeff wrote himself a note to check the date of the speech. Apparently, he did.

Jeff is being, perhaps, just a little too brief here.

Here is his thesis.

The nation is more correctly referred to as the United States. "America" also includes Canada and Mexico.

Jeff will also need to review how to incorporate quotations in his writing.

He needs to be careful here; he seems to be letting his essay deteriorate into a simple rehashing of the speech, allowing the reader to arrive at his or her own conclusion.

In November of 1863, a portion of the battlefield at Gettysburg, Pennsylvania, was consecrated as a cemetery. President Abraham Lincoln had been invited at the last minute to address the crowd. Knowing he had only a few words to inspire his war-weary audience, Lincoln carefully chose his words and structured his speech to appeal to the listeners' idealism, reminding them of what America was originally supposed to do, and what it was that they were still fighting for.

The speech can be divided into three paragraphs that span the past, present, and future of America. The famous beginning of the first paragraph establishes the past, the founding of America. "Fourscore and seven years ago, our fathers <u>brought forth</u> upon this continent a new nation."

The second paragraph describes the present. "<u>Now</u> we <u>are engaged</u> in a great civil war... We <u>are met</u> on a great battlefield of that war." Clearly, the present tense indicates that Lincoln is saying "[Today] we are met on a field..." This is the present. The "new nation" that was "bought forth" is "engaged in a great civil war." The third paragraph takes the reader to a future of hope. The nation established in the first paragraph can experience a "new birth." Granted, the completion of the war still "remain[s] before us." Lincoln looks to the future when he says of his own speech that the "world <u>will</u> little note, nor long remember" the speeches, but it "can never forget" the battle that was fought and the men who died there. This is all future tense, the future of the nation. If Lincoln can inspire his audience with this speech as he wants, then perhaps the "new nation" of paragraph 1 "shall not perish from the earth."

Not only do the three paragraphs structurally take us from the past to the present and into the future, but Lincoln's word choice traces the development of "American ideals." The new nation established in the first paragraph is "conceived in liberty and dedicated to the proposition that all men are created equal." This establishes the ideals of the nation. Lincoln refers to the Civil War as "testing whether that nation, or any nation so conceived and so dedicated, can long endure." His words unite the first and second paragraphs, the past and the present. His words also indicate what is happening to that American ideal. It is being threatened by the Civil War. In the third paragraph, there is hope that those ideals will survive if the spectators present can remember those ideals and hold onto that dream ("that we here highly resolve that these dead shall not have died in vain; that this nation, under God, shall have a new birth of freedom, and that Government of the people, by the people and for the people, shall not perish from the earth."). So, the three paragraphs of the speech tell the history of America. They also show the progress of the American ideals of liberty and equality.

The speech also achieves unity by the words Lincoln uses to express his ideas and show how they develop. Of the 262 words in the entire address, he repeats "dedicate" or "dedicated" six times. In the third paragraph, as Lincoln gives his audience a peek at the future, he uses the words "dedicate," "consecrate," and "hallow"

Notice that these two paragraphs are based on the material Jeff included in Roman numeral I of his outline. It is a gross oversimplification to claim that each Roman numeral in an outline corresponds to a paragraph in the essay. The conventions of paragraphing and outlining rarely coincide.

Earlier, Jeff called this the "American dream." The fact that he has changed his word choice and his use of quotation marks suggests that he is not quite certain exactly what he wants to say.

This string of simple sentences is becoming tedious to read and making part of his point obscure. It is not clear whether Jeff is talking about structural unity, thematic unity, or both. The way he simply inserts the quotation is invasive, almost distracting.

This essay still reads as if Jeff is simply marching his reader through the Gettysburg Address, making comments and illustrating them with quotations.

This is a good example of a place filler. It reads like a topic sentence, but it says nothing. "Lincoln uses words to express ideas…"

This might be an accurate observation, but it does not really give the reader any worthwhile, concrete information.

as synonyms. They are synonyms, but they have different shades of meaning so that "hallow" and "consecrate" mean to make something almost holy. Lincoln uses these words to connect the ideas that they are consecrating the battlefield into the hallowed ground of a cemetery, and he is asking them to dedicate themselves to the ideals that were at the founding of the nation in the first paragraph. "It is for us, the living, rather to be dedicated here to the unfinished work that they have thus far so nobly carried on. It is, rather for us to be here dedicated to the great task remaining before us." America was originally "dedicated to the proposition..." and now Americans must "dedicate [themselves] to the great task remaining before [them]." The word "dedicate" and its synonyms give the speech a very strong structure.

A lot of the power of the speech is not only in the structure, but also in the language itself. The speech starts out in idealistic language, "a new nation, conceived in liberty, and dedicated to the proposition that all men are created equal." This is in the first paragraph where Lincoln wants to remind his audience of the ideals that the country was founded on. In the third paragraph, he wants his audience to remember the ideals of the nation at its beginning, and he wants them to hold on to those ideals to see the war through to a successful end for the Union. "[T]hat Government of the people, by the people and for the people." The nation that was "dedicated to the proposition" becomes "this nation under God," and the Americans to whom Lincoln is speaking are being asked "to be dedicated here" to see the war through to a successful victory. It is, therefore, important that he talk about the War as a Holy Cause more than a personal tragedy for his listeners.

There are some pronoun-antecedent problems here.

Jeff began this paragraph introducing the sub-topic of "word choice," but it would have been more accurate for him to have identified the topic as "repetition" or "use of the word 'dedication.'"

This topic sentence more accurately introduces the next part of Jeff's outline than the previous paragraph's did.

Throughout the essay—and this is a particularly strong example—Jeff has used supporting quotations fairly well, but he frequently incorporates the quotation incorrectly into the sentence or paragraph.

As was the case in the first paragraph, Jeff sacrifices some of his own effectiveness by not allowing his reader to know the full impact of the war and the Battle of Gettysburg on the nation.

He calls the war a "civil war," which is what most Northerners called it. Most Southerners called it the "War Between the States." By calling the war a civil war, Lincoln is saying that America is a single nation, not a collection of small, independent states. It is the single nation that he talks about in the idealistic terms we've already discussed.

Jeff is assuming his reader understands the denotation of "civil war."

Lincoln also doesn't want to bring up any of the causes of the war, the issues that made the South want to secede in the first place. Instead, he simply calls the war a "test whether [America] can long endure." It is a Holy Cause, a test of whether American ideals can survive. When challenging his audience to keep themselves dedicated to the Cause, he calls the war a "great task." It is a "cause." "That cause for which they here gave the last full measure of devotion." The words elevate a long and bloody war that almost seemed as if we might lose to a Holy Cause, which his listeners cannot abandon.

His ideas are sound, but Jeff's sentence structure is getting careless. He'll have to address this in the revision stage.

The choice of first-person here might seem like an innocent decision, but Jeff has identified himself with the Union and lost any sense of factual objectivity he might want to keep all factions of his readers engaged.

Abraham Lincoln's Gettysburg Address is treasured as one of the most powerful and memorable speeches in American history. Its power is in the tight structure and masterful word choice of the speech.

Granted, this is a problem that can be fixed in revision, but this is a very disappointing ending to a potentially good essay.

Analysis of First Draft

What is this writer's purpose? The writer's purpose is essentially to inform his reader of some of the possible reasons that the Gettysburg Address is such a powerful and beloved document in United States history.

What is this writer's thesis? The thesis has to do with the impact of the speech's structure and language on its power and endurance.

What key points has the writer identified to *clarify* the thesis? This is one of Jeff's weaknesses. One key point that needs more development is the emotional and psychological significance of this particular dedication. What did Gettysburg represent? Why did Lincoln need this speech to be particularly inspiring?

Jeff also needs to clarify the definitions of a few key words, especially the distinction between a "civil war" and a "war between states."

What key points has the writer identified to support the thesis?

- The writer asserts that the three paragraphs of the address span Lincoln and his listeners' past, present, and future.

- The idealistic language of the address establishes the United States as unique and worth preserving.

- The idealistic language takes on an almost sacred tone when Lincoln talks about the war and the need to persevere.

What verifiable facts does the writer provide to illustrate and support his key points? This writer provides a number of direct quotations to support his points. He could provide a little more verifiable information from reference tools when he makes claims about denotations and connotations.

Among the quotations he provides to support his key points are:

- Three paragraphs...span...past, present, and future.

  "Fourscore and seven years ago..."

  "Now we are engaged..."

  "[Today] we are met..."

  "world will little note, nor long remember..."

  "it can never forget..."

  "the great task remaining before us..."

  "shall have a new birth..."

  "shall not perish..."

- Idealistic language...establishes the United States as unique and worth preserving.

  "a new nation, conceived in liberty, and dedicated to the proposition that all men are created equal"

  "this nation, under God," "that Government of the people, by the people and for the people"

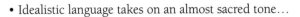

• Idealistic language takes on an almost sacred tone…

"brave men living and dead"

"nobly"

"great task"

"honored dead"

"increased devotion"

"last full measure of devotion"

NOW plan your own nonfiction literary analysis, following the same process by which Jeff arrived at his first draft.

STEP 1: Select a Topic

STEP 2: Brainstorm, Discuss, Research

What specific details, facts, etc., will provide sufficient background, definitions, and evidence to support an argument?

What specific details, facts, etc., will help you achieve your purpose (i.e., inform, persuade)?

What specific details, facts, etc., will help you achieve a desired tone (i.e., academic, authoritative, humorous, etc.)?

STEP 3: Draft a Thesis

Make sure your thesis is arguable—neither simple fact nor pure opinion.

Make certain you have or know you can find sufficient evidence and examples to explain and support your key points.

STEP 4: Outline

STEP 5: First Draft

STEP 6: Peer Edit

What is this writer's purpose?

What is this writer's thesis?

What key points has the writer identified to *clarify* the thesis?

What key points has the writer identified to support the thesis?

What verifiable facts does the writer provide to illustrate and support his or her key points?

STEP 7: Revised/Final Draft

- Twice, Jeff wrote himself a note to check the date of the speech. Apparently, he did.

- Jeff is being, perhaps, just a little too brief here.

- Here is his thesis.

- The nation is more correctly referred to as the United States. "America" also includes Canada and Mexico.

- Jeff will also need to review how to incorporate quotations in his writing.

- He needs to be careful here; he seems to be letting his essay deteriorate into a simple rehashing of the speech, allowing the reader to arrive at his or her own conclusion.

- Notice that these two paragraphs are based on the material Jeff included in Roman numeral I of his outline. It is a gross oversimplification to claim that each Roman numeral in an outline corresponds to a paragraph in the essay. The conventions of paragraphing and outlining rarely coincide.

- Earlier, Jeff called this the "American dream." The fact that he has changed his word choice and his use of quotation marks suggests that he is not quite certain exactly what he wants to say.

- This string of simple sentences is becoming tedious to read and making part of his point obscure. It is not clear whether Jeff is talking about structural unity, thematic unity, or both. The way he simply inserts the quotation is invasive, almost distracting.

- This essay still reads as if Jeff is simply marching his reader through the Gettysburg Address, making comments and illustrating them with quotations.

- This is a good example of a place filler. It reads like a topic sentence, but it says nothing. "Lincoln uses words to express ideas…"

- This might be an accurate observation, but it does not really give the reader any worthwhile, concrete information.

- There are some pronoun-antecedent problems here.

- Jeff began this paragraph introducing the sub-topic of "word choice," but it would have been more accurate for him to have identified the topic as "repetition" or "use of the word 'dedication.' "

- This topic sentence more accurately introduces the next part of Jeff's outline than the previous paragraph's did.

- Throughout the essay—and this is a particularly strong example—Jeff has used supporting quotations fairly well, but he frequently incorporates the quotation incorrectly into the sentence or paragraph.

- As was the case in the first paragraph, Jeff sacrifices some of his own effectiveness by not allowing his reader to know the full impact of the war and the Battle of Gettysburg on the nation.

- Jeff is assuming his reader understands the denotation of "civil war."

- His ideas are sound, but Jeff's sentence structure is getting careless. He'll have to address this in the revision stage.

- The choice of first-person here might seem like an innocent decision, but Jeff has identified himself with the Union and lost any sense of factual objectivity he might want to keep all factions of his readers engaged.

- Granted, this is a problem that can be fixed in revision, but this is a very disappointing ending to a potentially good essay.

And here are Jeff's responses:

> "America to "the United States" is an easy fix.
>
> I can explain what a "civil war" is, and I have information about how bloody the Battle of Gettysburg was...the North was almost ready to just give up...DISCOURAGED
>
> I'll review all of my sentence structure and all uses of first- and second-person to make this essay as neutral as possible.

Analysis of First Draft

What is this writer's purpose? The writer's purpose is essentially to inform his reader of some of the possible reasons that the Gettysburg Address is such a powerful and beloved document in United States history.

What is this writer's thesis? The thesis has to do with the impact of the speech's structure and language on its power and endurance.

What key points has the writer identified to *clarify* the thesis? This is one of Jeff's weaknesses. One key point that needs more development is the emotional and psychological significance of this particular dedication. What did Gettysburg represent? Why did Lincoln need this speech to be particularly inspiring?

> The Battle of Gettysburg had been one of the bloodiest battles of the war so far. The North was discouraged because the war had lasted a lot longer than they had expected and it seemed as if the South might actually win. Luckily the North won at Gettysburg, so Lincoln can use this victory as a rallying point.

Jeff also needs to clarify the definitions of a few key words, especially the distinction between a "civil war" and a "war between states."

> A civil war is between factions in a single nation. War Between the States implies a war between separate and individual entities. (Maybe like the countries of Europe.)

What key points has the writer identified to support the thesis?

- The writer asserts that the three paragraphs of the address span Lincoln and his listeners' past, present, and future.

- The idealistic language of the address establishes the United States as unique and worth preserving.

- The idealistic language takes on an almost sacred tone when Lincoln talks about the war and the need to persevere.

What verifiable facts does the writer provide to illustrate and support his key points? This writer provides a number of direct quotations to support his points. He could provide a little more verifiable information from reference tools when he makes claims about denotations and connotations.

Here is Jeff's second draft:

In November of 1863, a portion of the battlefield on which one of the bloodiest battles of the Civil War had been fought was consecrated as a national cemetery, an honored burial ground for those soldiers who had fought and died in the battle. The Civil War, which everyone had thought would be an easy victory for the North, had been raging for three years, and until the Union victory at Gettysburg, it seemed as if the South was going to win the war. President Abraham Lincoln was invited at the last minute to address the crowd that would assemble at Gettysburg for the dedication. Knowing he had only a few words to inspire his war-weary audience, Lincoln carefully chose those words and structured his speech to appeal to the listeners' idealism, reminding them of what the United States

This little bit of information is probably just enough to explain why the sentiment was so high at the occasion of this address.

Here is a subtle change Jeff has made in his own word choice.

was originally supposed to be, and what it was that they were still fighting for.

The speech can be divided into three paragraphs that span the past, present, and future of the United States. The famous beginning establishes the past, the founding of the United States: "Fourscore and seven years ago, our fathers brought forth upon this continent a new nation." Lincoln uses the past tense and specifies the time in the past when the nation was established.

The second paragraph begins, "Now we are engaged in a great civil war," establishing the present situation. Lincoln continues in the present tense, "We are met on a great battlefield of that war." Clearly, the present tense indicates, and historical fact supports, that Lincoln is saying "[Today] we are met on a field..." This is the present. The "new nation" that was "bought forth" is now in peril, "engaged in a great civil war." In the third paragraph, Lincoln offers a glimmer of hope for the future. The nation established in the first paragraph and threatened in the second can experience a "new birth." Granted, the completion of the war still "remain[s] before us." Lincoln looks to the future when he says of his own speech that the "world will little note, nor long remember" the speeches, but it "can never forget" the battle that was fought and the men who died there. This is all future tense, the future of the nation. If Lincoln can inspire his audience with this speech as he wants, then perhaps the "new nation" of paragraph 1 "shall not perish from the earth."

Not only does Lincoln guide his listeners from the past to the present and into the future, but his word choice traces the development of "American ideals." The new nation established in the first paragraph was "conceived in liberty and dedicated to the proposition that all men are

Interesting that Jeff would appeal to "historical fact." This adds strength to his analysis of the verb tense.

This is a little better; at least Jeff offers his reader a sense of what to think about the "now we are engaged…" quotation.

This is an improvement. It is the speaker, not the speech, that is guiding the audience.

created equal." This establishes the ideals of the nation. When Lincoln refers to the Civil War as "testing whether that nation, or any nation so conceived and so <u>dedicated</u>, can long endure," his words structurally unite the first and second paragraphs, the past and the present. His words also indicate what is happening to that American ideal. It is being threatened by the Civil War. In the third paragraph, there is hope that those ideals will survive if his audience can remember those ideals and hold onto that dream. He stresses how important it is "that we here highly resolve that these dead shall not have died in vain; that this nation, under God, shall have a new birth of freedom, and that Government of the people, by the people and for the people, shall not perish from the earth." So, the three paragraphs of the speech not only tell the history of the United States, but they describe the progress of the ideals of liberty and equality.

Lincoln also successfully unifies the ideas and structure of his speech by repeating other key words and substituting key synonyms to indicate progress or development. Of the speech's 262 words, the words "dedicate" or "dedicated" appear six times. The United States is "dedicated to the proposition" of equality. Later, it is the "nation so dedicated" that is threatened by the Civil War. The second-paragraph repetition of the first-paragraph word adds unity. The word "dedicate" appears again when Lincoln acknowledges that the reason they are all there is to <u>dedicate</u> the battlefield as a cemetery. Finally, in the third paragraph, as Lincoln gives his audience a peek at the future, he uses the words "dedicate," "consecrate," and "hallow" to suggest to his listeners that the United States had a Holy Cause, and the war was therefore a Holy War. "Hallow" and "consecrate" mean to set

Another good choice on Jeff's part; he has subordinated the quotation to stress the unity. He also clarifies the type of unity achieved.

This is much better than Jeff's previous attempt.

Much better! Rather than simply tell his reader that there are six repetitions of the word, Jeff points each out and explains why it is significant.

something aside for a holy purpose or to make it holy. Lincoln uses these words to connect the ideas that they are consecrating the battlefield into the hallowed ground of a cemetery, and he is asking his audience to dedicate themselves to the ideals that founded the nation in the first paragraph: "It is for us, the living, rather to be dedicated here to the unfinished work that they have thus far so nobly carried on. It is, rather for us to be here dedicated to the great task remaining before us." The United States was originally "dedicated to the proposition..." and now Americans must "dedicate [themselves] to the great task remaining before [them]." The word "dedicate" and its synonyms help Lincoln move his address forward toward the inspirational conclusion he wants.

Much of the power of the speech is not only in the structure, but also in the language itself. The speech starts out in idealistic language: "a new nation, conceived in liberty, and dedicated to the proposition that all men are created equal." Lincoln begins by reminding his audience of the ideals on which the country was founded. In the third paragraph, he wants his audience to reaffirm those ideals, to hold on to their principles and see the war through to a successful end for the Union, so that "that Government of the people, by the people and for the people" will survive. The nation that was "dedicated to the proposition" becomes "this nation under God," and the Americans to whom Lincoln is speaking are being asked "to be dedicated here" to the war that has dragged on and cost the United States so much. Lincoln's idealistic language applies to not only the names he calls the United States, but also to the way he talks about the war itself. He knows the people are tired of the war, and that they could easily be persuaded to allow the South to win and secede

This final sentence is an improvement over the one in the previous draft. It reminds the reader of the actual topic of the essay, the power of the speech.

Throughout the essay—and this is a particularly strong example—Jeff has used supporting quotations fairly well. Now, in this revised draft, he correctly incorporates those quotations into the text.

from the Union. It is, therefore, important that he talk about the War as a Holy Cause more than a personal tragedy for his listeners.

He calls the war a "civil war." This might not seem like that big a deal, but the difference between "civil war," which is what most Northerners call the war, and "the War Between the States," which is what most southerners call it, is important. A civil war is a war between two different factions in the same country. A war between states would be like most wars when one independent country (or state) wages war against another. By calling the war a civil war, Lincoln is saying that America is a single nation, not a collection of small, independent states. It is this single nation that he refers to in the first paragraph.

Lincoln also doesn't want to bring up any of the causes of the war, the issues that made the South want to secede in the first place. Instead, he simply calls the war a "test whether [the United States] can long endure." It is a Holy Cause, a test of whether American ideals can survive. When challenging his audience to keep themselves dedicated to the Cause, he calls the war a "great task." It is a <u>cause</u>, "that cause for which they here gave the last full measure of devotion." These words elevate a long and bloody war that seemed like an inevitable Union defeat to a Holy Cause, which his listeners cannot abandon.

Abraham Lincoln's Gettysburg Address is treasured as one of the most powerful and memorable speeches in American history. At a time when the nation was discouraged and the ideals of the past seemed all but forgotten, the president used the dedication of a cemetery to rededicate himself and his listeners to their holy purpose. The speech is short, but structured and worded perfectly to inspire the people and give them the strength to finish the war.

This is a vast improvement. Knowing the nation was tired of the war and almost ready to give up helps Jeff's reader appreciate the impact of Lincoln's speech.

The sentence structure is not great, and Jeff would be well advised to take this essay into a third draft, but this paragraph is a huge improvement over the previous draft. The reader now has enough information to appreciate the distinction Jeff is noting.

Much better.

Analysis of Final Draft:

What is this writer's purpose? The writer's purpose is essentially to inform his reader of some of the possible reasons that the Gettysburg Address is such a powerful and beloved document in United States history.

What is this writer's thesis? The strength of the speech lies mainly in its structure and language.

What key points has the writer identified to *clarify* the thesis? The writer establishes the emotional and psychological need of the people to be inspired by alluding to the historical context of the speech.

He also clarifies the denotations and connotations of key terms like "civil war." By grounding his assertions in non-arguable fact, this writer maintains a strong, authoritative position.

What key points has the writer identified to support the thesis?

- The writer asserts that the three paragraphs of the address span Lincoln and his listeners' past, present, and future.

- The idealistic language of the address establishes the United States as unique and worth preserving.

- The idealistic language takes on an almost sacred tone when Lincoln talks about the war and the need to persevere.

What verifiable facts does the writer provide to illustrate and support his key points? This writer does provide a brief explanation of the historical context of the speech: the significance of Gettysburg, the mindset of the people. He also establishes the denotation of the phrase "civil war."

POSSIBLE STEP 8: Rewrite Opportunity

MINI-LESSON 2:

The Reading Check Essay: Interpretation

You already know, even if it is a difficult principle to remember and apply, that a summary allows for no interpretation or commentary. In a summary, précis, or synopsis, you are merely telling your reader what something you've heard or read said. Rarely will you be asked simply to summarize, unless—as was the case in the earlier Mini-lesson in this chapter—it is a homework assignment or study aid, or you are required in your job to brief a co-worker or superior or prepare an encapsulation for someone else's benefit.

At other times, however, in addition to simply reporting what the source has said, you may actually be asked to make a statement of what it means or what the person to whom you're reporting is supposed to think of it. This is what editorial writers, columnists, commentators—even attorneys arguing their sides of the case—do.

They don't only repeat the data; they guide their readers or hearers toward a particular interpretation of that data.

Do not confuse interpretation and analysis. Interpretation is a statement of meaning. Good interpretation is grounded closely in the text, but analysis examines the elements of the text and how it is constructed, *how* it conveys its meaning. Interpretation explains the meaning.

As an "outside reading" assignment, **Jeff's** class was allowed to chose from a list of short novels. Jeff chose Joseph Conrad's *Heart of Darkness*. Here is the brief report he submitted as evidence that he had indeed read and understood the book. None of these outside reading assignments was discussed in class, and there were no tests, quizzes, or other assignments associated with them.

Reading Check Essay: Interpretation

Title: Heart of Darkness

Author: Joseph Conrad

Source Information (publication, publishing company, copyright date, etc.):
Prestwick House SAT Words from Literature edition, copyright 2007

Genre: Novel; novella

What is the general subject or topic of this piece?: the dark side of human nature explored metaphorically through a criticism of British colonialism

What is the author's intent?: Because it is a novel, Conrad, of course, wants to entertain his reader with a tale of adventure and suspense. He also wants to plant the seeds of a couple of ideas in his readers' minds.

What is the message, lesson, "moral," or theme of this reading? (Remember that a moral or literary theme cannot be communicated in a single word.):
There are two main themes: (1) British Colonialism is harmful to indigenous peoples, and (2) the idea that the British or Europeans in general are somehow "better" or "more sophisticated" than other peoples is wrong and potentially destructive to both the European and native psyches.

Brief interpretation of reading (explain and support your statement of theme or meaning):

In this type of essay, a statement like "can be interpreted on many levels" is essentially meaningless. If the text couldn't be, it wouldn't be possible to write this type of essay.

On the one hand, this is not a bad introduction, but Jeff needs to be careful that he does not rely too heavily on clichés like "Dark Continent" and simply repeating the title in a slightly different use.

Joseph Conrad's Heart of Darkness is a troubling book that can be interpreted on many levels. On the surface, it is an adventure story, a travelogue about a journey up the Congo. On a deeper level, it uses the stereotypical idea of Africa as the "Dark Continent" and explores what happens both to individual people and to an entire society when they venture too far and come too close to their own "heart of darkness."

The book's title, Heart of Darkness, refers to both the story's journey up the Congo, to the "heart" of "deepest, darkest Africa" and to the dark corruption the main character, Kurtz, finds in his own heart in his treatment of the Africans. By extension, Kurtz's darkness becomes Imperial Europe's darkness because Kurtz is merely an extension of the Company's policies and Europe's overall goals in trading in Africa and colonizing the continent. Historically, the two primary purposes of colonizing Africa were to "trade" with the indigenous people for things that the Europeans treasured, like ivory, and to bring the "light of civilization and Christianity" to the "dark heathen." These seem like worthy goals, and I think Kurtz's "intended" firmly believes in them when she insists at the end of the book that the now-dead Kurtz was a great man, possessing a "generous mind ... [and a] ... noble heart." Because she does not know what Marlow and the reader know about Kurtz's life and actions in Africa, she can hold onto the naive belief that men like Kurtz were exemplary. The Intended says to Marlow, "Men looked up to him—his goodness shone in every act." To the European mindset, men like Kurtz were to be admired and imitated.

It is vital to support an interpretation with direct quotations or close paraphrases to the text. Jeff's reader might be able to argue with his understanding of the Intended's words, but they cannot argue with the actual words themselves.

However, Marlow knows the truth, and through Marlow, so does the reader. Kurtz originally went to the Congo idealistically planning to convert the trading stations into outposts of civilization and European morality. By reputation, he is known to be an excellent trader, sending the Company's agents only the finest ivory. Marlow later learns, from the Russian and from Kurtz himself, that there was more "raiding" than "trading" in Kurtz's methods, and that rather than bring the light of civilization to the Africans, Kurtz has succumbed to the darkness of brutality. At the end of the apparently idealistic pamphlet by Kurtz on how to "civilize" the African, Kurtz handwrote, "Exterminate all the brutes!" His dying words are, "The horror! The Horror!" While the meaning of

By not dealing more conclusively with the novel's two most problematic lines, Jeff weakens his interpretation a bit. His ability to turn a phrase like "gospel of extermination" adds tone but does not remedy the weakened content.

Accurate summary can be as effective as direct quotation. No one can argue that this is how Marlow's conversation with the Intended goes.

Jeff is trying to make a biblical allusion. The idea might work, but for a concluding sentence, this is a bit awkward and still inconclusive. Still, for a simple reading check, this essay does indeed provide evidence that Jeff has read the novel and understood much of what he has read.

both of these is ambiguous, it is clear that Kurtz has devolved from a missionary-like idealist whose goal is to civilize and save as well as trade into a man who allows himself to be worshipped as a god and preaches a gospel of extermination.

The novel ends with the suggestion that the world has not learned from Kurtz's example, since the one man who can reveal the truth, Marlow, chooses instead to maintain the myth. Rather than break the Intended's heart with the truth of Kurtz's decline, he agrees with her that Kurtz was a remarkable man and tells her that Kurtz's dying words were her own name.

Heart of Darkness, then, is a puzzling book. It is an adventure story of a trip up the Congo River complete with shrunken heads and battles with the natives. It is a story that illustrates the brutality of European colonialism and the hypocrisy of Europeans' claims that their purpose in Africa was to enlighten and save. It is also a story that illustrates the depths to which a man, even a brilliant, well-intended man, can sink when faced with what he perceives to be the deepest and darkest evil. Kurtz and Marlow both face darkness, and they are both—though maybe to different extremes—more overcome by the darkness than they are able to overcome the darkness with their light.

PART III:

Persuasive Writing

[asserting and defending claims]

By now, the ideas of persuasion and argumentation are not new to you. You've gone from factually supporting a relatively simple claim to making a case for that claim, like a criminal prosecutor, with supporting claims and evidence. You've learned that support can come in the form of facts, examples or illustrations, or expert opinions. You know that you are not likely to find much evidence to prove your general claim outright, but you will search for—and present to your reader—evidence for all of your supporting claims. As you establish their validity, you will strengthen the credibility of your general claim.

Probably most importantly, you've learned that that general claims cannot be mere fact or mere opinion. Established fact simply cannot be argued. When you expose someone to a new fact, you are not "winning" an argument; you are merely verifying the fact.

Opinion cannot be argued either, especially if it is sound opinion based on actual knowledge and experience. Although you will find it difficult to persuade someone to give up a well-thought-out and informed opinion, you should approach argumentation as if your one goal were to persuade your reader to agree with your viewpoint.

The central claim of your argument then must be something arguable, something for which you can make a case, support with evidence, and at least get your reader to concede that you make a good point.

It is precisely this aspect of the argumentation process that this book is going to address.

Since it is extremely difficult to persuade a reader to abandon a thoughtful and informed opinion, you know even before you begin to present your argument that at least some of your readers are going to "argue back." And you know that many of your opponents are going to provide thoughtful and informed counter-arguments, or rebuttals. You should, therefore, *anticipate* readers' objections and opportunities to rebut from the beginning of your process.

By the same token, you should also consider others' arguments from the standpoint of finding opportunities to refute or rebut—making certain that your rebuttal will be thoughtful and informed *and based on a valid understanding of your opponent's initial argument.*

ASSIGNMENT 1:

The Initial Argument

The first two assignments in this chapter emphasize the process of initiating a claim and then arguing back. You will more than likely have to do both at one time or another, whether it be an academic assignment or the case of defending (or opposing) a project proposal in your work. You will use both skills when you speak in favor (or against) a candidate for office. In fact, the very process of argument is not complete without both sides of the case being represented.

Remember that the basis of the argument is the *claim*. In a criminal trial, the prosecution's claim is that the defendant is guilty of a crime.

In order to be valid, the claim must be supportable by *evidence*. You don't have to watch too many episodes of *Law and Order* to know that, without enough evidence of the right kind, the prosecutors won't even press the charges. If they can't "win" the argument, they won't press their claim.

In addition to the evidence are the *warrants*. These are the statements of interpretation, the prosecutor's addresses to the jury, explaining how the evidence supports the claim. In the case of your own persuasive writing, the warrants will be your necessary explanation, interpretation, and so on.

In other words, you cannot simply allow the evidence to speak for itself. You are initiating the debate, and you must make your case.

STEP 1: Select a Topic

If a topic is not assigned to you, consider any open-ended or controversial topics you've covered in any of your classes. For example, **Chandra** reviewed her notes and came up with the following possible persuasive topics:

- Federal funding for Planned Parenthood—this might be too political? But if I'm supposed to find a topic that's controversial, politics will come into it anyway.

- Pro Life vs. Pro Choice—links into the above. I know how I feel about women's reproductive rights, but I'm unresolved about abortion. Don't think I could make a strong argument because of that.

> Chandra actually could, if she thought about it, make a persuasive argument that endorses women's reproductive rights, but stops short of advocating abortion. A strong argument doesn't steer clear of gray areas—it embraces them.

- Increased security against terrorism—does it impinge on our civil rights?—I feel strongly about this one, I might be able to argue it pretty well.

- Balancing the federal budget or jump starting the economy—which is more important?—I hear this hashed over every night on television. I don't think I want to spend more time and attention on this one.

> Chandra is wise to avoid a topic that is already overexposed in the media, especially if she herself is tired of hearing about it. You should choose a topic that genuinely holds your interest and that you have strong opinions on, but it's a good idea to stay away from a subject that is dominating the national debate to the point of tedium.

- Gun control laws in the U.S.—or the lack of them. I could get into this one, make a pretty strong argument.

STEP 2: Develop an Argument

You learned last year that the basis of a persuasive essay is the *claim*, the central point or argument that you want to establish. Claims are similar to theses in other essays.

- Claims cannot be mere fact because while a fact might need to be verified, it cannot be argued.

- Claims cannot be mere opinion because even an informed and reasonable opinion cannot be argued beyond stating the opinion and the reasons for holding it.

While some claims are specific enough that they can be argued directly (as Jacob did in his essay last year), most claims will be too broad to throw evidence at them and expect the reader to be convinced. Instead, the central argument will be broken down into smaller claims that can be proven directly. The model we introduced last year still holds. In a society in which an accused is *presumed innocent until proven guilty*, the burden of proof is on the prosecution.

Since you are the person advancing the claim, *you* are the prosecution. *You* bear the burden of proof, and neither your reader nor those who might disagree with you are obligated to treat your central claim, your supporting claims, or your evidence mildly. In court, the prosecution must prove the defendant's guilt "beyond a reasonable doubt."

That should be your standard as well.

Remember also that, according to the criminal trial model, the prosecution does not merely hammer away at its central claim that the defendant is guilty. Instead, the prosecution builds a case of supporting claims: the defendant had motive; the defendant had opportunity; the defendant had means... and so on.

Each individual bit of evidence, then, does not need to point to the "big picture," the central claim, the defendant's guilt. Each bit of evidence simply needs to support one of the supporting claims. By establishing each of the supporting claims, you build the validity of your central claim.

For Chandra and her classmates, then, developing the argument involves both clarifying her central claim and drafting those supporting claims that will be provable and will collectively point to the validity of that central claim. Like many of her classmates, she has carried a few of her possible topics into the next step. She realized that the process of generating and supporting claims would help her exclude topics that wouldn't work and assist in identifying the argument she was most interested in pursuing.

> Increased security against terrorism—does it impinge on our civil rights?—
> While it is important to protect citizens against acts of terror, there is a
> distinct line between what is necessary for national security and what represents
> an invasion of privacy and a violation of our civil rights.
> - Racial profiling is frequently engaged in by the FBI to try and
>   identify terrorists, resulting in harassment and arrests of innocent
>   citizens merely because of race and/or religion.
> - Increased monitoring of electronic communications is leading law
>   enforcement down a slippery slope toward a "Big Brother" mindset
>   and unreasonable invasion of our privacy.
> - High-resolution body scanners that allow airport security a kind of
>   virtual strip-search are a definite violation of our rights.

Chandra is making a very strong argument here. She needs to be prepared for the rebuttal, which will doubtlessly also be a strong counterargument.

Gun control laws in the U.S.—We don't have enough of them, and the ones we do have aren't strong enough.
- The NRA, with its power, funds, and resources, has intimidated our lawmakers and politicians, even our presidential candidates, none of whom are willing to advocate for gun control laws, despite increasing gun violence.

This sounds like opinion more than fact, and Chandra needs facts to back up her opinion. She should see if she can find some data relating to the NRA's expenditures for Washington lobbyists.

- The number of gun-related deaths has skyrocketed since the Republican-controlled Congress allowed Clinton-era gun restrictions to expire.

- Allowing the general public access to automatic weapons such as the one used in the movie theater shooting in Colorado makes it too easy for disturbed people to cause mass killing and mayhem. No deer hunter needs an AR 15 to pursue the sport.

Again, Chandra is making a good argument here. As strong as it is, she needs to always back her opinions up with supporting facts and not confuse her argument with the data she needs as backup.

STEP 3: Brainstorm, Discuss, Research

Chandra decided she was most interested in the gun control argument, since it was especially topical and certainly controversial, and she was certain the data she needed to back up her opinion would be readily available. Her research will be largely on the Internet, since this is not a formal research paper; a few blogs and news articles will give her the necessary factual backup for her assertions.

STEP 4: Outline

Central Claim: Gun control laws in the United States are too weak to protect the citizenry from random acts of violence, largely because the gun lobby exerts too much influence and power over lawmakers.

I. Gun violence in the U.S. has been on the rise for the last decade.

  A. Statistics

   1. Number of gun-related deaths over the last ten years

   2. Increase in occurrence of mass shootings

  B. Gradual weakening of gun control laws over that same period

   1. Comparative look at gun control laws in the '80s and '90s

   2. How do the statistics from those periods compare to present day?

    a. Show the correlation

    b. Compare the political climate of both decades to the present

II. The undue political clout of the NRA and the gun lobby

This might seem like a trivial point for an outline, but Chandra is actually *begging the question* here. Certainly she can show that the NRA has an influence, and she can argue that the influence is inappropriately strong, but the way she states it here, she is presuming that her reader also sees the influence as "undue."

  A. Use of lobbyists

  B. Fundraising clout

  C. Intimidation of politicians—lawmakers afraid to set policy that NRA doesn't approve of; gun control becoming a "third rail" in the political environment

III. Why stronger gun control laws are needed in the U.S.

Again, Chandra is begging the question. In this essay, she needs to establish that stronger laws *are* needed.

  A. Assault weapons—should they really be available to anyone other than the military?

  B. Compare statistics of gun violence in countries with stronger gun control laws

  C. Need for longer waiting periods

   1. To be sure guns are not getting into the hands of terrorists or criminals

   2. To be sure guns are not getting into the hands of disturbed people

   3. To be sure anyone purchasing a gun is doing so for a legitimate reason

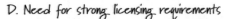

D. Need for strong licensing requirements

   1. Just like driving a car, owning a gun should be seen as a privilege that comes with certain responsibilities and requirements.

   2. Need for identity verification

   3. Need for education in safe handling of weapons

> For some reason, Chandra has abandoned the supporting claims she developed as the framework for her argument in Step 2. This might spell trouble for the essay itself.

STEP 5: First Draft

Here is Chandra's first draft. Read it and consider its strengths and weaknesses. How successfully does Chandra develop her supporting claims and, thus, establish her argument?

The statistics on gun-related violence in the United States reveal a grim reality: the U.S. leads in deaths from firearms among developed countries by an alarming ratio. That ratio shows the U.S. has fully 19.5 times the number of gun-related homicides than Europe, Canada and China, according to the _Journal of Trauma-Injury Infection & Critical Care_. In the past ten years 30,000 people per year have died from gun violence—300,000 homicides in all. There has also been a pronounced increase in mass shootings such as the recent Aurora, Colorado movie theater massacre and the attack on a Sikh temple in Wisconsin shortly thereafter. There have, in fact, been at least sixty mass murders in the United States since 1982, according to the National Institute of Justice, many employing assault weapons and semiautomatic handguns that served to increase the number of deaths and injuries inflicted.

Chandra is parsing her data in a risky way here, one that her opposing arguer will definitely call her on. She is trying not to weaken her argument by admitting that other countries, such as those in Latin America and the Caribbean, have much higher rates of gun violence than the U.S. does. "Developed countries" implies that, for instance, Venezuela and Brazil are somehow undeveloped, which is not the case and seems pejorative. She needs to rethink how to present this data.

Chandra is wise to back up her claims, which gives her questionably worded argument some needed credibility, but with the statistic and source cited here, Chandra has essentially no introductory paragraph.

This is Chandra's most dramatic statistic so far; she would be well to cite her source here.

It's good that Chandra is backing up each claim she makes, but the end of this sentence presents an assumption, that while reasonable, also needs some support.

Comments like these actually weaken Chandra's argument. Her conclusion is not "without a doubt" or there could be no rebuttal. Chandra needs to stick to facts and careful interpretation of facts. Otherwise, she comes close to begging the question, a serious logical fallacy in argument.

Again, Chandra tends to sensationalize and oversimplify a complex event. Her use of the word "senseless" likewise continues her tendency to beg the question.

This sentence is overlong and awkward and packed with information that needs to be presented in a better organized fashion.

The lobbying efforts of the National Rifle Association have been, without a doubt, the biggest obstacle to increased gun control legislation. The NRA wants laws that would extend the right to carry concealed weapons across state borders. They also lobbied for the "Stand Your Ground" law in Florida that resulted in the senseless death of Trayvon Martin, as well as efforts to allow guns to be carried everywhere from college campuses to bars and restaurants, even elementary schools, state mental hospitals, and daycare centers. Conversely, legislative efforts to require background checks for buyers at gun shows, the ability of the government to revoke licenses of dishonest gun dealers, and even the banning of sales to persons on the federal government's terrorist watch list have been blocked or opposed by the organization.

A little more than ten years ago, the political climate in the United States was very different on the issue of gun control. In his first term, President Bill Clinton lobbied for and then signed both the Brady Bill and the 1994 Violent Crime Control and Law Enforcement Act (also known as the Crime Bill), which included the federal assault weapons ban. The Brady Bill was named for James Brady, press secretary to Ronald Reagan, who had been seriously wounded in the assassination attempt on Reagan; Brady's wife Sarah had been advocating for the bill for years. Public opinion favored the bill, which included background check requirements for gun purchases, as well as a five-day waiting period. The Crime Bill was passed one year later, which along with the assault weapons ban, prohibited the manufacture of ammunition magazines that held over ten rounds. During this period, crime dropped sharply in the U.S.; homicide rates dropped to 5.5 from 9.8 per 100,000 (Steven D. Levitt, <u>Understanding Why Crime Fell in the 1990s: Four Factors that Explain the Decline and Six that Do Not</u>).

The Crime Bill, however, did not settle the question once and for all. It energized the NRA and its Republican supporters. The 1994 mid-term elections resulted in Republicans taking control of both the Senate and the House. They very quickly eliminated restrictions on gun and ammunition purchasing. In 2004, Congress allowed the 1994 federal assault weapons ban to expire. The result in gun violence statistics was obvious; between 2004 and 2010, 370,401 people died from gun-related violence, according to the Centers for Disease Control.

> Chandra wants to parse this a little more carefully; right now, it sounds as if she's blaming Republicans directly for gun violence. While she is right to take a strong stand in her argument, if she comes across as overly partisan, she will weaken her case.

In the 2008 presidential election, the NRA spent ten million dollars, all of it earmarked to defeat Barack Obama. In 2011, Wayne LaPierre, the CEO, refused to meet with President Obama to discuss gun control, stating flatly, "Why should I or the NRA go sit down with a group of people that have spent a lifetime trying to destroy the Second Amendment in the United States?" That same year, the NRA spent $2,905,000 on lobbying and $974,006 in campaign contributions. (http://www.opensecrets.org/orgs/summary.php?id=D000000082). In the face of the

> Chandra's presenting good facts and backing them up here; she's making her case effectively.

NRA's undue power, politicians who had previously championed gun control are now too intimidated to even bring the issue up for discussion, let alone a vote. As Heidi Przybyla writes in Bloomberg News, "Most Democrats say they aren't trying anymore. The NRA's 'political muscle' has 'silenced pro-gun-control voices even to the point where we can't have a reasonable discussion about reasonable measures to try to take, really, weapons of war off the streets,'" said Representative Gerry Connolly, a Virginia Democrat who, in his 2010 election campaign, favored tightening registration requirements for gun show dealers.

> Again Chandra begs the question. She is doing a decent job demonstrating that the NRA has influence, but if her point is that the NRA's influence is *excessive* or *unwarranted*, she needs to support this claim as well.

> It is unclear here who exactly is Chandra's source. She should quote Connolly here and then cite Przybyla parenthetically.
>
> This is a start, but Chandra needs a good bit more to lead her reader to conclude that the NRA's lobbying efforts are excessive.

For most gun control advocates, the least understandable of the NRA's positions is its opposition to the banning of assault weapons and high-capacity ammunition magazines. Plainly, these weapons are not designed for use by anyone other than the military; moreover, their use in mass shootings, such as the event in Aurora, has resulted in dramatically increased death and injury. Trying to make the case that if the shooters had not had access to automatic weapons, they simply would have found other guns, the NRA and gun lobby shows that it is tone deaf on the issue. Their party line does not counter the argument that if no civilian had these weapons there would be far fewer deaths. The United Kingdom, which enacted strict gun control laws in response to the Dunblane Massacre of 1997, the worst mass shooting in British history, the entire country saw only fifty deaths from shootings in 2006; during the same period, there were 25,423 such deaths in the U.S. (Donial Dastgir, <u>The Cornell Daily Sun</u>, April 23, 2008).

Along with the return of the assault weapons ban, longer waiting periods for gun ownership need to be reinstated to ensure guns do not get into the hands of such disturbed individuals as James Holmes, or into the hands of terrorists and criminals. We need to know that anyone purchasing a weapon is doing so for a legitimate reason and is going to handle that weapon responsibly. Strong licensing requirements need to be obeyed, for all of the above reasons; owning a gun should be perceived, not as a birthright, as the NRA and its supporters do, but a privilege, like driving an automobile, that comes with responsibilities and rules. The identity of everyone purchasing a weapon should be verified, and education in the safe handling of weapons should be a pre-requirement.

Chandra is being redundant here; she hit on this point earlier. Also, the sentence about the NRA being "tone deaf" on the issue is awkward and needs to be reworked.

Another long, unwieldy, and grammatically problematic sentence.

Chandra is apparently assuming the reader already knows who James Holmes is.

Chandra is either mistaken or has chosen her words carelessly. It sounds as if she is suggesting that there is no Second Amendment.

Chandra makes an impassioned argument, but she has left herself vulnerable to rebuttal on several points; for instance, she fails to engage in any discussion of the Second Amendment and its constitutional application in the modern day. Her opponent will jump on this if she fails to address it in her next draft. She also needs to rework the final paragraph; the need for education in the safe handling of firearms is not the most compelling issue to conclude her argument. It would also be a good idea to cite some other sources who agree with her assertions.

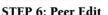

STEP 6: Peer Edit

What is this writer's point? Chandra's point is that stronger gun control legislation in the United States is needed but cannot be passed because of the undue political and lobbying efforts of the gun lobby, chiefly the NRA.

What is this writer's angle? Her angle is that, in the face of such violent crimes as the mass shooting in Aurora and the Sikh Temple shooting in Wisconsin, stronger gun control is needed more than ever. She misses the opportunity, however, to fully engage the political aspect of the issue, most especially the constitutional interpretation of the Second Amendment, what its original intent may have been, and whether that intent remains relevant in the 21st century.

How strong is this writer's support? How authoritative is her overall argument? She provides, overall, fairly solid support for her assertions, but could benefit in certain sections with increased citations. She comes across as informed rather than authoritative and leaves her argument open to challenge in several key areas.

What techniques has this writer used to establish this authority? She cites sufficient sources to back up her basic argument, but is plainly selective in the sources she uses, some of which are more partisan than is ideal.

What specific details, facts, etc., make this argument convincing? Chandra cites a fair amount of data to further her argument, culled from the internet, scholarly papers, and newspaper articles. These include:

- the U.S. has fully 19.5 times the number of gun-related homicides than Europe, Canada, and China

- 30,000 people per year have died from gun violence

- 300,000 homicides in all

- the recent Aurora Colorado movie theater massacre and the attack on a Sikh temple in Wisconsin

- at least 60 mass murders in the United States since 1982

- measures to allow carrying concealed weapons across state borders are backed by the NRA
- NRA supports efforts to allow guns to be carried everywhere from college campuses to bars and restaurants, even elementary schools, state mental hospitals, and daycare centers.
- specific sums of money spent on recent lobbying efforts
- between 2004 and 2010, 370,401 people died from gun-related violence

She could benefit from also citing some expert opinion, particularly in the final paragraph.

NOW plan your own argumentative essay. Remember that Chandra brainstormed and took notes on several possible topics and developed each of them to see which one would yield the best essay.

STEP 1: Select a Topic

What topics or issues have you read about or discussed in school that might make for an interesting argument?

What issues or controversies in your school, community, state, or nation have attracted your interest?

What trends or movements might have a direct impact on you or those you love?

STEP 2: Develop a Slant/Angle/Hook

What aspects of your indicated issues are most important? Why?

What aspects of your indicated issues are most interesting? Why?

What ideas or insights do you have that others seem not to have noticed or seem to undervalue?

STEP 3: Brainstorm, Discuss, Research

What sources are likely to provide the most accurate and authoritative support for your argument?

What specific details, facts, etc., are likely to make your argument convincing?

STEP 4: Outline

STEP 5: First Draft

STEP 6: Peer Edit

What is this writer's point?

What is this writer's angle?

How strong is this writer's support? How authoritative is his or her overall argument?

What techniques has this writer used to establish this authority?

What specific details, facts, etc., make this argument convincing?

STEP 7: Revised/Final Draft

Here are Chandra's editor's comments and analysis as well as her responses:

- Chandra is parsing her data in a risky way here, one that her opposing arguer will definitely call her on. She is trying not to weaken her argument by admitting that other countries, such as those in Latin America and the Caribbean, have much higher rates of gun violence than the U.S. does. "Developed countries" implies that, for instance, Venezuela and Brazil are somehow undeveloped, which is not the case and seems pejorative. She needs to rethink how to present this data.

- Chandra is wise to back up her claims, which gives her questionably worded argument some needed credibility, but with the statistic and source cited here, Chandra has essentially no introductory paragraph.

- This is Chandra's most dramatic statistic so far; she would be well to cite her source here.

- It's good that Chandra is backing up each claim she makes, but the end of this sentence presents an assumption that, while reasonable, also needs some support.

- Comments like these actually weaken Chandra's argument. Her conclusion is not "without a doubt" or there could be no rebuttal. Chandra needs to stick to facts and careful interpretation of facts. Otherwise, she comes close to begging the question, a serious logical fallacy in argument.

- Again, Chandra tends to sensationalize and oversimplify a complex event. Her use of the word "senseless" likewise continues her tendency to beg the question.

- This sentence is overlong and awkward and packed with information that needs to be presented in a better organized fashion.

- Chandra wants to parse this a little more carefully; right now, it sounds as if she's blaming Republicans directly for gun violence. While she is right to take a strong stand in her argument, if she comes across as overly partisan, she will weaken her case.

- Chandra's presenting good facts and backing them up here; she's making her case effectively.

- Again Chandra begs the question. She is doing a decent job demonstrating that the NRA has influence, but if her point is that the NRA's influence is *excessive* or *unwarranted*, she needs to support this claim as well.

- It is unclear here who exactly is Chandra's source. She should quote Connolly here and then cite Przybyla parenthetically.

- This is a start, but Chandra needs a good bit more to lead her reader to conclude that the NRA's lobbying efforts are excessive.

- Chandra is being redundant here; she hit on this point earlier. Also, the sentence about the NRA being "tone deaf" on the issue is awkward and needs to be reworked.

- Another long, unwieldy, and grammatically problematic sentence.

- Chandra is apparently assuming the reader already knows who James Holmes is.

- Chandra is either mistaken or has chosen her words carelessly. It sounds as if she is suggesting that there is no Second Amendment.

- Chandra makes an impassioned argument, but she has left herself vulnerable to rebuttal on several points; for instance, she fails to engage in any discussion of the Second Amendment and its constitutional application in the modern day. Her opponent will jump on this if she fails to address it in her next draft. She also needs to rework the final paragraph; the need for education in the safe handling of firearms is not the most compelling issue to conclude her argument. It would also be a good idea to cite some other sources who agree with her assertions.

And here is Chandra's reaction:

Wow, I thought I had a lot of good facts and statistics. I'm not sure I understand the "begging the question" comments. The argument is supposed to be based on my opinion, right? And arguments are supposed to be slanted. Otherwise, they're not arguments.

Maybe I need to think a little like my reviewer and predict where I am inviting rebuttal and how I can counter or prevent it.

I also know that I can be more careful citing my sources.

Chandra is correct; an important part of effective argument is anticipating opposing arguments and addressing them. She also needs to redouble her efforts and find more information, especially on how the Second Amendment has been interpreted on both sides of the argument; in doing so, she will most likely become more authoritative on the issue.

Analysis of First Draft

What is this writer's point? Chandra's point is that gun control legislation in the United States is needed but cannot be passed because of what she calls undue political and lobbying efforts of the gun lobby, chiefly the NRA.

That's my point but stated almost backwards. I want my point to be about rising gun violence and the fact that the NRA is part of the problem, not part of the solution.

> It's a little disappointing that Chandra wants this to be her point. Her goal is ultimately to persuade her reader, not to preach.

What is this writer's angle? Her angle is that, in the face of such violent crimes as the mass shooting in Aurora and the Sikh Temple shooting in Wisconsin, stronger gun control is needed more than ever. She misses the opportunity, however, to fully engage on the political aspect of the issue, most especially the constitutional interpretation of the Second Amendment, what its original intent may have been, and whether that intent remains relevant in the 21st century.

> *Oh, okay, they got that. I can't believe I totally missed the constitutional argument; I need to address that.*

> Chandra is making the common mistake of confusing her point with her slant, but now she understands. Knowing that she needs to engage on the constitutional issue will definitely strengthen her argument.

How strong is this writer's support? How authoritative is her overall argument? She provides, overall, fairly solid support for her assertions, but could benefit in certain sections with increased citations. She comes across as informed rather than authoritative and leaves her argument open to challenge in several key areas.

> *I thought I gave enough statistics; do I actually need to give more?*

> It isn't necessarily more statistics that Chandra needs; she could also cite some expert opinion on the subject, which would lend her argument some weight and believability.

What techniques has this writer used to establish this authority? She cites sufficient sources to back up her basic argument, but is plainly selective in the sources she uses, some of which are more partisan than is ideal.

> *What do you do when almost all you can find on the subject is partisan? Maybe using OpenSecrets.org was a tipping point? Okay, back to research.*

> Chandra's confusion is understandable. One solution to her problem would be to include an acknowledgment of some of her sources' bias, as well as more analysis of the data, sharing her conclusions, not just her sources'.

What specific details, facts, etc., make this argument convincing? Chandra cites a fair amount of data to further her argument, culled from the Internet, scholarly papers, and newspaper articles. These include:

- the U.S. has fully 19.5 times the number of gun-related homicides than Europe, Canada, and China
- 30,000 people per year have died from gun violence
- 300,000 homicides in all
- the recent Aurora Colorado movie theater massacre and the attack on a Sikh temple in Wisconsin
- at least 60 mass murders in the United States since 1982
- measures to allow carrying concealed weapons across state borders are backed by the NRA
- NRA supports efforts to allow guns to be carried everywhere from college campuses to bars and restaurants, even elementary schools, state mental hospitals, and daycare centers.
- specific sums of money spent on recent lobbying efforts
- between 2004 and 2010, 370,401 people died from gun-related violence

She could benefit from also citing some expert opinion, particularly in the final paragraph.

> Oh, that's a light bulb moment. Expert opinion—so I can cite opinions on the issue, but just make sure they're the opinions of experts and from respected sources.

Here is Chandra's revised draft. Since her reviewer noted some problems with her outline, she has revised it, as well and based her revised essay on the new outline.

Central Claim: Gun-related violence is a growing problem in the United States, and organizations like the National Rifle Association, which could champion the cause of safe and responsible gun use, have become part of the problem rather than the solution.

> Stated like this, Chandra has a much clearer and defensible argument. She also tones down the "NRA is evil and powerful" tone of her earlier argument.

I. Gun violence in the U.S. has been on the rise for the last decade.

   A. Statistics

      1. Number of gun related deaths over the last ten years

      2. Increase in occurrence of mass shootings

   B. Gradual weakening of gun control laws over that same period

      1. Comparative look at gun control laws in the '80s and '90s

      2. How do the statistics from those periods compare to present day?

         a. Show the correlation

         b. Compare the political climate of both decades to the present

II. NRA could be part of the solution.

   A. History and purpose of the NRA

   B. Second Amendment concerns and interpretations of the Second Amendment

III. Instead, the NRA is part of the problem.

   A. Use of lobbyists

   B. Fundraising clout

   C. Intimidation of politicians—lawmakers afraid to set policy that NRA doesn't approve of; gun control becoming a "third rail" in the political environment

IV. Strong gun laws could protect citizens from violent crime while not restricting their Constitutional right to guns.

   A. Assault weapons—should they really be available to anyone other than the military?

   B. Compare statistics of gun violence in countries with stronger gun control laws

   C. Need for longer waiting periods

      1. To be sure guns are not getting into the hands of terrorists or criminals

      2. To be sure guns are not getting into the hands of disturbed people

      3. To be sure anyone purchasing a gun is doing so for a legitimate reason

   D. Need for strong licensing requirements

      1. Just like driving a car, owning a gun should be seen as a privilege that comes with certain responsibilities and requirements.

      2. Need for identity verification

      3. Need for education in safe handling of weapons

The United States is approaching another presidential election, and many of the issues facing the nation have divided the population into warring camps, each unwilling to find a middle ground or compromise. One of those issues, one that must be settled for the safety and well-being of every American citizen, is the issue of gun control. Gun-related violence is a growing problem in the United States, and organizations like the National Rifle Association, which could champion the cause of safe and responsible gun use, have become part of the problem rather than the solution. Gun violence in the U.S. has been on the rise for the last decade. Strong gun laws could protect citizens from violent crime while not restricting their Constitutional right to guns. However, massive efforts on the part of wealthy and politically powerful organizations like the National Rifle Association have blocked all efforts to control the sale and ownership of even the most dangerous and least necessary of firearms.

Chandra has written a decent introduction and laid out an argument that will probably be more reasoned and less passionate than her first draft was.

The statistics on gun-related violence in the United States reveal a grim reality: the U.S. sees more deaths from firearms annually than Australia, Canada, and the United Kingdom do—combined. The "ScienceBlogs" website, a partner of National Geographic online, calls United States gun violence a "public health problem." The number of combined homicides in all other G12 nations is only slightly higher than the rate in the U.S. alone—3.02 per 100,000 for G12, 2.98 for the U.S. (http://scienceblogs.com/thepumphandle/2012/07/23/gun-violence-is-a-u-s-public-health-problem/). According to the Baltimore Sun, over the last decade in the United States, roughly 30,000 people per year have died from gun violence—300,000 homicides in all. There has also been a pronounced increase in mass shootings such as the recent Aurora, Colorado,

Chandra is presenting her data much more effectively and dramatically here, and even better, citing a supporting source.

Chandra is giving an additional source for her startling data here; so far, she is doing a good job of increasing her source citing and backing up her assertions.

The Aurora shooting occurred on 20 July 2012, and the Sikh temple shooting on 5 August, only weeks before Chandra wrote this persuasive piece.

Chandra is backing up her assertion here with a powerful example, which strengthens her argument.

Chandra may be introducing a valid supporting claim, but this sentence is a bit overwritten, relying on exaggeration rather than allowing the facts to speak for themselves.

This is good information and just what Chandra needs to establish her point, but without some reference to valid and reliable sources, her credibility is weakened. Readers who disagree with her have no real reason to alter their views.

movie theater massacre and the attack on a Sikh temple in Wisconsin shortly thereafter. There have, in fact, been at least sixty mass murders in the United States since 1982, according to the National Institute of Justice, many employing assault weapons and semiautomatic handguns that served to increase the number of deaths and injuries inflicted. James Holmes, the now-notorious perpetrator of the Aurora, Colorado, shootings, would not have been able to shoot 72 people, killing 12 of them, if he had only had access to conventional weapons.

The National Rifle Association, which was originally an advocate for the safe, responsible, and legitimate use of firearms, could take the lead in efforts to control the flow of guns into the hands of criminals and the mentally disturbed. The NRA was established during the Civil War as a program to teach marksmanship to Union soldiers whose shooting skills were not equal to the newly accurate and powerful guns they had been given. After the war and in the early twentieth century, the National Guards of several states contracted with NRA chapters to teach marksmanship to their troops. In 1903, Congress authorized the creation of the Civilian Marksmanship Program. Under this program, the United States Army distributed obsolete and surplus firearms to civilians. The purpose of this program was not only to put guns into the hands of civilians but to teach those civilians marksmanship as well as gun safety and use. The stated purpose of the CMP was to create and maintain a body of qualified citizens in case they were ever called into military service.

The NRA also organized gun clubs and became a strong advocate of safe and responsible gun use, as well as an organizer and supporter of hunting and other gun sports. In 1934, the NRA supported the National Firearms Act and later the Federal Firearms Act of 1938. These acts established licensing procedures for gun dealers, imposed taxes on the sale of guns, prohibited the sales of certain types of guns, and required that all civilians register the firearms they owned. Today, the NRA and similar organizations criticize the 1938 act as a violation of the Second Amendment. Such claims, however, miss the point of both the Second Amendment and the gun-control lobby.

The Second Amendment reads: "<u>A well regulated militia being necessary to the security of a free state</u>, the right of the people to keep and bear arms shall not be infringed." The origin of the NRA and its earliest activities all have to do with arming and training soldiers and potential soldiers. The recreational aspects of the NRA developed later.

But even those who recognize the NRA's strong support of the rights of Americans to own and use guns for recreational purposes acknowledge that from its beginning, the NRA has been associated with gun safety, providing safety programs even for women and children. Such a group would surely want to be at the forefront of any movement to protect safe and appropriate gun ownership. Instead, they choose to be part of the problem, keeping inappropriate weapons in the hands of criminals and the mentally ill and facilitating violence and crime.

The National Rifle Association has been the biggest obstacle to gun control laws in this nation over the last decade or more. They have consistently advocated measures that would extend the right to carry concealed weapons across state borders, as well as the infamous "Stand Your Ground" law in Florida. The organization is currently lobbying vigorously for the right of

Again, Chandra has a lot of information here that is relevant to her point, but she offers no citation or documentation to verify that what she is saying is accurate.

Chandra does succeed in tying her argument to the Second Amendment, but except for the text of the amendment itself, Chandra does not verify any of the information she provides.

What had been an overlong and awkward sentence has been broken down into three, and the data presented is more effectively showcased.

private citizens to carry weapons onto college campuses, as well as into bars, restaurants, and even elementary schools, state mental hospitals, and daycare centers. Conversely, legislative efforts to require background checks for buyers at gun shows, the ability of the government to revoke licenses of dishonest gun dealers, and even the banning of sales to persons on the federal government's terrorist watch list, have been blocked or opposed by the organization. (http://www.guardian.co.uk/world/2012/apr/13/nra-weakened-gun-control-laws).

A little over a decade ago, there was a considerably different political climate on the issue of gun control. In his first term of office, President Bill Clinton successfully lobbied for and signed both the Brady Bill and the 1994 Violent Crime Control and Law Enforcement Act (also known as the Crime Bill), which included the federal assault weapons ban. The Brady Bill was named for James Brady, press secretary to Ronald Reagan, who had been seriously wounded in the assassination attempt on Reagan; Brady's wife Sarah had been advocating for the bill for years. Public opinion favored the bill, which included background check requirements for gun purchases, as well as a five-day waiting period. The Crime Bill was passed one year later, which along with the assault weapons ban, prohibited the manufacture of ammunition magazines that held over ten rounds. During this period, crime dropped sharply in the U.S.; homicide rates dropped to 5.5 from 9.8 per 100,000 (Steven D. Levitt, Understanding Why Crime Fell in the 1990s: Four Factors that Explain the Decline and Six that Do Not).

The Crime Bill, however, came with a steep price for gun control advocates; it energized the NRA, as well as the Republican base. The 1994 mid-term elections resulted in Republicans taking

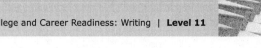

control of both the Senate and the House, and the NRA began to aggressively lobby to eliminate restrictions on gun and ammunition purchasing.

In 2004, the NRA, after years of effort, was finally successful in influencing Congress to allow the 1994 federal assault weapons ban to expire. The unforeseen consequence was a pronounced spike in gun violence; between 2004 and 2010, 370,401 people died from gun-related violence, according to the Centers for Disease Control.

In the 2008 presidential election, the NRA spent ten million dollars, all of it earmarked to defeat Barack Obama (Eunice Moscoso, "NRA Campaign Against Obama Carries $10 Million Price Tag," Palm Beach Post, October 21, 2008). In 2011, Wayne LaPierre, the CEO, refused to meet with President Obama to discuss gun control, stating flatly, "Why should I or the N.R.A. go sit down with a group of people that have spent a lifetime trying to destroy the Second Amendment in the United States?" That same year, the NRA spent $2,905,000 on lobbying and $974,006 in campaign contributions. (http://www.opensecrets.org/orgs/summary.php?id=D000000082). In the face of the NRA's clout, politicians who had previously championed gun control are now too intimidated to even bring the issue up for discussion, let alone a vote. According to Representative Gerry Connolly, a Virginia Democrat who, in his 2010 election campaign, favored tightening registration requirements for gun show dealers, "Most Democrats say they aren't trying anymore. The NRA's 'political muscle' has silenced pro-gun-control voices even to the point where we can't have a reasonable discussion about reasonable measures to try to take, really, weapons of war off the streets" (Przybyla, Heidi. Bloomberg News).

The cornerstone of the NRA's political position is a radical interpretation of the Second Amendment.

Chandra has made a small but significant change to the last sentence; stating the violence was an "unforeseen consequence" is a clever and effective way of not seeming to blame Congress for the rise in deaths, but at the same time laying the responsibility at their feet. This statement no longer reeks of partisanship and, therefore, becomes a stronger indictment.

Chandra's correct to leave this section as it was in the previous draft; it's well presented and gives good backup.

While Chandra has cleaned up many of the problems that were apparent in her first draft, much of her new information reads like first draft material and could stand to be edited and revised.

The amendment represents to the NRA what the First Amendment represents to the American Civil Liberties Union—an absolute principle. The ACLU will go to court to protect the rights of white supremacists to engage in what many of us would see as hate speech; the NRA will go to court for the right to carry a rifle onto a playground. But is it the same thing? Gun control advocates and opponents interpret the key phrases, "well regulated militia" and "shall not be infringed" very differently. The NRA sees them as a validation of their ideal for totally unregulated gun ownership, while others see them as relating only to a particular period in history and a particular reason for gun ownership. The founders could not have foreseen a future in which technology had created firearms capable of firing up to thirty or forty rounds of ammunition per minute. (http://www.military-sf.com/ROF.htm) They also cannot have foreseen the realities of the world we currently live in, the kind of internal violence it is confronted with, nor the effect of pervasive media, which can propel deranged individuals to commit violent acts in a depraved play for attention.

It's good that Chandra stresses the constitutional issue in this draft, and she makes some excellent points. However, she lists only one source for backup on her assertions and ends with a very big assumption that she leaves unsupported—and it goes off point.

For most gun-control advocates, this is the hardest of the NRA's positions to understand—its opposition to banning assault weapons and high-capacity ammunition magazines. When it is suggested that shootings like Aurora, Colorado, would not have happened if the assault weapons weren't available, the NRA responds that the shooters would have simply found other guns. Clearly, the NRA and the gun lobby in general either does not understand the control advocates' point, or they are indifferent to it. The NRA party line does not counter the argument that if no civilian had these weapons there would be far fewer deaths. The United Kingdom, which enacted strict gun control laws in response to the Dunblane Massacre of 1997, the worst mass shooting in British history, saw only 50 deaths from shootings in 2006. During the same period, there were 25,423 such deaths in the U.S. (Donial Dastgir, The Cornell Daily Sun, April 23, 2008.)

Stronger gun laws could protect citizens from violent crime while not restricting their constitutional right to guns. Along with the return of the assault weapons ban, longer waiting periods for gun ownership need to be reinstated to ensure guns do not get into the hands of such disturbed individuals as James Holmes, or the hands of terrorists and criminals. Society needs and has the right to know that anyone purchasing a weapon is doing so for a legitimate reason and is going to be responsible in the handling of that weapon. None of this is contrary to the original values of the National Rifle Association, which used to be the strongest proponent of gun safety and actually supported appropriate control legislation. Nor do these suggestions represent a restriction of the constitutional right of the citizenry to bear arms, since that right is clearly tied to the need to maintain a militia for the purpose of national security. These suggestions represent the government performing its responsibility to protect its citizens. As President Obama stated in his comments to the Urban League, "...AK-47s belong in the hands of soldiers, not in the hands of criminals...they belong on the battlefield of war, not on the streets of our cities. I believe the majority of gun owners would agree that we should do everything possible to prevent criminals and fugitives from purchasing weapons; that we should check someone's criminal record before they can check out a gun seller; that a mentally unbalanced individual should not be able to get his hands on a gun so easily. These steps shouldn't be controversial. They should be common sense." Appropriate control of the availability of guns never intended for civilian use and ownership simply makes sense, and the United States gun lobby, especially the National Rifle Association, should champion the cause of sense and safety instead of insane violence and murder.

Chandra has excised the redundant sentence from the previous draft and revised the awkward sentence about the "tone deafness" of the NRA. The paragraph is improved because of those changes.

This is a stronger argument than Chandra's previous draft. She refers to the history of the NRA and the actual wording of the Second Amendment, which lend incontrovertible support to her case.

Obviously, it has been hard for Chandra to find many expert opinions on gun control in her online search, but at least she has found the President's comments, which help bring her argument to a more powerful conclusion. His reflection of her assertions gives them somewhat more of a needed gravitas, and she is obviously more ready for debate, given the overall improvement of this draft.

Analysis of Revised Draft

What is this writer's point? The point has not changed from the first draft. Chandra has, however, strengthened it in this draft.

What is this writer's angle? Her angle has also not changed, but it has been tweaked; in the face of such violent crimes as the mass shooting in Aurora and the Sikh Temple in Wisconsin, stronger gun control is needed more than ever. The constitutional argument for unfettered ownership of firearms is invalid, and reasonable gun control is not contrary to the principles on which organizations like the NRA were founded. By including these new insights, Chandra has considerably strengthened her argument.

How strong is this writer's support? How authoritative is her overall argument? Overall, Chandra has found good additional support for her assertions, and she seems much more authoritative on the topic. Her argument is not perfect, especially the material that is new for this draft, but her point is considerably improved.

What techniques has this writer used to establish this authority? Chandra presents statistics, other data, and expert opinion, and does a mostly admirable job of establishing her authority.

What specific details, facts, etc., make this argument convincing?

- The U.S. sees more deaths from firearms annually than Australia, Canada, and the United Kingdom—combined.

- The number of combined homicides in all other G12 nations is only slightly higher than the rate in the U.S.—3.02 per 100,000 for G12, 2.98 for the U.S.

- There have been at least 60 mass murders in the United States since 1982, according to the National Institute of Justice.

- During the period after the Crime Bill was passed in 1994, crime dropped sharply in the U.S.; homicide rates dropped to 5.5 from 9.8 per 100,000.

- After the assault weapons ban was allowed to expire in 2004, 370,401 people died from gun-related violence between that time and 2010, according to the Centers for Disease Control.

- Great Britain saw only 50 deaths from shootings in 2006; during the same period, there were 25,423 such deaths in the U.S.

POSSIBLE STEP 8: Rewrite Opportunity

ASSIGNMENT 2:

The Rebuttal

In this series, we've been using a comparison of the argument process with a criminal trial in which the argument belongs to the prosecution, and it bears the burden of proof. It is not inaccurate to say, then, that any responses to the prosecution, especially *refutation* or the *rebuttal,* mimic the role of the defense.

It's a simple scenario:

- The prosecution states its central claim, *the defendant is guilty.* It then lays out its case in terms of supporting claims and evidence—motive, opportunity, means, and so on.

- The defense responds to the charge—a *refutation* would be the equivalent of a *not guilty* plea.

    —A *rebuttal* might also be a plea of not guilty, but the *rebuttal* allows the defense to admit the defendant's guilt while arguing for a lesser charge, a more lenient sentence, or an acquittal based on a more complete knowledge of the case.

In both the refutation and the rebuttal, the defense will want to examine the evidence presented by the prosecution in a new way and present new evidence that the prosecution may have missed or simply chosen to ignore in trying to make its case.

The rebuttal, then, is a response to the initial argument; but it is not an outright contradiction, not the debater's saying, "You're wrong." Instead it is the equivalent of saying, "You make an interesting case, but…"

STEP 1: Select and Analyze the Argument You Are to Rebut

There are countless sources for arguments to rebut—editorials and letters to the editor in both print and electronic periodicals, nonfiction essays, both contemporary and historical (consider, for example a rebuttal of Patrick Henry's famous "Give me Liberty or Give me Death!" speech).

Chandra and **Eleanor's** teacher assigned them to consider several of their classmates' initial argument essays from Assignment 1 of this chapter. Every student's essay was published anonymously, so the rebuttal would be fair and not biased by the students' personal feelings for one another.

After considering several of her classmates' arguments, Eleanor has chosen to rebut Chandra's essay on gun control. Eleanor is reminded that her assignment is not simply to refute Chandra's thesis—Chandra has proposed and supported a valid thesis, and Eleanor will not be able simply to assert that Chandra is wrong.

Instead, Eleanor is assigned to point out to the reader another side of the story.

- Eleanor's thesis might simply be the *antithesis* of Chandra's, that all efforts at gun control legislation represent a violation of the Second Amendment, or that the National Rifle Association is actually fulfilling a necessary role as the guardian of American rights.

- It might be a *qualification* of Chandra's thesis—that while gun control measures are necessary, the NRA is not the "bad guy" and should be courted rather than condemned. Eleanor might want to suggest that, while Chandra's crime statistics are incontrovertible, the cause is not gun availability, and the solution is not gun control.

Eleanor will, of course, need to provide her own evidence in support of her thesis, but she will also need to counter Chandra's arguments, reinterpret Chandra's data, cast new light on Chandra's insights. That is all part of a rebuttal—a response of, "You make an interesting case, but…"

In order to offer a suitable essay, Eleanor needs to be intimately familiar with her opponent's argument and with the facts that will support her view.

Read the essay—at least twice, making notes on any points that seem inadequately supported, weakly argued, or that lead to questionable conclusions.

Analyze the thesis—does the essay address and support it sufficiently? What could strengthen the author's arguments? What has been missed or ignored? Are the sources cited reliable and solid? Are there enough sources to support the author's argument?

Independently research the topic—with special attention to any data that weakens, refutes, or contradicts the data presented by the author, especially anything missed or ignored by the author that would have strengthened his or her argument.

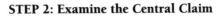

STEP 2: Examine the Central Claim

Eleanor looks at Chandra's central claim and how Chandra has broken her larger claim into smaller supportive claims. She needs to critically examine the structure of Chandra's argument, how well she proves both her central claim and smaller claims, and ferret out any weak points, lazy research, or missed or ignored data.

Central Claim: Gun-related violence is a growing problem in the United States, and organizations like the National Rifle Association, which could champion the cause of safe and responsible gun use, have become part of the problem rather than the solution.

Gun violence in the U.S. has been on the rise for the last decade.

Check the statistics, see if they add up
   — How solid are the numbers given?

   — Any contradictory or missing data?

   — See how effective gun control laws in the '80s and '90s really were

   — Check the statistics given then and now. Any problems?

      — Is there a true correlation? How could it be refuted? How to refute the refutation?

      — Is the political climate of the two eras given truly relevant?

NRA could be part of the solution.

History and purpose of NRA—check... how else can it be interpreted?

Find out exact wording and intent of 1934 and '38 acts.

Chandra mentions that 1938 law is criticized... check this out, criticized by whom and in what terms?

Instead, the NRA is part of the problem.

   — How influential are lobbyists really?

   — How much fundraising clout does the NRA really have, as compared to other organizations?

   — Intimidation of politicians—this is probably true, but how well does she prove it?

Strong gun laws could protect citizens from violent crime, while not restricting their constitutional right to bear arms.

Chandra's statement on assault weapons—look at possible refutation and counter it.

Check the statistics of gun violence in countries with stronger gun control laws—is what's given in the essay accurate?

Need for longer waiting periods—again, see what the refutation might be, and refute the refutation.

Need for strong licensing requirements—this one could probably be better supported. Again, counter the refutations for all the below:

   — Need for identity verification

   — Need for education in safe handling of weapons

Eleanor has done a reasonably good job of outlining how she will rebut Chandra's essay. She may find some challenges in doing so, since Chandra's final draft was fairly well supported, but any reasonable argument can be reasonably debated.

STEP 3: Refine Your Argument

This is the brainstorm and research step. In step 2, Eleanor took Chandra's outline and indicated every fact she wanted to verify, qualify, or counter. This is the step in which she does exactly that.

This is also the step in which she allows the information she finds to tweak the central focus of her rebuttal:

- Will the facts allow her to contradict Chandra?

- Can she demonstrate bias or incomplete research on Chandra's part?

- Does she have to concede Chandra's central point but challenge some of her other conclusions?

Below are some of Eleanor's notes gathered during her research:

Gun violence in the U.S. has been on the rise for the last decade.

- Actually, according to the Guardian UK, the occurrence of gun-related murders was down in 27 states from 2009-2010 by as much as a 41% decrease (Alabama).

- According to the Pew Research Center (2009), the percentage of U.S. households owning at least one gun reached a high of 54% in 1977 and decreased steadily thereafter, reaching a low of 33% in 2009. So, the Clinton-era decline might simply have been part of this 22-year trend and had nothing to do with gun control legislation.

> Eleanor is about to commit a fatal error here. She is equating a drop in gun ownership with a drop in gun crime. They are two separate phenomena.

On 1 October 1987, Florida's right-to-carry law took effect. Anyone licensed to carry a concealed weapon must:
- be 21 or older

- have clean criminal and mental health records

- complete a firearms safety training course

—probably not too different from those offered by the NRA

As of 31 July 2010, Florida has issued:

- 1,825,143 permits

- 746,430 active licensees

- representing approximately 5.4% of the state's age-eligible population

Murder rate <u>decreased</u> down from 11/100,000 in 1988 to 6.5/100,000 in 2008.

Texas also saw its murder rates go down after its "right-to-carry" law took effect.

Declines in murder rates mirrored the national trend for those periods, and both states' numbers were higher than the national.

Check the statistics, see if they add up

- How solid are the numbers given?

- Any contradictory or missing data?

- See how effective gun control laws in the '80s and '90s really were

- Check the statistics given then and now. Any problems?

  - Is there a true correlation? How could it be refuted? How to refute the refutation?

  - Is the political climate of the two eras given truly relevant?

NRA could be part of the solution.

History and purpose of NRA—check...how else can it be interpreted?

Find out exact wording and intent of 1934 and '38 acts

Chandra mentions that 1938 law is criticized...check this out, criticized by whom and in what terms?

Instead, the NRA is part of the problem.

Winnie Stachelberg of the Center for American Progress (panel After Aurora: Dispelling the Myth of NRA Power): "The NRA's influence, in fact, is waning and is rarely significant in any election." (Washington Post, 25 July 2012)

Paul Waldman, The American Prospect. "...gathered data on the outcome of every House and Senate election, including the margins of victory, the money spent by each candidate, the partisan character of each district, and whether the NRA made an endorsement in the race and how much money they spent. The conclusion to be drawn from these data will be surprising to many: The NRA has virtually no impact on congressional elections....In short, when it comes to elections, the NRA is a paper tiger."

- How influential are lobbyists really?

- How much fundraising clout does the NRA really have, as compared to other organizations?

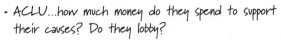

- ACLU...how much money do they spend to support their causes? Do they lobby?
- Maybe environmental groups?
- Intimidation of politicians—this is probably true, but how well does she prove it?

Strong gun laws could protect citizens from violent crime while not restricting their constitutional right to bear arms.

A 1982 survey of male felons in 11 state prisons dispersed across the U.S. found:
- 34% had been "scared off, shot at, wounded, or captured by an armed victim."
- 40% had decided not to commit a crime because they "knew or believed that the victim was carrying a gun."
- 69% personally knew other criminals who had been "scared off, shot at, wounded, or captured by an armed victim."

(Wright, James D. and others. <u>Armed and Considered Dangerous: A Survey of Felons and Their Firearms.</u> Transaction Publishers, 1986)

Washington, D.C.'s, 1976 ban on handguns...struck down by SCOTUS 26 June 2008
- Violent crime actually increased from 28/100,000 in 1976 to a high of 80/100,000 in 1995
- Sharp decline 1995—2008, but still higher in 2008 when the law was struck down than when it was passed in 1976
- Decline continued to a low of 22 in 2008

Rise and fall mirrored a national trend, but rates were always still higher than the national.

(Uniform Crime Reporting Program, District of Columbia, 1960-2008. Federal Bureau of Investigation, Criminal Justice Information Services Division.)

Chandra's statement on assault weapons—look at possible refutation and counter it.

Check the statistics of gun violence in countries with stronger gun control laws—is what's given in the essay accurate?

Need for longer waiting periods—again, see what the refutation might be, and refute the refutation.

Need for strong licensing requirements—this one could probably be better supported. Again, counter the refutations for all the below:

- Need for identity verification

- Need for education in safe handling of weapons

Second Amendment Arguments

26 June 2008, <u>D.C. v Heller,</u> SCOTUS, 5-4 ruling struck down Washington, D.C.'s, 1976 ban on handguns. Quotation from the majority decision: "The Second Amendment is naturally divided into two parts: its prefatory clause and its operative clause. The former does not limit the latter grammatically, but rather announces a purpose. The Amendment could be rephrased, 'Because a well regulated Militia is necessary to the security of a free State, the right of the people to keep and bear Arms shall not be infringed.' "

28 June 2010, <u>McDonald v Chicago,</u> SCOTUS, 5-4 ruling struck down Chicago's 1982 ban on gun ownership. Quotation from the majority decision: "it is clear that the Framers and ratifiers of the Fourteenth Amendment counted the right to keep and bear arms among those fundamental rights necessary to our system of ordered liberty."

STEP 4: Outline Your Draft

After doing her own independent research on gun violence and gun control laws, Eleanor looks at Chandra's outline and decides to basically follow it point by point. Unfortunately, her reliance on Chandra's argument will not serve her well.

Central Claim: Gun control laws in the United States are too weak to protect the citizenry from random acts of violence, largely because the gun lobby exerts too much influence and power over lawmakers.

I. Gun violence in the U.S. has been on the rise for the last decade.

   A. Yes, but the U.S. is far from number one in gun violence.

      1. Top three countries are all developing, third world nations

      2. High degree of drug trafficking and crime-related violence

      3. Bigger issue: ratio of weapons to citizenry in U.S.—88 per 100 people

   B. Weakening of gun control laws represents a cultural shift.

      1. Political polarization makes gun control a harder sell.

      2. Statistics can be easily manipulated by either side to support its positions.

         a. An armed populace does not result in lower crime statistics.

         b. The political climate of the two eras is relevant because the '80s and '90s represented the beginning of extreme polarization between the parties.

II. The undue political clout of the NRA and the gun lobby

   A. More statistics on the influence of lobbyists

   B. The cultural clout of the NRA is actually more influential than its fundraising powers

   C. Intimidation of politicians—more about this being one of the "third rails" of politics

III. Why stronger gun control laws are needed in the U.S.

   A. Wide availability of assault weapons and the mass shootings that have occurred—correlation

   B. More detail on gun violence in countries with stronger gun control laws

   C. Why longer waiting periods are appropriate and needed—more detail if possible

   D. Need for strong licensing requirements—more detail:

      1. The government requiring a license to drive a vehicle is not an infringement of personal liberty, but necessary for public safety.

      2. In the post 9/11 world, identity verification is necessary and appropriate.

      3. Education on safe handling should include information on why it is actually safer not to own a handgun.

IV. The Second Amendment

   A. Strengthen the counter-constitutional argument

   B. Less relevant today than in the eighteenth century

   C. NRA use of it as a branding tool

Because Eleanor is adhering so closely to a plan laid out by someone else, it is difficult for a reader to anticipate what Eleanor's point will be and which of Chandra's points she will concede, which she will refute, and which she will rebut. Ultimately, however, what will be the core of Eleanor's argument?

STEP 5: First Draft

Read Eleanor's first draft and consider its strengths and weaknesses. How success-fully does Eleanor rebut Chandra's assertions, and does she find any points that Chandra missed or ignored that actually strengthen Chandra's claims?

From the beginning, Eleanor makes a common error. While it is true that her essay is written to rebut another writer's argument, this argument must stand on its own. By phrasing her opening sentence as a response, she has already undermined the independence of her own essay.

Eleanor is still phrasing her sentences as if she is already in the middle of a discussion. She has made no claim, introduced no argument, simply jumping in with her statistics to counter statistics she *assumes* her reader has seen.

Notice that Eleanor more or less dismisses a key point. The crux of Chandra's issue becomes merely a peripheral concern. This strategy might backfire on Eleanor.

If we are still in Eleanor's introduction, then this is a valid statement of her central claim. None of the previous material has read like an introduction, however, so "mere availability" reads more like another dismissal than a rebuttal.

"Little doubt" among whom? Again, Eleanor is presuming knowledge on the part of her reader that she may actually need to establish.

While it is a fact that the U.S. sees more deaths from firearms annually than Australia, Canada, and the United Kingdom combined, this is a selective statistic. According to an article in the Guardian UK online magazine, the United States is not even close to being number one in gun-related violence—it is actually number twenty-eight; the highest rates are seen in Honduras, El Salvador, and Jamaica. And while one can also point to the number of combined homicides in all other G12 nations as only slightly higher than the rate in the U.S. alone, there is perhaps a more compelling statistic to consider—the number of firearms owned by United States citizens: 88 firearms per every 100 people. A Reuters.com article from 28 August 2007 claims that the U.S. owns 270 million of the world's 875 million known firearms. Given the alarming ratio of guns to citizens, it is hardly surprising that over the last decade, there have been roughly 300,000 homicides due to gun-related violence; the question that needs to be asked is what, other than the mere availability of guns, is the root cause of gun violence. In the nations with the highest rates, all Third World, developing nations, there is little doubt of the root cause—the drug trade, organized crime, human trafficking, and political instability, as reported to the General Assembly of the United Nations. With a much smaller share of the world's weaponry, these nations nevertheless are responsible for a disproportionate amount of its mayhem. The argument is thus frequently made by gun advocates that the number of weapons a nation is armed with has nothing to do with the amount of violence it is victim to. The recent mass shootings in Aurora, Colorado, and at the Sikh temple in Wisconsin would seem to belie that assertion, but gun rights advocates insistently contend that if more people were armed, they would be better able to protect themselves. This position is countered by the fact that, according to the American Bar Association, the presence of a firearm in a household triples the likelihood that a member of that household will become a victim of homicide.

While the NRA is most frequently singled out as the largest, most powerful obstacle to gun control laws in the U.S., there is a bigger picture that is being missed—the increased political polarization between the political parties, which has steadily risen over the last two decades. In fact, its influence may actually not be equal to its reputation, as Winnie Stachelberg of the Center for American Progress said at a panel discussion last July titled, After Aurora: Dispelling the Myth of NRA Power. "The NRA's influence in fact is waning and is rarely significant in any election." (Washington Post, 25 July 2012). In fact, the NRA's funding and endorsements historically can be seen as far less decisive than believed, according to Paul Waldman, contributing editor for The American Prospect. "...I gathered data on the outcome of every House and Senate election, including the margins of victory, the money spent by each candidate, the partisan character of each district, and whether the NRA made an endorsement in the race and how much money they spent. The conclusion to be drawn from these data will be surprising to many: The NRA has virtually no impact on congressional elections. The NRA endorsement, so coveted by so many politicians, is almost meaningless. Nor does the money the organization spends have any demonstrable impact on the outcome of races.

It has taken Eleanor a long and torturous route to get to something like her central claim.

Eleanor is still responding to Chandra more than writing her own essay. This error probably originates in her deciding to follow Chandra's outline rather than draft her own based on her own central and supporting claims.

This is an interesting rebuttal to Chandra's claims about the NRA's power, but it bears no relevance to Eleanor's stated claim—that gun availability is not the cause of gun violence.

Eleanor should remember from last year that rhetorical questions are so overused as to be virtually ineffective and should be avoided whenever possible.

Eleanor should revise to eliminate this cliché.

Again, Eleanor has lost sight of the claim she is rebutting, the influence of the gun lobby, especially the NRA.

Eleanor loses her focus in this long sentence. While it is true...*what?*

Eleanor does have these figures in her notes, but she needs to cite her sources since she is offering hard numbers.

In short, when it comes to elections, the NRA is a paper tiger." (http://prospect.org)

Why do politicians still cower in fear of the NRA, particularly Democrats and progressives, who are unlikely to be affected by the organization? Poll numbers may well be a part of that picture; they show steadily declining public support of gun control laws from 66% in May 1999, shortly after the Columbine shootings, to only 44% in October of 2010. Perhaps even more important, according to a poll reported in the Huffington Post in July, support for gun rights among Republicans and Independent voters was an incredible 72%. In an increasingly divided electorate, where Independents are critical to any Democrat's election strategy, it's not surprising that gun-control legislation is pushed to the back burner, even in the face of recent violence.

While it is true that, in 1994, President Bill Clinton signed into law both the Brady Bill and the Violent Crime Control and Law Enforcement Act (the Crime Bill), known principally for the federal assault weapons ban, this was also the era that saw the beginning of deep political polarization between the parties, and the NRA was energized into action. And while crime did indeed drop sharply in the U.S. after the Brady and Crime bills were passed, there are those who felt the legislation did not have significant impact on the statistics. Clinton was inaugurated in 1993, but states like Florida and Texas and the District of Columbia had been seeing a decrease in gun violence since the late 1980s. Florida's "right-to-carry law" took effect in 1987. That state's murder rate has decreased steadily from 11 murders per 100,000 persons in 1988 to 6.5 murders per 100,000 persons in 2008. It is not logical to credit Clinton's gun and crime bills with a decline in crime that began long before he even took office.

Alternate explanations for the steep drop in crime, as explored in <u>Understanding Why Crime Fell in the 1990s: Four Factors that Explain the Decline and Six that Do Not</u> by Steven D. Levitt, include increased police, a rising prison population, the lessening of the crack epidemic, and even the legalization of abortion.

Since this is fairly surprising information that runs counter to conventional wisdom, Eleanor needs to do more than merely provide the title of the book she consulted.

In 2004, when the NRA's lobbying efforts induced Congress to allow the 1994 federal assault weapons ban to expire, there actually was a pronounced spike in gun violence. According to the National Institute of Justice, during 2010, an estimated 18.7 million citizens were victims of violent crime; this statistic becomes more alarming when one considers that only an estimated 50% of violent crimes were actually reported to the police. Despite these alarming statistics, the NRA has continued to spend much of its capital in support of or against candidates, depending on their positions on gun ownership. The $10 million they spent in an attempt to defeat Barack Obama in 2008 will almost certainly be exceeded in the 2012 campaign. <u>Business Week</u> reports that it had already raised that amount between August 2011 and June 30, 2012. It has also heightened its own propaganda campaign. After the shootings in Aurora, NRA president Wayne LaPierre sent out a fundraising letter claiming an Obama victory would result in the confiscation of all handguns and the repeal of the Second Amendment. LaPierre ended his letter saying: "The night of November 6, 2012, you and I will lose more on the election battlefield than our nation has lost in any battle, anytime, anywhere. Or, we will win our greatest victory as NRA members and freedom-loving Americans." (http://www.businessweek.com/news/2012-08-07).

Does this information contradict the claims of a steady decrease that Eleanor made earlier? She does not seem concerned with this apparent contradiction.

On a grammar and mechanics note, Eleanor must decide whether she is going to address the NRA as a singular or a plural.

The timing of this letter, immediately after the Aurora shootings, brought immediate controversy and criticism, as from Eileen McCarron, the president of the Colorado Ceasefire Capitol Fund, calling the letter and the timing of its release "very insensitive...Couldn't they have waited at least a week, especially here? People's souls are really wounded." Does it also betray a degree of desperation, in the face of a possibly lessening degree of influence over elections and policy?

Eleanor seems to have almost completely lost her focus. In her rebuttal of Chandra's pro-gun-control essay, she seems to want to bolster Chandra's arguments.

The Second Amendment is definitely the core of the NRA's political position. It reads: "A well regulated militia being necessary to the security of a free state, the right of the people to keep and bear arms shall not be infringed." The meaning of these words, whether or not they are still relevant, and what the nation's founders may have meant when they wrote them is a source of heated debate. Gun lobbyists interpret the amendment as granting any citizen the right to own and carry any kind of weapon with virtually no restriction whatsoever. The basis of their claim is the second part of the sentence, "the right of the people to keep and bear arms shall not be infringed." The beginning of the sentence, however, which refers to "A well regulated militia being necessary to the security of a free state..." seems to point to military, rather than civilian armament. Put into a historical context, that argument is strengthened. The Founding Fathers had just brought the nation through the Revolutionary War, and did not want to start a United States army, but rather turned the defense of the nation over to the individual states' militias. The Supreme Court has only rarely taken up the question of the Second Amendment; in the 19th century, it ruled that it does not bar state regulation of firearms. In 1939, the Court actually used a collective rights approach in interpreting the amendment, ruling that the state had the right to enforce the National Firearms Act of 1934 in regard to regulating a sawed-off shotgun that had been involved in interstate commerce. In contrast, in 2008, the Court ruled in District of

Eleanor is wrong here. Article 1, Section 8 of the Constitution grants Congress the power "To raise and support Armies," and Article 2 of the Constitution establishes the President of the United States as the "Commander in Chief of the Army and Navy of the United States, and of the Militia of the several States, when called into the actual Service of the United States." Thus, the Constitution makes provision for both a national army *and* state militias.

Columbia v. Heller that a District of Columbia law banning handguns and another requiring all lawful handguns in the home be either disassembled or trigger locked, were unconstitutional, and violated Second Amendment rights. The decision was 5 to 4—an indication of the political and cultural divide of the nation on the issue. The majority decision was based upon the following interpretation of the Second Amendment:

> The Second Amendment is naturally divided into two parts: its prefatory clause and its operative clause. The former does not limit the latter grammatically, but rather announces a purpose. The Amendment could be rephrased, "Because a well regulated Militia is necessary to the security of a free State, the right of the people to keep and bear Arms shall not be infringed."

Now Eleanor is talking about assault weapons with no transition from her discussion of the Second Amendment.

The NRA and the entire gun lobby are, without a doubt, most frequently taken to task for their opposition to the banning of assault weapons. But what is behind the propaganda and demagoguery? In a word, profit. A recent report by Reuters notes that the conventional weapons industry is a $60 billion business, and sales have spiked in the wake of each recent shooting. The NRA gets a great portion of its over $200 million lobbying budget directly from gun manufacturers. Assault weapons are big business, and the gun lobby does not want a major profit point to disappear.

In stark contrast, The United Kingdom, with its stringent gun control laws saw only 50 deaths from shootings in 2006; during the same period, there were 25,423 such deaths in the U.S. (Donial Dastgir, The Cornell Daily Sun, 23 April 2008.) Additionally, in Japan, which has even stricter gun control laws—the only weapon a citizen is allowed to own is a shotgun—the country has as few as two gun-related homicides a year.

Eleanor still seems more interested in building Chandra's argument than rebutting it.

The return of the assault weapons ban would certainly be an important step, along with longer

Toward what?

- 201 -

waiting periods for gun ownership. But closing the loophole that allows private sellers at gun shows to engage in their business without proper licenses would also be important, as well as increased regulation at all gun shows, of which there are anywhere from 2,500 to 5,200 annually.

It is an uphill battle, particularly in the current political climate, to get the populace, which does not currently favor increased gun control laws in high numbers, to perceive gun ownership as privilege rather than a right. The NRA has been allowed for far too long to dominate the national conversation on guns and gun control; more effective public education is needed on the topic, and politicians need to grow more backbone when confronted with the gun lobby. Michael Bloomberg, mayor of New York City, put it this way: "There is one particular fear the NRA manufactures with great success: fear of electoral defeat. Romney has walked away from the assault-weapons ban he once supported, and in nearly four years, Obama has offered no legislation to rein in illegal guns. In Congress, the NRA threatens lawmakers who fail to do its ideological bidding, although its record in defeating candidates is much more myth than reality..." It is time to stop fear and the gun lobby from dominating an important national subject and subverting the nation's interests for its own.

Here is another contradiction. This is not the point on which Eleanor closed her discussion of the Second Amendment.

STEP 6: Peer Edit

Analysis of First Draft:

What is this writer's point? It is nearly impossible to discern Eleanor's point. On the one hand, she claims to be offering a rebuttal to Chandra's pro-gun-control argument. However, much of the evidence and her interpretation of the evidence seems to support gun control. Much of her own argument is implied as a response to something Eleanor's readers may or may not have read. Thus, Eleanor does not really make her own claims clear or show how her evidence supports her claims—or counters the claims that she is supposed to be rebutting.

What is this writer's angle? It is premature to talk about an angle without a clear point. Eleanor's angle is equally uncertain. At first, she seems to take the position that she will not debate the problem of violence but will debate its cause and cure. Later, however, she abandons that angle and does not really replace it.

How strong is this writer's support? How authoritative is her overall argument? Eleanor has facts, and she is pretty careful with citing sources, but most of her evidence supports the point she is supposed to be rebutting. Because her central point is unclear, she does not strike the reader as terribly authoritative.

What techniques has this writer used to establish this authority? Eleanor provides facts and cites sources.

What specific details, facts, etc., make this argument convincing? Among the specific facts, statistics, and quotations Eleanor provides are:

- Specific poll numbers showing changes in gun control support
- Specific homicide rates before and after Florida's "right to carry" law passed
- Quotation of entire Second Amendment
- Quotation from *District of Columbia vs. Heller*
- NRA gets a great portion of its over $200 million lobbying budget directly from gun manufacturers.
- United Kingdom had only 50 deaths from shootings in 2006; during the same period, there were 25,423 such deaths in the U.S.

NOW plan and write your own rebuttal of someone else's argument.

STEP 1: Select a Topic

What topics or issues have you read about or discussed in school that might make for an interesting argument?

What issues or controversies in your school, community, state, or nation have attracted your interest?

What trends or movements might have a direct impact on you or those you love?

STEP 2: Develop a Slant/Angle/Hook

What aspects of your indicated issues are most important? Why?

What aspects of your indicated issues are most interesting? Why?

What ideas or insights do you have that others seem not to have noticed or seem to undervalue?

STEP 3: Brainstorm, Discuss, Research

What sources are likely to provide the most accurate and authoritative support for your argument?

What specific details, facts, etc., are likely to make your argument convincing?

STEP 4: Outline

STEP 5: First Draft

STEP 6: Peer Edit

What is this writer's point?

What is this writer's angle?

How strong is this writer's support? How authoritative is his or her overall argument?

What techniques has this writer used to establish this authority?

What specific details, facts, etc., make this argument convincing?

STEP 7: Revised/Final Draft

Here are Eleanor's editor's comments and analysis as well as her responses:

- From the beginning, Eleanor makes a common error. While it is true that her essay is written to rebut another writer's argument, this argument must stand on its own. By phrasing her opening sentence as a response, she has already undermined the independence of her own essay.
- Eleanor is still phrasing her sentences as if she is already in the middle of a discussion. She has made no claim, introduced no argument, simply jumping in with her statistics to counter statistics she *assumes* her reader has seen.
- Notice that Eleanor more or less dismisses a key point. The crux of Chandra's issue becomes merely a peripheral concern. This strategy might backfire on Eleanor.
- If we are still in Eleanor's introduction, then this is a valid statement of her central claim. None of the previous material has read like an introduction, however, so "mere availability" reads more like another dismissal than a rebuttal.
- "Little doubt" among whom? Again, Eleanor is presuming knowledge on the part of her reader that she may actually need to establish.
- It has taken Eleanor a long and torturous route to get to something like her central claim.
- Eleanor is still responding to Chandra more than writing her own essay. This error probably originates in her deciding to follow Chandra's outline rather than draft her own based on her own central and supporting claims.
- This is an interesting rebuttal to Chandra's claims about the NRA's power, but it bears no relevance to Eleanor's stated claim— that gun availability is not the cause of gun violence.
- Eleanor should remember from last year that rhetorical questions are so overused as to be virtually ineffective and should be avoided whenever possible.
- Eleanor should revise to eliminate this cliché.
- Again, Eleanor has lost sight of the claim she is rebutting, the influence of the gun lobby, especially the NRA.

- Eleanor loses her focus in this long sentence. While it is true…*what*?

- Eleanor does have these figures in her notes, but she needs to cite her sources since she is offering hard numbers.

- Since this is fairly surprising information that runs counter to conventional wisdom, Eleanor needs to do more than merely provide the title of the book she consulted.

- Does this information contradict the claims of a steady decrease that Eleanor made earlier? She does not seem concerned with this apparent contradiction.

- On a grammar and mechanics note, Eleanor must decide whether she is going to address the NRA as a singular or a plural.

- Eleanor seems to have almost completely lost her focus. In her rebuttal of Chandra's pro-gun-control essay, she seems to want to bolster Chandra's arguments.

- Eleanor is wrong here. Article 1, Section 8 of the Constitution grants Congress the power "To raise and support Armies," and Article 2 of the Constitution establishes the President of the United States as the "Commander in Chief of the Army and Navy of the United States, and of the Militia of the several States, when called into the actual Service of the United States." Thus, the Constitution makes provision for both a national army *and* state militias.

- Now Eleanor is talking about assault weapons with no transition from her discussion of the Second Amendment.

- Eleanor still seems more interested in building Chandra's argument than rebutting it.

- Toward what?

- Here is another contradiction. This is not the point on which Eleanor closed her discussion of the Second Amendment.

And here is Eleanor's reaction:

> It never occurred to me to structure this like an independent essay, but that makes sense to me now. I need to redo my outline and make up my own central claim and supporting claims. It's just that what I'm claiming in these claims will rebut what Chandra says in hers. I guess I also need to be more careful not to lose my focus. Although I am pretty much in favor of gun control, I should be able to build a case rebutting Chandra's, or at least to qualify her point.
>
> Rather than supporting Chandra's pro-control position, I need to find holes in her arguments and evidence to disagree with her.

Analysis of First Draft

What is this writer's point? It is nearly impossible to discern Eleanor's point. On the one hand, she claims to be offering a rebuttal to Chandra's pro-gun-control argument. However, much of the evidence and her interpretation of the evidence seems to support gun control. Much of her own argument is implied as a response to something Eleanor's readers may or may not have read. Thus, Eleanor does not really make her own claims clear or show how her evidence supports her claims—or counters the claims that she is supposed to be rebutting.

> Central Claim: There may or may not be a problem in the United States with violent crime, but guns are not the problem, and new gun control legislation is not the answer.
>
> Maybe I should suggest what the problem is... like America's "Culture of Violence" or something, but how much effort would I have to put into supporting that?
>
> Supporting Claims:
>
> — Many studies suggest that, contrary to common belief, crime in the United States is actually decreasing.
>
> — The NRA and the gun lobby in general are no more powerful or influential than any other lobbying organization.
>
> — Even in places with liberal gun laws or where gun control legislation has been overturned by SCOTUS, gun-related crime has gone down.
>
> These are actually direct refutations of Chandra's supporting claims, but I think I can finesse them to be more independent but still address these points.

> Maybe I should add something like: "Current bestselling movies, television shows, and books show that American society enjoys a "Culture of Violence" that clearly contributes to our rate of violent crime."

What is this writer's angle? It is premature to talk about an angle without a clear point. Eleanor's angle is equally uncertain. At first, she seems to take the position that she will not debate the problem of violence but will debate its cause and cure. Later, however, she abandons that angle and does not really replace it.

> Maybe I can do a "contrary to popular belief" or "contrary to conventional wisdom" type of thing.

How strong is this writer's support? How authoritative is his or her overall argument? Eleanor has facts, and she is pretty careful with citing sources, but most of her evidence supports the point she is supposed to be rebutting. Because her central point is unclear, she does not strike the reader as terribly authoritative.

> I think I've got the support. I'm just not using it to my advantage.

What techniques has this writer used to establish this authority? Eleanor provides facts and cites sources.

> Clarifying my point and writing my essay as a more stand-alone piece will help my authority.

What specific details, facts, etc., make this argument convincing? Among the specific facts, statistics, and quotations Eleanor provides are:

- Specific poll numbers showing changes in gun control support

- Specific homicide rates before and after Florida's "right to carry" law passed

- Quotation of entire Second Amendment

- Quotation from District of Columbia vs. Heller

- NRA gets a great portion of its over $200 million lobbying budget directly from gun manufacturers.

- United Kingdom had only 50 deaths from shootings in 2006; during the same period, there were 25,423 such deaths in the U.S.

> I have lots of evidence I can use.

Here is Eleanor's revised outline:

Central Claim: There may or may not be a problem in the United States with violent crime, but guns are not the problem, and new gun control legislation is not the answer.

I. Many gun control arguments are based on incomplete, misinterpreted, or misstated data.

    A. Gun ownership and gun-related crime

        1. Gun-control arguments

            a. National Geographic online calls United States gun violence a "public health problem."

            b. 3.02 per 100,000 for all G12 nations combined compared to 2.98/100,000 for the U.S.

            c. "between 2004 and 2010; 370,401 people died from gun-related violence, according to the Centers for Disease Control." But what does that translate to in x/100,000?

        2. Truth of the situation

            a. Gun ownership is down.

                (i). percentage of U.S. households owning at least one gun reached a high of 54% in 1977

                (ii). decreased steadily reaching a low of 33% on 2009

                (iii). Clinton-era decline was part of this 22-year trend

            b. Gun-related murders were down in 27 states from 2009—2010 by as much as 41%.

    B. Gun control as a deterrent to crime

        1. Even in places with liberal gun laws or where gun-control legislation has been overturned by SCOTUS, gun-related crime has gone down.

            a. <u>D.C. vs. Heller</u>

            b. <u>McDonald vs. Chicago</u>

            c. Florida's "Right-to-Carry" law

            d. Texas murder rates down after "right-to-carry" law

        2. Gun-control arguments

            a. James Holmes (Aurora) would not have been able to shoot 72 people, killing 12 of them, if he had access only to conventional weapons.

            b. Gun owner most likely to be victim of own gun

3. Truth of the situation

    a. Timothy McVeigh killed 168 (including 19 children) injured 680 using materials from a garden center: fertilizer and motor oil.

    b. September 11 attacks carried out using simple box cutters.

    c. 1982 survey of male felons in 11 state prisons

        (i). 34% had been "scared off, shot at, wounded, or captured by an armed victim."

        (ii). 40% had decided not to commit a crime because they "knew or believed that the victim was carrying a gun."

        (iii). 69% personally knew other criminals who had been "scared off, shot at, wounded, or captured by an armed victim."

II. NRA receives a lot of blame and/or credit for swaying Congress.

    A. The NRA and the gun lobby in general are no more powerful or influential than any other lobbying organization.

        1. Center for American Progress: "The NRA's influence in fact is waning and is rarely significant in any election."

        2. The American Prospect: "The NRA has virtually no impact on congressional elections....when it comes to elections, the NRA is a paper tiger."

        3. In the 2008 presidential election, the NRA spent ten million dollars, all of it earmarked to defeat Barack Obama...but Barack Obama was elected.

    B. Other lobbying agencies spend as much, if not more, money to influence elections and sway politicians' views.

        1. AARP (American Association of Retired Persons) = $27.9 million in 2008 compared to NRA's $10 million

        2. United States Chamber of Commerce = $91,955,000 in 2008

III. Our choices in movies, books, and television programming clearly show that the United States enjoys a Culture of Violence that is probably at the heart of both gun ownership and violent crime rather than the ownership being the cause of the crime.

    A. Television shows

        1. "Police Procedural"

        2. "Real Crime"

    B. Movies

        1. The Expendables

        2. Batman—Dark Knight

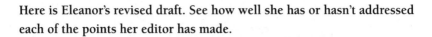

Here is Eleanor's revised draft. See how well she has or hasn't addressed each of the points her editor has made.

Whenever something bad happens, people rush to find a scapegoat. Nowhere is this more true than in the United States in which every act of violence committed is blamed on the gun lobby and the fact that United States citizens are allowed by law to own guns. A quick study of our society's most popular and successful books, television shows, movies, and other forms of entertainment media shows that we are a society that is fascinated by violence. We love reality-TV-style re-creations of sensational crimes. We love "police procedural" programs like Criminal Minds, any one of the countless subsets of Law and Order, Flashpoint, Burn Notice—the list is endless. Blockbuster Hollywood films and franchises prove a cultural obsession with crime, criminals, fast cars, big explosions, and powerful guns. The simple fact is that, in a capitalist society, producers make only what they know they can sell. If guns and violence didn't make a profit, there would be no guns and violence on television, in the movies, or in the books we read.

Eleanor did not specifically outline this insight, but it's valid, and there's no reason she shouldn't use it. Notice also how much more confident Eleanor's language is. This is probably due to the fact that she has a much clearer sense of the point she is going to argue and how she is going to argue it.

It is illogical and unfair to look at incidents of real violence in the United States, like the recent mass shootings in the Aurora, Colorado, movie theater and the Sikh temple in Oak Creek, Wisconsin, and immediately point the finger of blame at the fact that Americans can legally own guns. Such events as these might suggest that there may or may not be a problem in the United States with violent crime, but guns are not the problem, and new gun control legislation is not the answer. Many arguments in favor of gun control are based on incomplete, misinterpreted, or misstated data. Though probably well-intended, gun control advocates are simply not looking at

Here is a clear statement of Eleanor's central claim.

the entire picture. These same supporters of gun control measures view the National Rifle Association (NRA) as the leader and spokesman of a powerful gun lobby. Therefore, the NRA is blamed for influencing elections and swaying legislators so that a rich and vocal minority makes the rules and places the law-abiding majority in danger. The fact is, however, that the NRA is no more powerful or active than any other lobbying organization. In fact, recent data shows that the NRA is considerably <u>less</u> successful in its supposed lobbying efforts than it is given credit for.

This is an excellent introduction. The reader knows exactly what Eleanor's point and supporting claims are.

Many of the most popular gun control arguments are based on incomplete, misinterpreted, or misstated information. Gun control advocates are not necessarily dishonest, but they have been badly informed and coaxed into an essentially indefensible position. Theirs is an argument they cannot win. First and foremost, is the issue of the relationship between gun ownership and gun-related crime. It is true that the U.S. sees more deaths from firearms annually than Australia, Canada, and the United Kingdom combined, but given the fact that we claim the highest number of citizens who own private firearms, the fact that we are only twenty-eighth in the world for gun-related deaths is significant. Obviously, guns are not the only cause of the problem if we have far more guns but fewer deaths than twenty-seven other nations do. An article in the <u>National Geographic</u> online might call gun violence in the United States a "public health problem," but this evaluation does not necessarily suggest a high amount of crime. <u>Any</u> gun violence in an economically-developed, civilized nation could be considered a "public health problem." The Centers for Disease Control claims that 370,401 people died from gun-related violence between 2004 and 2010, but they do not explain whether this is an exceptionally high or relatively

This phrase is a cliché, but it does help Eleanor establish the order in which she is going to address her opponent's arguments.

low number. Other violence statistics are stated as ratios, so many incidents per 100,000 people. All of the G12 nations combined suffer 3.02 gun-related deaths per 100,000 people per year. The United States suffers 2.98 deaths per 100,000 people. Our <u>number</u> of deaths might be higher, but our <u>rate</u> is lower. Keep in mind that the United States also has more privately owned guns, even as it has fewer gun-related deaths.

It is also a fact that gun ownership in the United States is down. According to a 2011 article in <u>The Guardian UK</u> online magazine, the percentage of U.S. households that owned at least one gun reached a high of 54% in 1977. That percentage has decreased steadily since then, reaching a low of 33% in 2009. Gun control enthusiasts like to cite a drop in gun-related crime that seemed to follow President Clinton's passing of the 1994 Brady Bill and Crime Bill, which included a federal ban on manufacturing and selling assault weapons. Whatever decline they cite, however, is most likely simply a part of this national trend. During this same period, the states of Florida and Texas were still enjoying a decline in gun violence that followed the passage of their "right-to-carry" bills. Florida alone witnessed a decline in gun deaths from 11/100,000 in 1988, the year after the law took effect, to 6.5/100,000 in 2008. This is according to a website called "Just Facts, a Resource for Independent Thinkers."

Despite what gun control advocates claim about the need for stronger gun control legislation, even in places with liberal gun laws or where gun control legislation has been overturned by the Supreme Court, gun-related crime has gone down. Washington, D.C.'s, 1976 ban on handguns is a perfect example. According to data from the Federal Bureau of Investigation, Criminal Justice

There are a few problems with this section. First, Eleanor is possibly misinterpreting the data herself by trying to make the distinction between rates and numbers. To prove this point, she would need to cite populations and then convert rates to numbers or vice versa. Second, even though she had gleaned this data from Chandra's essay, she must still cite her sources. Finally, Eleanor is still being careless with first-person and direct address.

Eleanor has not noticed her reasoning error, but the Florida statistic helps her some.

Information Services Division, after the law took effect, the rate of violent crime actually increased from 28/100,000 in 1976 to a high of 80/100,000 in 1995. A sharp decline that occurred from 1995 to 2008 can hardly be attributed to the strict law that had been in place for almost twenty years. It is ironic, however, that even with the decline, when the Supreme Court overturned Washington, D.C.'s law in 2008, the crime rate was still higher than when the 1976 law went into effect. And contrary to what some might believe, the 1995–2008 decline continued after the ban was overturned.

Gun control advocates argue that gun availability must lead to gun crime. After all, if James Holmes in Aurora, Colorado, hadn't been able to get his hands on high-powered assault weapons—if he'd had access only to conventional weapons—he would not have been able to slaughter as many people as he did in as short a time. The fact remains, however, that Timothy McVeigh killed 168 people and injured 680 more using readily-available garden fertilizer and motor oil. Perhaps we need to pass stronger legislation to limit the availability of Miracle-Gro and WD-40.

Advocates of gun control also cite figures that seem to suggest gun owners put themselves and their families at risk by owning a firearm. Instead of increasing the owners' safety, gun control advocates argue that the owners themselves are more likely to be wounded or killed by their own weapon than by any intruder. A 1982 survey of male felons in eleven state prisons across the country, as described in their book, Armed and Considered Dangerous: A Survey of Felons and Their Firearms, James D. Wright and Peter H. Rossi report that 34% (one-third) of the surveyed convicts had been "scared off, shot at, wounded, or captured by an armed victim." Nearly

Sarcasm can be amusing, and sometimes it is difficult to resist, but it is always a risk. Eleanor stands as much chance of alienating her reader as she does of bolstering her argument.

half (40%) had decided not to commit a crime because they "knew or believed that the victim was carrying a gun." More than two-thirds (69%) said they <u>personally knew</u> other criminals who had been "scared off, shot at, wounded, or captured by an armed victim." Clearly, there is some security in owning and carrying a gun. If those potential victims had <u>not</u> been armed, they would have been mugged or their houses would have been burglarized.

When it comes to lobbying for or against gun control legislation, and in the minds of gun-control advocates lobbying for or against gun crime, the National Rifle Association (NRA) comes under special attack as the face and voice of the gun lobby. The fact is, however, that the NRA and the gun lobby in general is no more active or powerful than is any other special interest group. Gun control advocates love the fact that, in the 2008 presidential election, the NRA spent $10 million to defeat Barack Obama. This <u>would</u> be an impressive example of excessive spending and undue political clout—if it were not for the simple fact that, in the 2008 presidential election, despite the NRA's $10 million, <u>Barack Obama was elected</u>. According to the Center for American Progress: "The NRA's influence in fact is waning and is rarely significant in any election." Paul Waldman of <u>The American Prospect</u> agrees. He claims to have gathered data on the outcome of "every House and Senate election, including the margins of victory, the money spent by each candidate, the partisan character of each district, and whether the NRA made an endorsement in the race and how much money they spent." He concludes, "The NRA has virtually no impact on congressional elections....when it comes to elections, the NRA is a paper tiger." The impact of their 2008 election spending clearly supports this conclusion.

Eleanor is making an important connection for her reader. Speaking in favor of gun control legislation, Chandra tacitly equated gun ownership with gun crime. Eleanor is making a case that the one is not the cause of the other.

Having unleashed her sarcasm, Eleanor is now having trouble controlling it.

If gun control is not the answer to a problem with gun violence in the United States, it is reasonable to ask what is. One doesn't need to be a brilliant sociologist or anthropologist to take a look at the popular culture of the United States and see that we enjoy what can only be described as a "Culture of Violence." The most popular, most anticipated, and most profitable books, television shows, and movies highlight—even glamorize—violence. It is more likely that this cultural love of violence is the source of both our high rate of gun ownership and our high rate of crime, than that the one causes the other.

A look at the television schedule of any cable or dish provider will show that at any given time of the day, it will be possible to see episodes of "police procedural" shows like <u>Law and Order</u>, <u>CSI: Crime Scene Investigation</u>, <u>NCIS</u>, <u>Flashpoint</u>, or a dozen of other programs or spin-offs that focus on crime. Other stations provide nearly 24/7 offerings of reviews, summaries, and re-enactments of "famous" or intriguing crimes.

Hollywood's offerings are similar. Two examples are the top-rated and moneymaking franchises <u>The Expendables</u> and <u>The Dark Knight</u> series. <u>The Expendables</u> debuted in the United States at 3,270 theaters. According to <u>Box Office Mojo</u>, after the debut weekend, the film ranked as the tenth-biggest independent film release of all time. It debuted as the number one box office hit and earned $34.8 million in its opening weekend—$13.3 million on its opening day. In praise of the film, a reviewer for <u>The Hollywood Reporter</u> wrote "the body count is high and the personalities click in this <u>old-school testosterone fest</u>" (emphasis mine). In a similar positive review, <u>Boxoffice Magazine</u> stated that the film was "filled with <u>literally explosive</u> excitement" (emphasis mine). Not to judge the film or the people who

"24/7" is a colloquial or slang expression. Eleanor should find a more formal way of expressing her meaning.

- 216 -

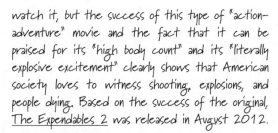

watch it, but the success of this type of "action-adventure" movie and the fact that it can be praised for its "high body count" and its "literally explosive excitement" clearly shows that American society loves to witness shooting, explosions, and people dying. Based on the success of the original, The Expendables 2 was released in August 2012.

Not to blame the victims, but it is a fact that the twelve people killed and the fifty-eight people wounded in the tragic Aurora, Colorado, shooting were at a special midnight showing of The Dark Knight Rises, the latest movie in another blockbuster franchise filled with explosions and gunfights. The fact that theaters all over the country held these special midnight showings on the day the film was to debut, and the fact that so many people attended them is more evidence of Americans' love of violence. Whether or not we admit it, we are a violent society, and it does not make any sense to ignore our Culture of Violence when looking for a cause of our high rates of gun ownership and gun-related crime.

As is often the case, Eleanor's new material is not as polished as what she composed earlier and edited and revised. This is a strong reason for taking even a revised essay into a third draft.

By the way, the film was so highly anticipated that it was predicted to make as much as $198 million on its opening weekend in the United States. Its actual opening figures are uncertain because Warner Brothers decided not to release the figures as usual in respect for the victims of the Aurora shooting. It is generally agreed that news of the shooting hurt opening weekend attendance and ticket sales, but even still, they are estimated to have been between $75 million and $77 million on its opening day. As of October 15, 2012, The Dark Knight Rises earned $446,247,060 in North America alone.

There are more academic phrases that can be used to introduce incidental, supplementary information. This is another argument for Eleanor's taking this essay into a third draft.

Clearly, even more evidence of a Culture of Violence that lies at the root of our rates of both violent crime and gun ownership.

This sentence fragment is another strong argument for a third draft.

Not only do gun control advocates search for the wrong cause—and therefore the wrong solution—to a national problem, they also tend to want to ignore the law of the land. The Second Amendment to the Constitution of the United States reads:

> "A well regulated militia being necessary to the security of a free state, the right of the people to keep and bear arms shall not be infringed."

While gun control advocates focus only on the first part of the amendment, the "militia" phrase, the Supreme Court of the United States has looked at the entire amendment, including the "right of the people" clause. In 2008, when the Supreme Court, by a 5 − 4 division, overturned Washington, D.C.'s, ban on handguns, the majority decision read in part:

> The Second Amendment is naturally divided into two parts: its prefatory clause and its operative clause. The former does not limit the latter grammatically, but rather announces a purpose. The Amendment could be rephrased, 'Because a well regulated Militia is necessary to the security of a free State, the right of the people to keep and bear Arms shall not be infringed.

The law, according to the Supreme Court, was that the right of the people was not to be infringed. Similarly, the Supreme Court's 2010 5−4 decision in McDonald vs. Chicago struck down Chicago's 1982 ban on gun ownership. To arrive at the court's decision, the majority justices looked to the Fourteenth Amendment, as well as the Second:

> it is clear that the Framers and ratifiers of the Fourteenth Amendment counted the right to keep and bear arms among those fundamental rights necessary to our system of ordered liberty.

Gun control is not just a matter of choice or convenience, it is a matter of law. Advocates of stronger legislation need to keep that in mind as they search for solutions to what they perceive as a severe problem.

Whether or not you personally like guns, own guns, or have ever shot a gun, there can be little doubt that gun ownership in the United States is a right guaranteed by the Constitution. It is really necessary, then, to keep that in mind in any discussion of crime in America and how to lower what few would disagree is an unacceptable rate of violent crime. Gun-related crime might be a problem in the United States, but it is just as likely that high crime and high gun ownership are both caused by the same "Culture of Violence" as that the gun ownership causes the crime.

Eleanor apparently likes the phrase "Culture of Violence," but she overuses it a bit. If it is, indeed, a quotation, she needs to provide her source. Overall, this is a much stronger essay than her previous draft, more focused and pointed and better supported.

Analysis of Revised Draft

Has the new draft strengthened the rebuttal? Yes, definitely. The author has tightened her focus and found additional support and data to back up her claims, and reinforced the central argument.

Has the angle of the rebuttal changed in any way? The earlier draft could not really be said to have a slant. Now, the slant is that gun control advocates miss the point in their desire to lower crime in the United States.

Has the author brought sufficient additional support for her claims in this draft? Yes, she has addressed the points in the critique that mentioned the need for additional detail, support, and data.

What else has this writer used to establish this authority? She has clarified her central claim and organized a focused and well-supported argument. She also writes with more confidence, occasionally slipping into sarcasm, which can work with some audiences but might be perceived as bullying or disrespect by others.

What additional details, facts, etc., make this argument more convincing? Eleanor's new information includes:

- Quotations from Supreme Court majority decisions.
- Data from a survey of convicted felons.
- Sales and attendance figures on *The Expendables* and *Dark Knight Rises*.
- Statistics on drops in gun ownership and crime rates to counter gun control advocate claims.

POSSIBLE STEP 8: Rewrite Opportunity

MINI-LESSON 1:

The Test or Exam Essay: (Support, refute, or qualify the thesis that...)

The exam essay—and this includes high-school and college mid-term and final exams, as well as any sample of writing you are required to produce in a formal test situation like the SATs, ACTs, an IB exam, or any of the numerous AP exams that require essays—is possibly the most important writing many students do, and it is ironically the writing they toss away as inconsequential, dismissing the need to produce a well-written essay in favor of an information mind dump.

While the scorer of your exam essay might truly be more concerned with the quality of the information than the quality of your presentation, there are still several reasons for wanting to take a step back from the gush of facts and insights and take some control as a writer over what information to share and how:

- Your scorer *must* be able to understand your answer. No matter how much information you dump into your answer, if that information appears only as it occurred to you, your answer will probably be a jumbled, incoherent mess—written babbling. All of your facts might be accurate, and all of your insights might be brilliant, but if your scorer cannot make sense of them, you cannot expect a high score on your exam.

- Giving some thought to presentation might prevent you from tossing in every fact you can think of, whether relevant to the issue or not. A little planning will help you weed out the irrelevancies and redundancies that will most certainly lower your score if they end up in your essay.

- Giving some thought to presentation might prevent you from leaving out important information. You don't get "credit" for knowing it if you don't state it. You won't receive a top score for an exemplary essay if you leave out crucial ideas or facts.

- Giving some thought to presentation might help you maintain your focus and ensure that you are answering the question that has been asked. No matter how chock full of information your mind dump is, if you're asked to analyze the character of Atticus Finch in *To Kill a Mockingbird*, a discussion of the similarities between Tom Robinson's trial and the historical Scottsboro Boys case—even a thorough and insightful study— would be off-topic and might actually net you a failing grade.

- Even on exams in which the information is valued above the writing, the well-written essay will probably receive a higher score than an equally informative but badly written attempt. If you want to maximize your score—assuming you do actually know the answer to the question—you want to show your ability to effectively communicate what you know.

This does not mean, however, that you can allow yourself the luxury of several days' planning, writing, conferencing with an editor, and revising. You will have time—in some exams, you will have *barely enough* time—to put together a decent first draft. Still, familiarity with—and confidence in—a development process will help you.

In **Eleanor** and **Jeff's** school, most of the eleventh graders study United States history from the European colonization of the Americas to the end of the Civil War and Abraham Lincoln's assassination. Here is the second and final essay prompt on their U.S. History final exam:

> *Read the following excerpts* [from two opposing views of federalism and the "success" of the Constitutional Convention of 1787]. *Choose either argument and write a carefully reasoned and well-supported essay that defends, challenges, or qualifies your chosen author's central thesis. Be certain to support all of your own assertions with evidence from material studied in class or your own reading.*

These students had a total of 3 hours (180 minutes) for their entire exam, so most students found they had about an hour (60 minutes) for this essay. Some standardized assessments allow for as little as 20 minutes to as much as 90 minutes for a single essay. How much time you spend on each step will obviously depend on how much total time you are allowed, but you can estimate a schedule by allocating a certain percentage of your time to each step.

STEP 1: Draft a Thesis (no more than 5 min out of 60)

For the above prompt, this is a relatively easy step since your thesis is simply a reaction to someone else's. You do need, though, to generate a new idea.

Always be aware of the possibility of borrowing words or ideas from the prompt in order to streamline your process. The scorer of your essay probably does not care about the side you take in the discussion as much as about how you argue that side.

Here are Eleanor's attempts at a thesis:

- [Author A] says that political maneuvering and excessive southern influence at the Constitutional Convention more or less guaranteed that the United States would fight something like the Civil War before the nation was even 100 years old.

- [Author B] argues that, far from being inevitable, the Civil War was the direct result of overzealous federalists and greedy northern industrialists whose goal was to expand their power and wealth at the expense of the individual sovereign state.

> From the beginning, Eleanor gets herself into trouble. These are merely restatements of the authors' points. Neither begins to address the point of the prompt.

Here are Jeff's:

- The number of compromises they had to make to draft a Constitution in 1787 and the types of compromises they made made it almost inevitable that the United States would break up in warring factions in less than a hundred years.

> Jeff is off to a slightly better start. He has an arguable thesis. Still, the reader must infer which source he is addressing and the extent to which he is "defend[ing], challeng[ing], or qualif[ying]" Author A's thesis.

- [Author A] is correct to claim that "political maneuvering" made division among the states and Civil War inevitable, but he is wrong to blame the South. The number of compromises made on both sides and the types of principles on which they compromised were the factors that doomed the new country to division and war.

> **TIME SPENT: 5 MIN—TIME REMAINING: 55 MIN**

STEP 2: Brainstorm, Jot Notes (no more than 10 min out of 60)

On a timed test, especially an "important" test—one on which you really want to do well—you will probably be tempted to jump right into writing your essay.

Such a strategy can only lower your score.

Since you want every point you can earn, and you know that this essay should be a thoughtful presentation of your knowledge and insight, you want to jot down all the facts, figures, examples, and specific sources you can remember.

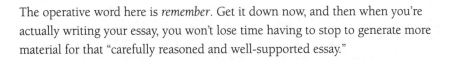

The operative word here is *remember*. Get it down now, and then when you're actually writing your essay, you won't lose time having to stop to generate more material for that "carefully reasoned and well-supported essay."

Here are Eleanor's notes:

- Virginia was largest state
- Pennsylvania
- Rhode Island did not attend
- Sovereign States
- Compare w/ Articles of Confederation
- Virginia Plan
- New Jersey Plan
- Electoral college

- James Madison
  Washington and Jefferson
- Federalists vs. Anti-Federalists
  Federalist Papers

- Connecticut Compromise

> Eleanor is still not thinking in terms of writing a coherent, cohesive essay and addressing the specific prompt she has been given. Her apparently random listing of information gives no indication of the point she intends to argue.

Here are Jeff's:

- representation: by population or per state?
- abolition of slave trade
- nullification... alienation/sedition... almost French Revolution here? (anti-federalists)
- North/South tariff issue... South felt disadvantaged.

- 3/5 compromise (representation vs. taxation)
- population growth patterns (irony here... 3/5 here, too)

> Notice that Jeff, without going into elaborate detail, is thinking about how he is going to use the information he has to address the assigned prompt.

> **TIME SPENT: 15 MIN—TIME REMAINING: 45 MIN**

STEP 3: Outline (no more than 5 min out of 60)

The inescapable truth is that writers do plan and organize their thoughts before committing to a draft. It almost doesn't matter what the outline looks like, but you don't want to have to be two-thirds through your essay, with five minutes left, and realize that you *should have talked about* some very important point much earlier in your essay.

Here is Eleanor's attempt at an outline:

I. [Author A]

    A. Virginia was largest state

    B. James Madison and Washington big leaders

        1. Madison afraid con would fail if Wash not go

    C. Rhode Island did not attend

II. Federalists vs. Anti-Federalists

    A. Sovereign States

    B. Federalist Papers

    C. Virginia Plan

    D. New Jersey Plan

    E. Connecticut Compromise

III. Electoral college

> Certainly, this outline represents an organizational plan, but given the problems with Eleanor's "thesis" and the vagueness of her notes, it is hard to predict whether this organization plan will lead to a "carefully reasoned and well-supported essay."

Here is Jeff's:

Issue of representation

    by population (favored by big states)

    equal per state (favored by small states)

    Connecticut Compromise satisfied small states

    3/5 compromise satisfied big southern states

    population shift to North... (irony)

Slavery

    3/5 compromise "legitimized" slavery

    no abolition of slave trade

Tariff of 1789 (Hamilton Tariff)

    advantaged North

    disadvantaged South

Although he is not using Roman numerals, upper case letters, etc., Jeff's outline is not a radical departure from the formal, academic outline. More important, though, is the fact that he centers the information he wants to present on issues. This will probably help him find and maintain a tight focus for his essay.

TIME SPENT: 20 MIN—TIME REMAINING: 40 MIN

STEP 4: Write Your Essay (35 min out of 60)

With a reasonably strong thesis, some clear and specific notes, and a sense of where you want to take your reader, writing the essay is almost a mere formality.

Here is Eleanor's essay:

Two famous historians and authors, [Author A], who sympathizes with the North, and [Author B], who is clearly a Southern sympathizer, claim two almost opposite reasons that the Constitutional Convention of 1787 caused the Civil War. [Author A] says that political maneuvering and excessive southern influence at the Constitutional Convention more or less guaranteed that the United States would fight something like the Civil War before the nation was even 100 years old. [Author B] argues that, far from being inevitable, the Civil War was the direct result of overzealous federalists and greedy northern industrialists whose goal was to expand their power and wealth at the expense of the individual sovereign state.

Eleanor is starting out weakly. She really has no thesis, only a vague recap of what the two authors claim.

In support of [Author A]'s claim is the fact that, at the time of the Convention, Virginia was the largest state in terms of population. Their proposal for a federal legislature, the Virginia Plan, bases state representation in both houses of the legislature on population. This proposal was popular with big states, like Virginia, who figured they could control the federal government because they would have more representation in Congress. Smaller states, like New Jersey, did not like the plan so much. With fewer representatives, they would have less representation.

New Jersey countered with the New Jersey Plan, which divided the legislature into a single house, based on one representative for each state. That way, all of the states, whether big or small, would be equally represented, and no one region would be able to dominate the government. Because they protested the whole idea of a federal government, the state of Rhode Island didn't send any delegates to the Convention.

The Federalists were the bloc of people who favored a strong federal government. Some even advocated abolishing the individual states and allowing the federal government to control everything. Their opposition was called the Anti-Federalists, and they supported states' rights. At the time of the Revolutionary War, individual states like Virginia, New Jersey, and Connecticut were not parts of a larger whole; they were their own whole. All of the Continental Congresses before the War and the United States Congress under the Articles of Confederation did not create a single, large nation. These congresses were meetings of representatives from all of the little "nations." Like the countries of Europe, the individual states considered themselves to be "sovereign states." The Anti-Federalists saw the Constitution as a threat to each state's sovereignty.

As her introduction suggested she would, Eleanor has embarked on a simple summation of everything she can remember from class. Certainly, her grade will reflect her understanding—which is not completely accurate—but she will not receive a top score for addressing the assigned prompt.

Nothing Eleanor is saying here is wrong, but there does not seem to be a point to it. She has fallen into the "mind dump" trap.

To satisfy the big states, who wanted to control Congress by having more representatives, and the small states that wanted equal power in the government, the Connecticut Compromise was adopted. This plan gave us the House of Representatives and the Senate that we know today. The House of Representatives is based on each state's population, so some individual neighborhoods in New York City have their own representative, while entire states like Delaware have only one. But the Senate gives each state, regardless of population, two representatives—two senators per state.

Because the Constitution says that the states elect the president and not the people, we have an electoral college. Each state has the same number of electors as representatives in Congress (Senate plus House of Representatives). The people of the state vote for whom to pledge their electors to. They do not vote for the president directly. Many people criticize the electoral college because they say it undermines our American democracy. Others say it is necessary because it maintains a balance between the sovereignty of each state and the federal government.

> All well and good, but Eleanor has still not addressed the Constitutional issues that led to the Civil War. Even if she were graded on content knowledge alone, she would receive a low passing grade at best because she is not demonstrating any knowledge beyond 1787.

> Eleanor clearly learned quite a bit about the Constitutional Convention and the process by which the Constitution was negotiated. Still, she has not really addressed the prompt at all and does not demonstrate any knowledge beyond the 1787 Convention that is implied by the prompt—the divisive issues that ultimately led to secession and Civil War.

Analysis of Exam Essay

What is this writer's point? In this essay, Eleanor seems to want to discuss the "almost opposite reasons that the Constitutional Convention of 1787 caused the Civil War." It is not clear whether she agrees or disagrees that these reasons did in fact cause the war.

In what way(s) does this thesis fulfill the requirements of the prompt? It doesn't. Students were instructed first to select one of the sources. Eleanor has not. They were then instructed to "defend, challenge, or qualify [their] chosen author's central thesis." Eleanor does not do this. Her essay is a narrative summary of a few of the issues facing the Constitutional Convention.

What information does the writer provide to demonstrate her understanding of the tested subject matter? Eleanor does do a nice job reviewing some of the key issues that faced the Convention:

- the issue of representation and how to balance the demands of the large and the small states

- the overall provisions of the Virginia Plan, the New Jersey Plan, and the Connecticut Compromise

- a reasonable encapsulation of the conflict between the Federalists and the Anti-Federalists

What techniques has this writer used to present this information in a coherent, cohesive essay? Eleanor's essay is written in a basic summative, chronological order. The information is clear to the reader, but there is no apparent point or purpose to the essay.

What type of score is this essay likely to receive? Why? Unfortunately, this essay is likely to earn, at best, a low- to middle-passing score.

- It does not address the requirements of the prompt: Choose one source and defend, challenge, or qualify...

- It deals only with issues facing the Constitutional Convention. Eleanor demonstrates no knowledge of the factors leading to the Civil War. Her score will have to reflect the extent to which the purpose of this exam was to test that knowledge.

Here is Jeff's essay:

The Civil War, or the War Between the States, depending on one's political views, was an enormous event, not only in United States history, but in the history of the modern world. Since the Declaration of Independence in 1776, the American defeat of the mightiest power in the world in the Revolutionary War, and the writing and ratification of the Constitution in 1787, the entire world watched to see whether this radical new form of nation would survive. Someone asked Benjamin Franklin what kind of government the Convention had given the people, and Franklin replied,

"A republic...if you can keep it." The warning "if you can keep it," was not just an empty expression, and [Author A] is correct when he claims that "political maneuvering" made division among the states and Civil War inevitable, but he is wrong to blame the South. The number of compromises made on both sides and the types of principles on which they compromised were the factors that doomed the new country to division and war.

Here is Jeff's thesis. His introduction is actually quite good, as it draws attention to the Constitutional Convention but also immediately brings in the topic of the Civil War. The Franklin quotation is also a nice touch, illustrating the precision and completeness of Jeff's understanding.

The issue of representation was the first big issue on which delegates from different states differed and that required a compromise that partially satisfied everyone but completely satisfied no one. The large states (large in population) favored the Virginia Plan, which allowed for two legislative houses. The number of members of both houses would be determined by each state's population. So, large states would enjoy more representatives than small states. Any vote on any issue would allow any individual state to overpower a smaller state. If representatives of large states formed alliances, especially on issues like tariffs and slavery, the smaller states would be so overpowered it would be almost as if they had no representation at all. Small states, of course, favored the New Jersey Plan, which established a single House with one representative per state. The compromise came in the form of the Connecticut Compromise, which established the two Houses, the lower one based on population, the higher one giving each state two representatives. It was a nice compromise, but small states still bristled at the fact that they had less power than large states in the House of Representatives, and the large states bristled that they didn't have <u>more</u> in the Senate.

This is a long sentence that Jeff might want to revise if he had time for a second draft, but it effectively keeps his reader's focus on the topic of compromise and inevitable conflict.

This passage of summary might seem relatively long for a short essay, but this is where Jeff demonstrates his knowledge, and he is careful to present the information from the angle that these are the facts that support the conclusion about compromise and conflict.

To complicate the issue and further divide the large and small states, Southern states demanded that their slave population be counted to determine representation. This would have given large states like Virginia (the largest state in the nation at the time)

Jeff himself uses the language of conflict to establish for his reader that he is not describing a peaceful or harmonious process.

Notice that Jeff determined early in his process that he wanted to note the irony of the population/representation debate. Any contradictions, inconsistencies, ironies, or unresolved points that you can honestly note and discuss will help your score.

[Author A] blamed "excessive southern influence" for the conflict. In his qualification of [Author A]'s thesis, Jeff does not want to sway his reader to the other extreme either.

and North Carolina huge power blocs in the House. Smaller states, and Northern states, which didn't have slaves to count, protested. The Constitutional compromise arrived at was that three out of every five slaves would be counted as "population." This increased the representation in Congress of Southern states and lessened the power of the North.

Ironically, however, as the eighteenth century ended, and the Industrial Revolution rolled in, population increased much faster in the North than in the South, and it was not too long before the North had the majority in the House of Representatives. With the North's growing power in the Legislature came the growing probability that eventually there would be a president from the North, and he would appoint non-Southern-sympathetic Supreme Court Justices. Eventually, the interests of Southern states would be ignored on the federal level.

So one of the compromises that allowed the Constitution to be approved may have made a Civil War more likely, but it actually in the long run placed the South at the disadvantage.

Slavery was another divisive issue that the Constitutional Convention handled in a way that made a future war more likely. On the one hand, the three-fifths compromise, which counted three out of every five slaves as "population" to be represented in Congress, seemed to legitimize slavery. This pleased the South but certainly not the abolitionists in the North. The Constitution also did nothing to end slavery in the South or to prevent its spread into new territory. It did not even guarantee an end to the slave trade. All it said was that Congress would do nothing to abolish the slave trade for at least twenty years. Once again, the South was pacified, but the North was agitated.

Still, it shouldn't seem as if the North was to blame for the war, either. The Constitution gave all power to levy tariffs on imports on the federal Congress. Before that, each state charged its own tariffs. The issue with tariffs is that they raise the cost of the imported goods. Immediately after the adoption of the Constitution, the majority of American imports was finished goods. The British especially wanted to keep their monopoly on textiles, so they made it illegal to export (from England) any loom, part of a loom, or instruction to build a loom. People who knew how to build or operate looms were not allowed to leave the country. The United States, then, produced the raw materials and imported the finished product.

Once the Industrial Revolution hit the North, however, people in Northern states could purchase locally made products. The South had no industry, so it still had to import finished goods from overseas. The tariff raised needed money for the federal government, didn't hurt the industrial North a bit, but placed the agricultural South at an economic disadvantage. When Southern states claimed the right to "nullify" federal laws that disadvantaged them, the Supreme Court of the United States declared their efforts unconstitutional.

Because the original Founding Fathers wanted so badly to write the Constitution and see it ratified, they were willing to ignore and to compromise on important issues that pitted state against state even in 1787. These compromises meant that the Union might be established in the short run, but the issues would have to be faced eventually. Something like the Civil War was definitely inevitable from the very founding of the United States, but [Author A] is wrong to suggest that it was Southern influence alone that created the threat. Both North and South wanted to protect their own interests and gain control of the government.

It was never the Union Made in Heaven that it was cracked up to be.

This ending might be a little excessive and overwrought, but this is an otherwise fine essay. Jeff has addressed the prompt, choosing one of the two authors and qualifying his thesis, and he has demonstrated considerable understanding of the process that resulted in the Constitution and the issues that eventually led to the Civil War. Some minor sentence structure and word choice errors will most likely be overlooked by the scorer who understands that Jeff had limited time to compose his answer and write his essay.

Analysis of Exam Essay

What is this writer's point? Jeff's point is a qualification of [Author A]'s thesis. Jeff agrees that the Constitution was the result of deep compromises that postponed the nation's having to face certain issues; that postponement made the Civil War essentially inevitable. He challenges [Author A]'s insistence that the primary blame for these compromises rests with the South and the "undue influence" it wielded during the Convention.

In what way(s) does this thesis fulfill the requirements of the prompt? This essay is a thorough response to the prompt. Jeff chooses [Author A]'s thesis. He qualifies the thesis to the extent that he agrees about the impact of the deep compromises made during the Convention, but he disagrees that the primary responsibility for those compromises lies with the South. He then writes an essay that is organized according to the various issues, with some essential background, an examination of how the issue was handled in the Convention, and then a reflection on how the issue eventually contributed to the War.

What information does the writer provide to demonstrate his understanding of the tested subject matter? Jeff presents information that successfully demonstrates his understanding of both the issues facing the Convention, including:

- the issue of representation and how to balance the demands of the large and the small states
- the impact of the representation compromise on the eventual makeup of the federal government
- suggestions that, rather than satisfying everyone, the compromises satisfied no one
- the role the Tariff Act of 1789 had in disillusioning Southern states with the new federal government

What techniques has this writer used to present this information in a coherent, cohesive essay? Jeff organizes his information around specific issues—representation, slavery, and the effect of the tariff—and discusses them with an eye to both how the issue was handled by the Convention and what the implications of the compromise were for an eventual conflict between states with different interests. Within his discussion of each issue, he looks at both the constitutional issue and its future impact.

What type of score is this essay likely to receive? Why? Jeff's essay should receive a very high score. He fully addresses the prompt: choose a source, qualify its thesis, write a "carefully reasoned and well-supported essay." He demonstrates an understanding of how various issues were handled by the Convention, as well as how the compromises arrived at left future conflict likely. He provides sufficient background information and explanation to allow his reader to appreciate his point and his understanding of the topic. The writing itself is clear, organized, and relatively free of surface errors.

TIME SPENT: 55 MIN—TIME REMAINING: 5 MIN

STEP 5: Review, Proof, and Edit (5 min out of 60)

Jeff clearly does not have enough time to take his essay into a complete second draft, but before he turns it in, he should give it one last quick look to correct any surface errors that might slowly erode his score. Misspellings of key words or prominent people's names are especially damaging.

Eleanor's essay has already been corrected for surface errors—because we wanted to model correct conventions use for you—but here is a portion of her actual submission with its cross-outs and insertions:

N   J   P

New Jersey countered with the new jersey plan, which

ture
divided the legislator into a single house, based on one representative for each state. That way, all of the states, whether big or small, would be equally represented, and no one region would be able to dominate the government. Because they protested the whole idea of a federal government, the state of Rhode Island didn't send any delegates to the Convention.

who
The Federalists were the block of people that favored a strong federal government. Some even

                  abolishing the

advocated ~~the abolishment of~~ individual states and allowing the federal government to control everything. Their opposition was called the Anti-Federalists, and they supported states' rights. At the time of the Revolutionary War, individual states like Virginia, New Jersey, and Connecticut were not parts of a larger whole; they <u>were</u> their own

                    c   c

whole. All of the Continental Congresses before the War and the United States Congress under the Articles of Confederation did not create a single, large nation. These congresses were meetings of representatives

               the countries of i

from all of the little "nations." Like ^ Europe., individual states considered themselves to be "sovereign states."

TIME SPENT: 60 MIN—TIME REMAINING:
0 MIN. It's over; time has expired.

ASSIGNMENT 3:

The Academic Thesis-Proof Essay

A little more than a persuasive essay, a little less than a research paper, this type of essay has probably comprised the bulk of your writing in school, whether you realized it or not. As with any other essay or writing assignment, including most of the ones modeled in this book, the *thesis* is the point, the central claim, the root of the argument, the *basic idea you want your reader to walk away with*.

The *proof* comprises the facts, examples, or illustrations, and expert opinions you will present to clarify, explain, define, and support that basic idea. The *proof* includes whatever warrants you provide to help your reader accept that your thesis is valid.

As we've said, if you accept the notion that every essay you write in school or on an exam or formal assessment should be a thesis-proof essay, you will find your confidence mounting and your scores climbing.

After spending much of the semester studying the relationship between character and theme in literature, during which they studied Tennessee Williams's *A Streetcar Named Desire*, Theodore Dreiser's *An American Tragedy*, and Shakespeare's *King Lear*, **Derek's** teacher assigned the following writing assignment in lieu of an end-of-unit exam:

> Tennessee Williams once made the following assertion on the nature of characters in theater:
>
>> The theatre is a place where one has time for the problems of people to whom one would show the door if they came to one's office for a job.
>
> In 1922, in his essay "On The Relation of Analytic Psychology to Poetry," Carl Jung had this to say about the nature of art and literature:
>
>> The impact of an archetype, whether it takes the form of immediate experience or is expressed through the spoken

word, stirs us because it summons up a voice that is stronger than our own. Whoever speaks in primordial images speaks with a thousand voices; he enthralls and overpowers, while at the same time he lifts the idea he is seeking to express out of the occasional and the transitory into the realm of the ever-enduring. He transmutes our personal destiny into the destiny of mankind, and evokes in us all those beneficent forces that ever and anon have enabled humanity to find a refuge from every peril and to outlive the longest night.

Consider both of these assertions and how they may relate to each other. Choose a character from the plays and novel you have studied this semester, and write a thoughtful, well-supported essay in which you use that character to support, refute, or qualify both Williams's and Jung's theses. Be certain to support all of your assertions with direct evidence from the text, as well as references to reliable literary criticism.

Because the purpose of this assignment is to assess your ability to discuss the literature studied in class, you may choose one of the following characters:

Blanche DuBois

Stanley Kowalski

Clyde Griffiths

Lear

STEP 1: Select a Topic

What does Tennessee Williams mean by someone "to whom one would show the door if they came to one's office for a job"? If we would kick them out of our office, I guess without interviewing them—well, even if we did interview them, we wouldn't give them the job—then they must be obviously unsuited or undesirable. Someone we don't want hanging around. Someone who doesn't fit in: a social outcast or misfit.

The key words and phrases to understand Jung's point seem to be <u>archetype</u>, <u>a voice that is stronger than our own, primordial images</u>—thousand voices (must be like a shared experience or collective unconscious or something). <u>Lift the idea .. out of the occasional and the transitory into the realm of the ever-enduring</u> (not relevant to today but relevant for all time...?)...<u>transmutes personal destiny into the destiny of mankind</u> (shared experience again). So the individual is interpreted to represent the entire class...

> Derek is right to make sure he understands the terms of the quotations before he tries to frame a response or reaction.

Blanche DuBois: the obvious choice, given the quote from Williams. Maybe it's too obvious? If I then think about the Jung quote, that may give me the chance to put more of an unexpected spin; Blanche isn't just this sad crazy lady, she represents something in society beyond herself. But will everybody write about Blanche?

> Derek is right to consider all aspects of the assignment, and what the pluses and minuses of each option would be.

Stanley Kowalski: a lot less obvious choice as social outcast; he is actually functioning in the world in a way Blanche is incapable of. But he is lower class, will probably never rise above where he is in the play, and what kind of marriage are he and Stella likely to have going forward? He doesn't, and probably never will, have a lot of advantages; how does he relate to Jung's quote? Can I make a case for him as an archetype for the economically and socially disadvantaged, and how that may foster the brutality that he shows at the end of the play?

Clyde Griffiths: definitely a social outcast; he's both poor and socially disadvantaged, and his ambition leads to murder or at least the initial intent to murder, so he has an archetypal quality that reflects a social reality and relates to Jung's ideas. The problem is, the book actually kind of bored me, and I don't feel like I could get excited writing about it.

> Derek's lack of enthusiasm for this subject is neither right nor wrong; none of us will like every piece of literature we are presented with or connect with it in a way that inspires. It's actually smart of Derek to rule out writing on a topic that doesn't excite him.

King Lear: He doesn't start out as a social outcast or misfit; he's King. But the journey of the play is his unraveling, until he is mad, or at any rate seen to be mad, by his court and family, and by the end of the play, he's certainly a misfit. Plus he does work as an archetype, the hubris of the highly placed and all that. But like Blanche, maybe a little too obvious?

> In the process of considering his options, Derek is discovering what he most wants to accomplish in this essay—an unexpected topic, an individual slant, and originality—good things to aim for in every essay.

STEP 2: Brainstorm, Discuss, Research

Derek has decided that choosing Stanley Kowalski to explore the ideas of Williams and Jung will help him write the most original essay he can. He knows he will have to support his ideas with material from the play itself and that he will have to be able to explain his assertions to someone else.

Stanley as social misfit or outcast:

Stanley is a manual laborer in a factory, not making much money, with few visible prospects or ambition for advancement, and largely uneducated.

He and Stella live in a run-down, dilapidated apartment in a poor section of New Orleans, near the railroad tracks.

Both Stella and Blanche, in unguarded moments, refer to him as their social inferior; Blanche even calls him a "Polack" in Act Two, and even Stella on occasion patronizes him, despite her passion for him.

In Scene 8, he reacts to Stella's attitude: "When we first met, me and you, you thought I was common. How right you was, baby. I was common as dirt. You showed me the snapshot of the place with the columns. I pulled you down off them columns and how you loved it, having them colored lights going! And wasn't we happy together, wasn't it all okay till she showed here? And wasn't we happy together? Wasn't it all okay till she showed here, hoity-toity, describin' me like a ape?"

At the end of Act One, Blanche describes Stanley this way: "There's even something sub-human about him, something not quite to the stage of humanity yet!...Thousands and thousands of years have passed him right by, and there he is, Stanley Kowalski, survivor of the Stone Age!..."

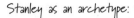

Stanley as an archetype:

Williams portrays him as brutal, raging, animalistic, a former Army officer returned from World War II. He represents the new working class—violent, crude, uneducated, and arrogant—the generation that is replacing Blanche's class and cares little for the ideals she holds.

In the first scene, he tosses raw meat to Stella.

He quotes Huey Long at one point: "Now just remember what Huey Long said—that every man's a king—and I'm the King around here, and don't you forget it."

His rape of Blanche at the end of the play can be seen as the triumph of the post-war, industrialized and increasingly insensitive culture over the old world of gentility, education and romantic ideals—or as the rage of the working class being directed at its former oppressors.

> The last part of this sentence is a provocative statement indeed. Derek may well be on his way to an original and unexpected essay, but he needs to be careful in how he presents his ideas. His thesis should not be that Williams is portraying rape as a rebellious, heroic act, although there may well be something to the class warfare angle that bears further exploration.

STEP 3: Draft a Thesis

Derek is aware that he has to take both Williams's and Jung's quotations, find a relationship or analogy between them, and come up with a thesis that will "support, refute, or qualify" both.

To be sure he stays close to the topic, he begins by restating both quotations:

The theatre is a place where one has time for the problems of people to whom one would show the door if they came to one's office for a job.

The impact of an archetype, whether it takes the form of immediate experience or is expressed through the spoken word, stirs us because it summons up a voice that is stronger than our own. Whoever speaks in primordial images speaks with a thousand voices; he enthralls and overpowers, while at the same time he lifts the idea he is seeking to express out of the occasional and the transitory into the realm of the ever-enduring. He transmutes our personal destiny into the destiny of mankind, and evokes in us all those beneficent forces that ever and anon have enabled humanity to find a refuge from every peril and to outlive the longest night.

Derek first considers how the two quotations relate to each other. Do they say the same thing? Are they complementary? Contradictory? Antithetical?

Williams is basically saying that the most interesting characters in a play are the misfits—people who are out of the mainstream, people who are low on the social scale or headed downward—people in desperate circumstances, people with self-destructive habits, addictions, or bad behavior.

> In this apparently minor relative clause, Derek has actually identified the issue that should motivate his discussion of Stanley Kowalski.

Jung's statement says that the characters that interest us most are those who represent something bigger than themselves, not "symbols" like a rose means love or a sunrise means hope, but the individual character represents or stands for a type of person—archetypes show <u>universal truths</u> about the <u>human condition</u>.

So...putting the two ideas together—truly interesting characters are those who do not exactly fit in with the rest of their society but somehow make us see ourselves and our lives (or maybe the lives of people we know) in them.

Derek then more or less customizes his fusion of the quotes into a statement about Stanley:

Stanley Kowalski, while often characterized as a brutal, cruel abuser, is also an archetype of the social outsider—a symbol of the postwar working class, crude but real, whose rage against upper class ideals and oppression leads to misdirected violence and tragedy.

> As he gets deeper into his process, Derek is leading himself further away from the actual assignment. Remember that this essay is the culmination of a unit on character and theme.

STEP 4: Outline

Thesis: Stanley Kowalski, while often characterized as a brutal, cruel abuser, is also an archetype of the social outsider—a personification of the postwar working class, crude but real, whose rage against upper class ideals and oppression leads to misdirected violence and tragedy.

> Derek has made a significant change here. Notice how his ideas are evolving.

I. Stanley Kowalski is not just a brutal, one-dimensional character.

    A. How he relates to the Williams quote about theater being about "people you would show the door" at a job interview

    B. How he is an archetypal figure, as outlined by Jung.

II. Social aspects of the play and how Stanley figures

    A. Postwar working class

    B. Rage against society and his place in it

        1. Leads to violence

        2. Rebelliousness

III. More detailed analysis of Stanley's character

    A. Low level of society

    B. Poorly paid, factory worker, little opportunity

    C. Frustrated, oversensitive, threatened

    D. Erupts in rage not just at Blanche and Stella, but what they represent

IV. Stanley as archetype and symbol of new generation

    A. First image of him tossing raw meat to Stella

    B. Blanche referring to him as "sub-human"

    C. Stanley and Blanche as opposite archetypes

    D. Stanley's violent speech to Stella and Blanche, referencing Huey Long

V. The rape as symbol

    A. Stanley's need to dominate because he is threatened

    B. Rape as way of tearing Blanche down, a weapon against her world

    C. How the act destroys Stanley, as well as Blanche

This is a well-organized outline, and it seems as if Derek is actually on his way to writing an original, strong essay with a unique viewpoint.

STEP 5: First Draft

Tennessee Williams once wrote, "The theatre is a place where one has time for the problems of people to whom one would show the door if they came to one's office for a job." Most people think of the character of Blanche DuBois in Williams's <u>A Streetcar Named Desire</u> in relation to that statement, but it could also apply to the other major character in that landmark play—Stanley Kowalski. Kowalski's character can also be seen in the light of Carl Jung's theory of the importance of the archetype in all forms of art: "The impact of an archetype, whether it takes the form of immediate experience or is expressed through the spoken word, stirs us because it summons up a voice that is stronger than our own."

> It is good that Derek has edited down the Jung quotation; the entire paragraph would be overlong and unnecessary here. However, by zeroing in on the quotations, Derek might be missing the point—that this is to be an essay about what makes literary characters memorable.

Stanley Kowalski, while often characterized as a brutal, cruel abuser, is also an archetype of the social outsider—a personification of the postwar working class, crude but real, whose rage against upper class ideals and oppression leads to misdirected violence and tragedy. Stanley is most often identified with the actor who originated the role onstage and in the film, Marlon Brando, whose magnetic sensual presence and forceful acting helped define the character as threatening, impulsive, violent, uneducated and crude, yet powerful and somehow perversely intriguing. Brando's performance also brought another aspect of the character to the forefront—the archetype of the rebellious post-World War II generation, frustrated by a lack of opportunity, a class structure that they were at the bottom of, and old-fashioned sexual and social values.

> Ironically, Derek's description of Brando is both a digression from a discussion of the *character* and a glimpse of the actual intent of the assignment—an exploration of what makes a literary character interesting; this sentence can probably be deleted in the next draft, but he needs to retain the intent.

If one looks at Stanley's character in relation to Williams's statement, it seems that Stanley isn't really much of an outcast. Unlike Blanche, he is actively employed—but he is a low-paid factory worker, with little opportunity for advancement; he

> Now Derek is really off course; he needs to prove his thesis by pointing to specific items in the script, not in Brando's performance.

> This is a miscue Derek slipped into very early in his essay. He does not have to defend Stanley as an outcast.

and Stella live in a dilapidated, run-down apartment in a poor section of New Orleans. Having been a Master Sergeant in the Army Engineer Corps has not yielded him anything better; Stella tells Blanche early in the play that she was not "...blinded by the brass. But of course there were things to adjust myself to later on." Stanley is especially oversensitive to any implication he is socially inferior. Some of his biggest explosions come in reaction to Blanche or Stella patronizing him for his common background. One of his more memorable speeches to Stella, in Scene 8, shows this rage:

> When we first met, me and you, you thought I was common. How right you was, baby. I was common as dirt. You showed me the snapshot of the place with the columns. I pulled you down off them columns and how you loved it, having them colored lights going! And wasn't we happy together, wasn't it all okay till she showed here? And wasn't we happy together? Wasn't it all okay till she showed here, hoity-toity, describin' me like a ape?

Here, Williams shows Stanley to be frustrated and resentful. He doesn't seem to mind being "common"; in fact, he seems almost proud to be "common as dirt" and to have "pulled [Stella] down off them columns." It is only after Blanche arrives that he feels as if he is being made to seem inferior. Blanche still pretends to be the wealthy Southern aristocrat, and in her "hoity-toity" view, a man like Stanley is less than human. Stanley resents Blanche, and he resents her attitude of feeling superior to him.

This conflict with Blanche also points out their archetypal significance. Stanley and Blanche are not two individual characters who do not get along; they are representatives of two different social classes and two different generations. Stanley represents the new, crude, uneducated

It's good that Derek is back to analyzing the play itself and quoting from it, but this is perhaps not the most salient point.

generation that is rapidly replacing Blanche's world of Southern belles. Both Blanche and Stanley are archetypes. From their first meeting, it is clear that the two cannot exist at the same time. One of them will have to conquer the other.

It is pretty clear that Williams wants the audience to see Stanley as not only a brutal man but as a type of character. One of the first things Blanche says about him is, "There's even something sub-human about him, something not quite to the stage of humanity yet!...Thousands and thousands of years have passed him right by, and there he is, Stanley Kowalski, survivor of the Stone Age!..." But Blanche herself is so weird, so stereotypical, that her description of Stanley becomes simply one stereotype describing another. When readers and audiences vividly remember these two characters, it isn't because they are so unique, it is because they tap into something in the audience: what Jung called "transmut[ing] our personal destiny into the destiny of mankind."

> Derek is making some excellent points, but he needs to keep referencing elements in the play to back up his conclusions.

It's not Stanley versus Blanche; it's what Stanley represents versus what Blanche represents.

And whatever they represent, Stanley and Blanche are polar opposites, absolute antitheses. For the poor, hard-working, and uneducated Stanley, Blanche represents everything wrong with his life. As he admits in the quote above when he says that he and Stella were happy until Blanche arrived, he doesn't only resent Blanche being an uninvited guest, he resents her influence over Stella. One time, after Stella insults him, he even says, "Don't you ever talk that way to me. 'Pig,' 'Polack,' 'disgusting,' 'vulgar,' 'greasy'— those kind of words have been on your tongue and your sister's tongue just too much around here. What do you think you are, a pair of queens?" For Williams and his audience, the conflict is not only between

> It is fine for Derek to refer to an earlier point, but it is bad style to refer to his own paper like this.

> Some summary here, but Derek is still being very careless with direct references to the play.

an annoying, snobby woman and her sister's vulgar husband. Blanche represents the aristocracy that has always oppressed the peasant. She is entitled to enter Stanley's home and eat his food and drink his beer without contributing anything or even saying thank you. She represents a class of person who considers others of lower classes to be inhuman. And he represents the peasant class that always rebels against the aristocracy and destroys them.

This is a very powerful conclusion. It may or may not be valid, but Derek certainly has not provided sufficient textual support to tempt the reader to accept it.

Evidence that Williams wants Stanley to represent a type is also clear in the fact that he quotes Huey Long: "Now just remember what Huey Long said— that every man's a king— and I'm the king around here, and don't you forget it." Granted, Huey Long was famous enough. He'd been governor of Louisiana (and the play takes place in New Orleans), talked of running for president, and his "Every man a king" campaign made him something of a national icon among the poor, but the only reason Williams would need Stanley to mention him by name and quote him would be to make his audience think of his "Share the Wealth" program that would have limited the wealth of a Blanche while increasing the wealth of a Stanley.

Derek is finally providing some concrete evidence from the play. In his second draft, he needs to make sure that *all* of his conclusions are supported this carefully.

It's almost like the French or the Russian Revolution.

The intensifying conflict between these archetypes reaches its peak in Stanley's rape of Blanche near the end of the play. On one level, this act is Stanley's brutal defeat of the woman who has invaded his home, insulted him, and destroyed his happiness. Uneducated and common, he defeats her the only way he knows how. On another level, however, this rape represents the oppressed class's final defeat of the oppressor. When Stanley says, "We've had this date with each other from the beginning," he is not just Stanley Kowalski talking about the many times

Having established the facts of (1) who Huey Long was, (2) what he attempted, and (3) that Stanley quotes him in this context now gives Derek the freedom to speculate about Williams's point in writing this exchange. Certainly, Derek's explanation of the allusion supports his argument about the archetypal values of these two characters.

Blanche has flirted with him and made suggestive overtures; he is the peasant class of every society in history talking to every aristocracy in history, saying that the fated revolution has come.

This is another strong statement, possibly overwritten. Derek can possibly get away with it if he leads to it more carefully with textual support for every conclusion that leads to this point.

Tennessee Williams's characters of Blanche DuBois and Stanley Kowalski from <u>A Streetcar Named Desire</u> are definitely characters that, as Williams would say, "one would show the door if they came to one's office for a job." They are outcasts or misfits that one wouldn't necessarily want to spend time with in real life. Audiences are attracted to them, however, and willing to spend time with them, because, in Carl Jung's terms, they speak "in primordial images [and] with a thousand voices...lift[ing] the idea he is seeking to express out of the occasional and the transitory into the realm of the ever-enduring." They are archetypes, and their story is the story of humanity's endless struggle to overcome adversity and oppression.

At the end, Derek does return to a sense of what he was assigned to write. Certainly, this is potentially an excellent essay, but Derek does have some work to do to support all of his conclusions and assertions with evidence from the play.

Analysis of First Draft

What is this writer's point? Derek's point is unclear. His thesis has to do with the strength of Stanley Kowalski as a memorable character, both a misfit and an archetype, but he also seems to want to compare Stanley with Blanche. By the end of his essay, he seems content to offer both characters as examples of the two quotations he was asked to address.

What is this writer's angle? At this point, his angle or slant is as unclear as his central point. One potential but undeveloped slant is the idea that while the status of the misfit and the archetype may seem antithetical, they are actually quite complementary.

How strong is this writer's support? How authoritative is his overall argument? By the end of the essay, Derek provides more and stronger support, but textual evidence is generally lacking. He does make several authoritative claims, and one gets the impression that Derek knows what he is talking about, but he does not provide enough material to convince a reluctant or skeptical reader to accept his thesis.

What techniques has this writer used to establish this authority? Derek makes very strong claims. When he does offer textual evidence, it is usually right on the mark.

What specific details, facts, etc., make this argument convincing?

- Blanche's and Stella's references to Stanley's lower-class background and his violent responses

- Stanley's entrance at the beginning of the play, tossing raw meat to Stella

- Stanley quoting Huey Long, Blanche's description of Stanley as "subhuman," etc.

- Stanley's own references to the disparity in his and Stella's backgrounds, his having dragged Stella down from "that place with the columns"

NOW plan an essay on one of the following prompts or one assigned by your teacher. Notice that not all of the prompts address English language arts or literature. A few rely on some understanding of multiple subjects and the way they interact.

> *For many readers, the most satisfying moment in a novel, movie, or play is not the climax, when the outcome is determined, but the later moment of redemption when a key character regains at least some of the reader's sympathy lost during the plot. Consider, for example, Sidney Carton's "far, far better thing," or Darth Vader's killing the Emperor in order to save Luke Skywalker. Critics have long noted that tragic heroes, modern heroes, and anti-heroes often experience a moment of redemption before their deaths and that this redemptive moment is essential to the emotional or psychological impact of the literature. Choose a character from a novel or play you have studied in class who experiences a redemptive moment and write a thoughtful and well-organized essay in which you analyze the impact of that character's redemption on the effect and overall meaning of the chosen literature.*
>
> *Be careful not to simply summarize the plot or describe the redemptive moment.*
>
> *Characters who lend themselves to this type of discussion include:*
>
> Jay Gatsby, *The Great Gatsby*
> Arthur Dimmesdale, *The Scarlet Letter*
> Amir, *The Kite Runner*
> Walter, *A Raisin in the Sun*
> Hamlet
> Macbeth

A key principle of the New Historicist approach to literature is that a reader should not wonder whether a text's portrayal of a culture is "accurate." Instead, readers should explore the kind of view the text presents. Choose a novel, play, or work of nonfiction studied in class and write a well-supported essay in which you analyze the nature of the view presented by the text and evaluate the impact this view has on your understanding of the culture represented.

Texts that lend themselves to this type of reading include:

Barbara Kingsolver, *The Poisonwood Bible*
Tim O'Brien, *The Things They Carried*
Kathryn Stockett, *The Help*
Khaled Hosseini, *The Kite Runner*
Donald Miller, *Blue Like Jazz*
Eric Schlosser, *Fast Food Nation*
Elie Wiesel, *Night*
James McBride, *The Color of Water*

Bestselling and award-winning science fiction author Isaac Asimov is often quoted as having said, "The saddest aspect of life right now is that science gathers knowledge faster than society gathers wisdom." Consider what Asimov might have meant in this observation. Then, write a thoughtful, well-organized essay in which you analyze the denotative and connotative differences between the words knowledge *and* wisdom *and how these terms determine Asimov's meaning.*

Below are several quotations that define history while challenging popular conceptions of the reasons, benefits, and purposes of documenting and studying history. Consider what these writers, historians, and historical persons claim and write a well-supported essay in which you examine the meaning of one of the quotations; then, support or rebut it. Make certain you support all of your own claims with direct references to historical persons, events, and trends.

> *To know the truth of history is to realize its ultimate myth and its inevitable ambiguity.*
> > *—Roy P. Basler, mid-twentieth-century historian, editor of* The Collected Works of Abraham Lincoln

> *Any fool can make history, but it takes a genius to write it.*
> > *—Oscar Wilde*

> *The farther backward you can look, the farther forward you are likely to see.*
> > *—Winston Churchill*

> *History is written by the winners.*
> > *—Napoleon Bonaparte*

> *If history were taught in the form of stories, it would never be forgotten.*
> > *—Rudyard Kipling*

STEP 1: Select a Topic

STEP 2: Develop a Slant/Angle/Hook

STEP 3: Brainstorm, Discuss, Research

STEP 4: Outline

STEP 5: First Draft

STEP 6: Peer Edit

What is this writer's point?

What is this writer's angle?

How strong is this writer's support? How authoritative is his or her overall argument?

What techniques has this writer used to establish this authority?

What specific details, facts, etc., make this argument convincing?

STEP 7: Revised/Final Draft

Here are Derek's editor's comments and analysis as well as his responses:

- It is good that Derek has edited down the Jung quotation; the entire paragraph would be overlong and unnecessary here. However, by zeroing in on the quotations, Derek might be missing the point—that this is to be an essay about what makes literary characters memorable.

- Ironically, Derek's description of Brando is both a digression from a discussion of the *character* and a glimpse of the actual intent of the assignment—an exploration of what makes a literary character interesting; this sentence can probably be deleted in the next draft, but he needs to retain the intent.

- Now Derek is really off course; he needs to prove his thesis by pointing to specific items in the script, not in Brando's performance.

- This is a miscue Derek slipped into very early in his essay. He does not have to "defend" Stanley as an outcast.

- It's good that Derek is back to analyzing the play itself and quoting from it, but this is perhaps not the most salient point.

- Derek is making some excellent points, but he needs to keep referencing elements in the play to back up his conclusions.

- It is fine for Derek to refer to an earlier point, but it is bad style to refer to his own paper like this.

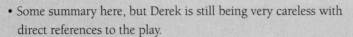

- Some summary here, but Derek is still being very careless with direct references to the play.

- This is a very powerful conclusion. It may or may not be valid, but Derek certainly has not provided sufficient textual support to tempt the reader to accept it.

- Derek is finally providing some concrete evidence from the play. In his second draft, he needs to make sure that *all* of his conclusions are supported this carefully.

- Having established the facts of (1) who Huey Long was, (2) what he attempted, and (3) that Stanley quotes him in this context now gives Derek the freedom to speculate about Williams's point in writing this exchange. Certainly, Derek's explanation of the allusion supports his argument about the archetypal values of these two characters.

- This is another strong statement, possibly overwritten. Derek can possibly get away with it if he leads to it more carefully with textual support for every conclusion that leads to this point.

- At the end, Derek does return to a sense of what he was assigned to write. Certainly, this is potentially an excellent essay, but Derek does have some work to do to support all of his conclusions and assertions with evidence from the play.

And here are Derek's reactions:

> So I need to clarify my point and support it more. Am I writing about Stanley? Blanche? Both? Is my big point that they are misfits or archetypes? Or both? Still, they do say that this is "potentially an excellent essay," so there must be some hope.

Analysis of First Draft

What is this writer's point? Derek's point is unclear. His thesis has to do with the strength of Stanley Kowalski as a memorable character, both a misfit and an archetype, but he also seems to want to compare Stanley with Blanche. By the end of his essay, he seems content to offer both characters as examples of the two quotations he was asked to address.

> Okay, I think I was assuming that everyone would look at Blanche as the misfit, but I never said that in my essay. I think I do want to discuss them both because it's hard to talk about one without having the other to compare. I think I started to realize that they are sort of the two sides of the same coin...archetypes for opposing forces...like oil and water.

What is this writer's angle? At this point, his angle or slant is as unclear as his central point. One potential but undeveloped slant is the idea that while the status of the misfit and the archetype may seem antithetical, they are actually quite complementary.

> That's it. I see that now.

How strong is this writer's support? How authoritative is his overall argument? By the end of the essay, Derek provides more and stronger support, but textual evidence is generally lacking. He does make several authoritative claims, and one gets the impression that Derek knows what he is talking about, but he does not provide enough material to convince a reluctant or skeptical reader to accept his thesis.

> More textual support and direct reference to the play. Got it.

What techniques has this writer used to establish this authority? Derek makes very strong claims. When he does offer textual evidence, it is usually right on the mark.

> Well, at least I did <u>something</u> right.

What specific details, facts, etc., make this argument convincing?

Blanche's and Stella's references to Stanley's lower-class background and his violent responses

Stanley's entrance at the beginning of the play, tossing raw meat to Stella

Stanley's quoting of Huey Long

Blanche's description of Stanley as "subhuman," etc.

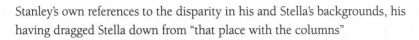

Stanley's own references to the disparity in his and Stella's backgrounds, his having dragged Stella down from "that place with the columns".

> Okay.

Here is Derek's revised draft. Notice how he has specifically addressed the notes he got from the peer edit.

One of the chief characteristics of great literature is that the character is supreme. Plots might be exciting, funny, or suspenseful, but it is the characters who live within the plot that makes it unique and memorable. About the role of character in literature, Tennessee Williams once wrote, "The theatre is a place where one has time for the problems of people to whom one would show the door if they came to one's office for a job." In other words, the characters that draw audiences and readers to plays reflect people of whom these audience members would disapprove in real life. Audiences don't want to watch <u>their</u> lives played out on stage, they want to watch the odd lives of odd people. This certainly seems true of Williams's popular Pulitzer-prize-winning <u>A Streetcar Named Desire</u>. The two main characters, Blanche DuBois and Stanley Kowalski, are both "people to whom one would show the door if they came to one's office for a job."

By starting out with a reflection about character-driven literature, Derek is returning to the unit his class has just completed and the purpose of the assignment he is completing.

On the other hand, psychologist Carl Jung argues <u>against</u> the difference between characters and audience members, especially the idea that successful literary characters are so different from the audience that the audience wouldn't like them if they were real. Jung, who wrote about the "collective unconscious" and psychological archetypes wrote, "The impact of an archetype... stirs us because it summons up a voice that is stronger than our own. Whoever speaks in primordial images...lifts the idea he is seeking to express out

Derek has successfully introduced the first of the two quotations he has been assigned to discuss, and he has managed to keep his focus on the role of character in literature rather than misleading himself to believe that this essay is supposed to be about Blanche or Stanley.

Structurally, this sentence has a few problems, but Derek's point is valid. The intent of this sentence is a nice way to bring in the Jung quotation that he is also assigned to discuss.

of the occasional and the transitory into the realm of the ever-enduring. He transmutes our personal destiny into the destiny of mankind..." Ironically, Jung's thesis can also apply to Blanche and Stanley. There is a good deal of evidence to suggest that, in addition to being a melodrama about a dysfunctional working-class family, A Streetcar Named Desire works on an archetypal level to represent the social conflict between a fading aristocracy and a rising lower class.

Most people immediately think of Blanche DuBois as the person they wouldn't want to work with in real life. Blanche drinks, lies, and is sexually promiscuous. She is a phony and a snob. She almost seems to deserve what happens to her at the end of the play. But Blanche is not the only memorable, misfit character in the play. Stanley Kowalski is coarse, hard-drinking, and prone to violence. He is also unkind and unfaithful to his wife. It would not be an exaggeration to say that very few in Williams's audience would want Stanley Kowalski working in their office, even if they are fascinated by his life and can't wait to see how the tension between him and his wife's sister plays out.

Ironically, it is their status as social misfits or outcasts that allows Williams to use Blanche and Stanley as archetypes. It is probably some combination of Williams's and Jung's ideas of what makes a literary character memorable and powerful that allow Blanche and Stanley to still be discussed and written about sixty years after the play was written. The first time the audience sees Blanche, it is obvious that she is out of her element.

Having already established the setting of the play—the physical set of an onstage performance—as a slum, Williams then describes Blanche as "daintily dressed in a white suit with a fluffy bodice, necklace and ear-rings of pearl, white gloves and hat, looking

These two paragraphs give Derek a much better start on his revised essay. It is now clear that he is discussing Stanley Kowalski and Blanche DuBois as examples of the type of character Williams described and as archetypes for two conflicting social classes.

Some of this is valid elaboration of points in his first draft. Hopefully, however, he will remember that he needs more than summative statements to support his points.

Ultimately, this paragraph repeats more than it elaborates on points already introduced.

as if she were arriving at a summer tea or cocktail party in the garden district." He actually specifies "Her appearance is incongruous to this setting."

The same passage of stage directions further describe what the audience sees:

> Blanche comes around the corner, carrying a valise. She looks at a slip of paper, then at the building, then again at the slip and again at the building. Her expression is one of shocked disbelief....

Her "shocked disbelief" is obvious enough for another character on stage to comment on it, inviting Blanche to explain her out-of-place feeling:

Eunice [finally]: What's the matter, honey? Are you lost?

Blanche [with faintly hysterical humor]: They told me to take a streetcar named Desire, and then transfer to one called Cemeteries and ride six blocks and get off at—Elysian Fields!

Eunice: That's where you are now.

Blanche: At Elysian Fields?

Eunice: This here is Elysian Fields.

Blanche: They mustn't have—understood—what number I wanted...

Eunice: What number you looking for?

[Blanche wearily refers to the slip of paper.]

Blanche: Six thirty-two.

Eunice: You don't have to look no further.

Blanche [uncomprehendingly]: I'm looking for my sister, Stella DuBois. I mean—Mrs. Stanley Kowalski.

Eunice: That's the party.—You just did miss her, though.

Blanche: This—can this be—her home?

Blanche is definitely a "fish out of water," an aristocrat in the slum.

Derek has taken to heart his editor's suggestion that he needs textual support, but he might have condensed the Eunice/Blanche exchange to include only the essential information.

Derek needs to be careful. It seems as if he is wandering from establishing the outcast status of his characters and beginning to discuss their archetypal values.

That means that Stanley, being Blanche's antithesis, should actually be <u>completely</u> in his element. However, once Blanche arrives, her presence changes the environment. Stella, being Blanche's sister, is a weaker representation of the Southern aristocracy than Blanche represents. With two of them in the apartment, Stanley is outnumbered. Almost from the moment of their reunion, Blanche criticizes the Kowalski home, and Stella does not defend it. By remaining silent, she almost seems to agree with Blanche. She also insults Stanley, suggesting that not only is he not a member of the Southern aristocracy from which she and Stella come, but he is possibly not even fully human. In Scene 4, she tells Stella:

> There's even something sub-human about him, something not quite to the stage of humanity yet!...Thousands and thousands of years have passed him right by, and there his is, Stanley Kowalski, survivor of the Stone Age!...

Stanley himself notices the change Blanche has caused in his home and marriage, and he says to Stella in Scene 8:

> When we first met, me and you, you thought I was common. How right you was, baby. I was common as dirt. You showed me the snapshot of the place with the columns. I pulled you down off them columns and how you loved it, having them colored lights going! And wasn't we happy together, wasn't it all okay till she showed here? And wasn't we happy together? Wasn't it all okay till she showed here, hoity-toity, describin' me like a ape?

Stanley is clearly complaining to his wife that Blanche has changed the feeling in their home and both Stella's and Stanley's happiness.

So, the New Orleans slum is the society in which Blanche is a misfit, but the presence of Southern-aristocrat Blanche DuBois and her onetime-Southern-aristocrat sister Stella create a society in which Stanley Kowalski is a misfit. These opposing societies and the characters who represent them are what move the play into an archetypal story of social conflict and change. Stanley and Blanche are not just two individual characters who do not get along, they are representatives of two different social classes and two different generations. Stanley represents the new, crude, uneducated generation that is rapidly replacing Blanche's world of Southern belles. Both Blanche and Stanley are archetypes. From their first meeting, it is clear that the two cannot exist at the same time. One of them will have to conquer the other.

All in all, this is a nice transition from one part of Derek's topic to the next.

For the poor, hard-working, and uneducated Stanley, Blanche represents everything wrong with his life. As he admits when he says that he and Stella were happy until Blanche arrived, he doesn't only resent Blanche being an uninvited guest, he resents her influence over Stella. One time, after Stella insults him, he even says, "Don't you ever talk that way to me. 'Pig,' 'Polack,' 'disgusting,' 'vulgar,' 'greasy'— those kind of words have been on your tongue and your sister's tongue just too much around here. What do you think you are, a pair of queens?" For Williams and his audience, the conflict is not only between an annoying, snobby woman and her sister's vulgar husband. Blanche represents the aristocracy that has always oppressed the peasant. She is entitled to enter Stanley's home and eat his food and drink his whiskey without contributing anything or even saying thank you. She represents a class of person who consider others of lower classes to be inhuman. And he represents the peasant class that always rebels against the aristocracy and destroys them.

Derek is making some excellent points, but he needs to keep referencing elements in the play to back up his conclusions.

Evidence that Williams wants Stanley to represent a kind of revolution is also clear in the fact that he

This is an important word change from Derek's first draft. Rather than simply repeat the archetype meme, Derek begins to bring in the idea that, on some level, this essay is about character and theme.

quotes Huey Long: "Now just remember what Huey Long said— that every man's a king— and I'm the king around here, and don't you forget it." Granted, Huey Long was famous enough as governor of Louisiana (and the play takes place in New Orleans) and as a candidate for president, and his "Every man a king" campaign, but the only reason Williams would need Stanley to mention him by name and quote him would be to make his audience think of his "Share the Wealth" program that would have limited the wealth of a Blanche while increasing the wealth of a Stanley.

There is also a strong suggestion of revolution in Scene 8 when Stanley, still railing against the way Blanche regards him as less of a human, something to be bred with to improve the aristocratic bloodline, says:

> I am not a Polack. People from Poland are Poles, not Polacks. But what I am is a one hundred percent American, born and raised in the greatest country on earth and proud as hell of it.

The rising of the peasants against the aristocracy reaches its peak in Stanley's rape of Blanche near the end of the play. On one level, this act is Stanley's brutal defeat of the woman who has invaded his home, insulted him, and destroyed his happiness. Uneducated and common, he defeats her the only way he knows how. On another level, however, this rape represents the oppressed class's final defeat of the oppressor. When Stanley says, "We've had this date with each other from the beginning," he is not just Stanley Kowalski talking about the many times Blanche has flirted with him and made suggestive overtures, he is the peasant class of every society in history talking to every aristocracy in history, saying that the fated revolution has come.

Tennessee Williams's characters of Blanche DuBois and Stanley Kowalski from <u>A Streetcar Named Desire</u> are definitely characters that, as

While it may be a little melodramatic, Derek's choice to once again change a reference to archetypes into a reference to the theme of social revolution helps this essay fulfill its purpose in the unit of study.

Williams would say, "one would show the door if they came to one's office for a job." They are outcasts or misfits that one wouldn't necessarily want to spend time with in real life. Audiences are attracted to them, however, and willing to spend time with them, because, in Carl Jung's terms, they speak "in primordial images [and] with a thousand voices...lift[ing] the idea he is seeking to express out of the occasional and the transitory into the realm of the ever-enduring." They are archetypes, and their story is the story of humanity's oppressed, specifically the American underclass, struggling to overcome its oppressors and come into its own.

Analysis of Final Draft

What is the writer's thesis? In response to the assignment, which was ultimately to support, refute, or qualify both Williams's and Jung's theses, Derek's *de facto* thesis is that the characters of Blanche DuBois and Stanley Kowalski from Tennessee Williams's *A Streetcar Named Desire* support both Williams's thesis that audiences attend the theater to spend time with misfits and outcasts *and* Jung's claim that the characters that most resonate with audiences and readers are those that transcend their individuality and approach the level of archetype.

Has the writer's new draft strengthened his point? Yes, most definitely. Having clarified the point in his own mind, he has been able to shift his focus from the characters and the plays to the role of character in general. He has then successfully used his characters as his *examples* rather than as his focus.

Has the rewrite strengthened the case for the thesis? Again, yes. He cites from the play authoritatively and consistently, and makes his point both compelling and convincing.

What new details, facts, etc., have been included to make the thesis more valid?

- Stella's inability or unwillingness to defend her living situation to Blanche

- Stanley's line about not being "Polack" but being "American"

- The description of Blanche and her behavior at her arrival in Scene One

Does the writer effectively establish the validity of the thesis to any greater degree than in the previous draft? Why or why not? Derek has most definitely established the validity of his thesis to a greater degree than in the previous draft. Not only does he provide support from the play itself more frequently and deftly, he has, in the process, shown a greater understanding of the purpose of the assignment and its role in the unit on the relationship between character and theme in literature, which his class has just completed.

POSSIBLE STEP 8: Rewrite Opportunity

MINI-LESSON 2:

The Test or Exam Essay:
(Develop a thesis and support it.)

While the "defend, refute, or qualify" essay prompt is popular among high school exam writers and standardized test makers, it is not the only kind of essay you are likely to be asked to write to demonstrate the extent to which you have learned the material in a given course or program of study. In fact, most of your course-related exam essays are likely to ask you simply to provide information. Explain what you learned. Demonstrate your understanding.

Still, do not allow a less structured prompt or question to lull you into the complacent assumption that you do not need an essay. Unless you are specifically told to "list" or "list and explain," your score can only be improved by framing your answer in a well-structured and well-organized essay.

Derek and **Chandra's** English final exam included this question, which was intended as a summation of the class's study of "works of literary quality":

> Despite millennia of study and debate, scholars, critics, even writers themselves, have not yet agreed on what constitutes "literary quality." Still, many criteria have been proposed. Consider the various views discussed this year of what constitutes a "literary work." Then, choose a full-length work from this year's syllabus and write a thoughtful, well-organized essay in which you demonstrate that the work meets some standard of literary quality and is, therefore, suitable for inclusion in a course curriculum.

As was the case in Mini-lesson 1, students had a total of 3 hours (180 minutes) for the entire exam, allowing about an hour (60 minutes) for this essay.

The process for writing this essay is not very different from that for any other timed, on-demand essay for which you want to receive a top score. You will, of course, need to pause and choose a topic, a novel or play about which to write.

STEP 1: (no more than 5 min out of 60)

The prompt establishes two criteria for the work to be chosen: It must meet some accepted standard of literary quality, and it must be something the students studied this year (or at least on the syllabus to be studied).

Here is a re-creation of Derek's thoughts on his topic:

> Macbeth—obviously it's "literary"…it's Shakespeare.
>
> I already wrote a paper about A Doll's House and The Glass Menagerie
>
> didn't like The Scarlet Letter. Too many words and…really, who cares?
>
> The Great Gatsby was kind of cool. We read it pretty recently, too, so I remember it pretty well.

Derek is making an important mistake right now. The prompt says to "consider the…views" and then pick the literature. There is a suggestion there that, perhaps, the criteria should govern the choice of literature. By focusing on the literature first, Derek might find himself handicapped in discussing the various views of literary quality.

> The Great Gatsby is literary, exciting, and there have been several movies. I can maybe do a "tragic hero" or "romantic hero" thing as part of my "literary discussion" and show that I learned those things this year, too.

The fact that Derek is even considering bringing the "…hero thing" into his essay suggests that he is not paying attention to what the prompt is instructing him to think about and write.

Here are Chandra's thoughts:

> Different definitions of "literary quality" included being
>
> - character-driven instead of plot-driven
> - universal in terms of themes and characters
> - beautiful, well-crafted like a painting or a sculpture
> - "ennobling" or "transcending"…getting us out of ourselves, focusing on bigger things…maybe tie that in to "universal"!

Chandra has taken an entirely different approach, thinking first about the qualities she wants to discuss. These qualities will then guide her choice of literature.

I think I can make a case for <u>The Great Gatsby</u> fulfilling just about all those criteria and being very suitable for school.

TIME SPENT: 5 MIN—TIME REMAINING: 55 MIN

STEP 2: Draft a Thesis (no more than 5 min out of 60)

We've said it elsewhere in this book and this series: even if the prompt does not specify that you need a thesis, even if you think you are to write a purely informative piece, always think in terms of a thesis and proof—that you are advancing an argument and need to convince your reader of the validity of your thesis.

Here are Derek's attempts at a thesis:

- Due to its many and unquestionable literary qualities, <u>The Great Gatsby</u> is one book that should definitely be included in any study of United States literature.

Derek is begging the question by assuming the reader already knows or agrees on Gatsby's literary qualities.

- <u>The Great Gatsby</u> meets many standards of literary quality and is, therefore, suitable for inclusion in a course on United States literature.

This thesis is better—at least it doesn't beg the question. However, it is vague. Derek may fall into the trap of believing he is supporting his thesis when all he is doing is listing the standards he believes Gatsby meets.

Here are Chandra's attempts:

- While they may disagree on specific details, writers and critics through the ages have determined that the main criterion of a literary book is its universal quality, that it helps its reader transcend the narrowness of an individual life and catch a glimpse of the human condition or a universal truth. The characters of F. Scott Fitzgerald's The Great Gatsby, especially the central four: Gatsby, Nick, Tom, and Daisy, illustrate how this literary quality plays out.

> This thesis has some potential, but Chandra has lost sight of the prompt a little. She also seems to be blending the criteria of universality and character-driven story into a single element.

- If, as critics and scholars suggest, a work's literary quality lies in its universal appeal and the power of its characters, then The Great Gatsby is truly a literary work that deserves to be taught in schools.

> This is generally a better attempt. It is still a little vague, almost begging the question of what constitutes literary quality. Still, it does at least specify the two qualities Chandra seems most eager to discuss.

TIME SPENT: 10 MIN—TIME REMAINING: 50 MIN

STEP 3: Brainstorm, Jot Notes (no more than 10 min out of 60)

Remember that you want every point you can earn. This essay has to be a thoughtful and thorough display of *both your knowledge and your ability to talk about it*. That will be the purpose of every exam you will ever take, from your first state assessment to the defense of your doctoral dissertation.

Here are Derek's notes:

The Great Gatsby

Literary qualities: theme: impossibility of the romantic ideal
                 conflict: Gatsby vs. self
                      Gatsby vs. Tom
                      Gatsby's dream vs. reality

setting: Long Island and New York City
realistic, realism...details
1920s "Jazz Age"
Gatsby's parties
plot: Gatsby's pursuit of Daisy
Tom's possessive jealousy

> Derek has apparently either misunderstood the prompt, or he truly has not learned the distinction between "literary element" (also called the "elements of fiction" and "literary quality," which has to do with artistry and breadth of appeal.

Here are Chandra's:

Literary qualities:

Character driven:

Gatsby's dream, every decision, his obsession

Daisy's selfish irresponsibility

Tom's cruelty

Nick's apathy—how does his refusal to do anything cause the tragic ending?

Universal/transcending—not just the story of these people, but the story of a generation (Jazz Age)

Not just the story of that generation, but America—think about that ending passage about the explorers first entering New York Harbor

> This is an excellent strategy. As she lays out her broader ideas, Chandra also makes notes of specific support from the text.

Romantic ideal might say something about the human condition—other great love tragedies: Romeo and Juliet? Lancelot and Guinevere? Heathcliff and Cathy?

> Bringing in other acknowledged literary works will bolster Chandra's thesis and help demonstrate that she understands the issue of "literary quality."

> **TIME SPENT: 20 MIN—TIME REMAINING: 40 MIN**

STEP 4: Outline (no more than 5 min out of 60)

Derek:

Whether he is experiencing test anxiety or has grown complacent because of his usually fine work, Derek is setting himself up for failure. Not only does he misunderstand the issue, he is also simply going through the motions with this planning process. This outline reflects the order in which the ideas occurred more than an intentional attempt at organization on Derek's part. One might expect, pending no overriding plan, to discuss plot first, as most basic, and theme, as most complex.

I. theme

    A. impossibility of the romantic ideal

II. conflict

    A. Gatsby vs. self

    B. Gatsby vs. Tom

    C. Gatsby's dream vs. reality

III. setting: Long Island and New York City

    A. realistic, realism...details

    B. 1920s "Jazz Age"

    C. Gatsby's parties

IV. plot

    A. Gatsby's pursuit of Daisy

    B. Tom's possessive jealousy

> It might be tempting to accept Derek's assigning Roman numerals and capital letters to his notes, but there is no sense of *why* he is going to discuss his ideas in this order. This outline does not suggest anything more than an overview of the novel—what one might find in a book report—not a pointed argument or evaluation.

Chandra:

On the other hand, Chandra had a handle on how she would probably organize her essay from the moment she thought of her topic.

I. Character driven

    A. Gatsby's dream, every decision, his obsession

    B. Daisy's selfish irresponsibility

    C. Tom's cruelty

    D. Nick's apathy—how does his refusal to do anything cause the tragic ending?

II. Universal/transcending

    A. not just the story of these people, but the story of a generation (Jazz Age)

    B. not just the story of that generation, but America—think about that ending passage about the explorers first entering New York Harbor

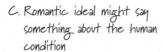

C. Romantic ideal might say
something about the human
condition

1. Lancelot and Guinevere

2. Romeo and Juliet

3. Heathcliff and Cathy

The key difference between Jeff's and Chandra's outlines, both of which mimic the order in which they jotted their notes, is that there is no compelling reason that Derek must present his ideas in the order he has set down. Chandra's can easily be interpreted to suggest an order of magnitude: she is first keeping her discussion in the novel and then gradually broadening her focus to well beyond the book itself.

TIME SPENT: 25 MIN—TIME REMAINING: 35 MIN

STEP 5: Write Your Essay (30 min out of 60)

Again, the suggested time allotment reflects the time you need to physically write or keyboard your essay. You should not need to pause to generate more ideas or think what you are going to say next.

Here is Derek's essay:

All short stories, novels, plays—actually, all fiction—have certain elements or qualities that determine their worth as literature. Those qualities are plot, theme, character, setting, and conflict. F. Scott Fitzgerald's The Great Gatsby has an intriguing and suspenseful plot, an important theme, well-drawn characters, and powerful conflicts. It is, therefore, fit to be included in a high school curriculum.

Clearly, Derek has misunderstood the prompt, confusing elements of fiction and literary qualities. To compound his weak start, he has disregarded his outline, again apparently mentioning his elements in no particular order but as they occur to him.

All fiction has plot, but to be considered "literary," the plot needs to be suspenseful and intriguing. There must be a sense of the action building to a climax, and there must be a satisfactory—even if unhappy—resolution. F. Scott Fitzgerald's The Great Gatsby has a plot that is both intriguing and suspenseful. It also has the rising action, climax and falling action required of all great literature. The intrigue is in the love story between Gatsby and Daisy. They'd been in love

This is confusing; perhaps Derek does understand the topic, but he is not clear what *qualities* he is being asked to discuss.

A common ploy for a student who does not have a strong grasp of the exam material is to repeat what has already been said. At least the essay will look long, even if it says nothing. Whoever scores Derek's essay will certainly see through this attempt.

five years earlier when Gatsby was in the Army. But Daisy had been from a wealthy, Old South family, and Gatsby was of questionable parentage. Now that Gatsby is rich, he wants Daisy back, and he wants her to admit that she never loved Tom, her husband. The suspense comes from both the uncertainty over whether Daisy and Tom will end up together. There is also the suspense of not knowing exactly who Gatsby is or how he came by such excessive wealth so quickly.

The events in the rising action include Nick's inviting both Gatsby and Daisy to his house so they can be reunited. The lunch at Daisy's house when we first learn of Tom's affair raises the stakes because maybe Daisy and Gatsby will get together. The climax is the confrontation in New York. Daisy will <u>not</u> say she never loved Tom. It is immediately after this incident that Daisy kills Myrtle and then Gatsby himself is killed. It is actually because of Gatsby's undying but misguided love for Daisy that he is killed. He takes the blame for driving the car, so when Myrtle's husband seeks revenge for his wife's death, he mistakenly kills Gatsby.

Another important and suspenseful plot is motivated by Tom's possessive jealousy. He treats Daisy like a possession, even to the extent of allowing his mistress to call him at his home while his wife is there. He boasts to Nick that he has a mistress and even takes Nick to meet her, even though <u>Nick is Daisy's cousin!</u> Tom likewise treats his mistress, Myrtle, like a possession, taunting George Wilson and even getting violent with Myrtle. After he learns of Gatsby's affair with Daisy, it is Tom's possessive jealousy that motivates his blaming Gatsby for Myrtle's death. With Gatsby dead, he is out of the way, and Tom and his prize possession, Daisy, can go on as if nothing ever happened.

There are two chief problems with Derek's essay so far. First, he is merely offering plot summary. Even if this were the topic he was supposed to be writing on, he would have to show how the cited events constitute rising action and lead toward the cited climax. Second, his summary is not completely accurate. Even though Gatsby did intend to take the blame for the accident, it was Tom who implicated Gatsby to Wilson.

Again, while it is true that Tom's implicating Gatsby leads directly to his death, it is not necessarily certain that Tom knew what Wilson intended and, thus, plotted Gatsby's murder.

The theme has to do with the American Dream, an individual's ability to raise himself from nothing to a wealthy man in a mere five years. It has to do with the undying and self-sacrificing quality of true love. These are universal themes, and it is their universality that helps The Great Gatsby achieve high literary status.

The conflicts are likewise universal. Character vs. self—Gatsby has to battle his own inner demons to convince himself that he is worth Daisy's love and that she is worth his. Nick suggests that Gatsby is a far superior person to all of the others.

> Derek seems to be running out of time and is panicking. He is no longer even providing references to the novel to clarify or support his summative statements.

Another plot-altering conflict is Gatsby vs. Tom. Here, we have the idealist versus the pragmatist, the lover versus the possessor. With Daisy as the fulcrum, Tom and Gatsby pivot up and down—who loves Daisy most, whom does Daisy love? And so on. The entire novel—right up to George Wilson's shooting Gatsby—is the result of this Gatsby-Tom conflict and who is going to "win" Daisy at the end.

> Derek brings up an interesting point about conflict here, but he does not establish the relevance either to the assigned topic or even to his interpretation of the topic.

The final important conflict in The Great Gatsby is the dream versus the reality of Gatsby's situation. For five years, Gatsby has chased an ideal, a memory of a Daisy he knew when he was in the Army. However, Daisy is not what Gatsby believes she is. She is irresponsible and selfish. The scene with the shirts almost proves that it is not Gatsby Daisy loves but his wealth. It's not Tom she loved and married but his money, the security he offered. That's why she so easily falls back into something like her former life after Gatsby is dead. He spent a night of vigil outside of her house in case she needed him, and he was willing to take the blame for her carelessness, and she did not even go to his funeral or ask Nick anything about him or his death. The dream destroys Gatsby, and that is the reality of his situation. This conflict points to the main theme of the novel.

> Derek is admittedly facing the clock here, but this next-to-last sentence says nothing.

This is where Derek ends his essay, most likely because he ran out of time. Notice that he did not follow the order of elements as he named them in his introduction. Quite possibly, when he knew he did not have enough time to discuss all of the elements introduced, he decided to write about the ones he thought were his strengths. This is actually a good strategy because in most exams and standardized assessments, scorers are instructed to reward what the student has done well at least as much as they penalize the student for his or her mistakes.

When faced with a ticking clock and a difficult topic, then, play to your strengths.

Analysis of Exam Essay

What is this writer's point? Derek has either misunderstood the prompt or does not understand the difference between elements of fiction and literary quality. In either case, the point evident in this essay is that all fiction contains the same elements, but what qualifies a work as literature is the uniqueness or excellence of those elements.

In what way(s) does this thesis fulfill the requirements of the prompt? Derek's thesis only marginally fulfills the qualities of the prompt. The root of the problem is most likely that he has confused elements of fiction and literary quality.

What information does the writer provide to demonstrate his understanding of the tested subject matter? It would be easier to list the information that suggests Derek's misunderstanding.

- Derek's introductory paragraph establishes that he is going to demonstrate how Gatsby contains all of the elements of fiction.

- Each point of discussion focuses on a specific element—plot, character, theme, etc.—as opposed to a characteristic that would contribute to an evaluation of a text as a work of literature.

What techniques has this writer used to present this information in a coherent, cohesive essay? This is another problem in Derek's essay. Even as he misunderstands his topic, he discusses the sub-points of this topic in an apparently random order.

What type of score is this essay likely to receive? Why? Unfortunately, this essay is most likely to receive a failing grade.

- It suggests a fundamental misunderstanding of the subject being assessed.
- There are factual errors in the discussion of the chosen text.
- The points in the essay are not organized in any discernable order.

Here is Chandra's essay:

If, as critics and scholars suggest, a work's literary quality lies in its universal appeal and the power of its characters, then The Great Gatsby is truly a literary work that deserves to be taught in schools. There isn't really one definition of "literary quality" that everyone agrees with, but most critics and writers seem to agree that "great literature" is more character driven than plot driven and that it somehow manages to transcend its own particular time, place, and characters and give the reader a glimpse of the universal. It is also generally agreed that the novels and plays studied in school should be more than "good stories" but "great literature." The Great Gatsby is this kind of book and is an appropriate book to be taught in school.

Just about everyone agrees that "great literature" is character driven rather than plot driven. There is a plot, but the characters' lives and backgrounds motivate the plot events. In fact, the characters in a character-driven story are so fully created that the plot events seem inevitable. They are what must happen to these people in these circumstances. Nothing in the plot is obvious or seems unnatural or too coincidental or happens just because the writer wanted it to happen. For example, Jay Gatsby is shown to be mysterious, but he is also revealed to be obsessive. It almost doesn't matter how he made all of his money, which is a major source of suspense in the book; the fact is that he made the money only so he could win Daisy. He intentionally takes the house in West Egg specifically because it is directly across the bay from Daisy's house. It's not actually stated, but it almost seems as if somehow Gatsby arranged for Nick to have the next-door house so he could arrange the reunion. The parties that

Not a bad introduction for an exam essay. Chandra addresses every aspect of the prompt and introduces the two literary qualities she is going to discuss.

Notice that Chandra does not simply use the term "character driven"; she explains in her own words what it means. This is how she demonstrates her understanding of the material tested by this prompt.

made Gatsby so famous were also only for the benefit of Daisy. Gatsby hoped Daisy might hear about the parties and come over. Then he could meet her. In short, everything Gatsby has done in making himself Gatsby is for one reason only: so he can be reunited with Daisy. He loved her five years earlier, and he has been obsessed with her ever since.

The key plot events are caused directly by this obsession. Once Gatsby and Daisy begin their affair, it is not enough only that she say she loves him. She must also say that she never loved Tom. This climactic scene in New York is what leads directly to the accident, Myrtle's death, Wilson's revenge, and Gatsby's death. The chain of events seems inevitable, the inevitable result of Gatsby's obsession.

Another well-developed character who makes the plot events seem inevitable is Tom Buchanan. Tom is a bully. He is cruel, jealous, and possessive. Nick says that he knew Tom a little in college, and this establishes Tom's primary character traits. It is Tom's cruelty and possessive nature that motivate his affair with Myrtle and his taunting of Wilson. It is his possessive nature that also makes him torment Gatsby. He probably does not <u>love</u> Daisy as much as he feels he <u>owns</u> her. And it is this sense of ownership that motivates his telling Wilson that it was Gatsby's car that killed Myrtle, clearly suggesting that Gatsby killed Myrtle, and this motivates Wilson's vengeance and Gatsby's death. So, the tragic end of the novel is presented as the inevitable result of the clash of two strong characters.

Great literature also appeals to something universal in its characters and themes. It might be the story of specific people in a specific time and place, but there is something in it that readers can identify with that makes it the story of

This is not a bad discussion. It is, perhaps, a little heavy on the plot summary, but Chandra does demonstrate a firm grasp of the subject and of the novel. She has departed from her outline, which included discussions of Daisy and Nick, but this might simply reflect a lack of time. Still, as scorers are generally instructed to reward what the student does well, these omissions should not result in a significant decrease in Chandra's score.

Again, Chandra not only mentions the quality but describes it.

everyone everywhere. The Great Gatsby is truly the story of Nick, Gatsby, Tom, and Daisy on Long Island in the 1920s. But details of the "valley of ashes," the parties, the cars, and the drinking of bootleg liquor make it also the story of a generation, a period in United States history. References to the "Swastika" company suggest the beginning of the situation that led to World War II. Fitzgerald also makes comments about the irresponsibility of this generation of people and of the social class represented by Tom and Daisy. The characters are not simply individual persons, they are symbols of a generation and a social class.

The novel is not only the story of a generation, but it is also the story of the United States. Gatsby's dream is the American dream. His optimism—that some poor boy from somewhere in the Midwest can win the heart of an old-money Southern Belle—reflects American optimism. Nick's too. He comes from the Midwest, to the East to make his fortune. The old-moneyed and indifferent upper class represents the corruption of the American Dream that disillusions and destroys the optimism of a Nick and a Gatsby. The interplay of Tom and the Wilsons reflects the disparity of wealth in pre-Depression America. The people represented by George Wilson do not really know who their enemies are. They blame and destroy the optimistic self-starters (Gatsby) and let their real oppressors (Tom) off the hook. Fitzgerald ends the novel with a reflection on the first explorers or settlers who came through the bay that separated Gatsby's and Daisy's houses. He reflects on what the New World represented to them, and there is a strong hint of regret that, what had been their pristine dream could have been so corrupted. Thus, the story of Jazz Age irresponsibility and corruption becomes the story of the corruption of the entire American ideal.

Chandra introduces a valid point. Ideally, she would be more specific in her references to the novel, but she is most likely using her memory to cite from a book she read weeks or months ago that she does not have with her. Still, she makes the strongest reference she can in order to support her point.

Chandra is offering something of a Marxist interpretation of the novel. It may or may not be a supportable interpretation, but she must be careful not to lose her focus of this discussion, which is the universality of the novel.

Finally, there is also the love story of Gatsby and Daisy. Daisy is, for Gatsby, an unattainable ideal. The Daisy that Gatsby pursues does not exist. She is an ideal, and their romance is doomed to failure from the very beginning. This makes <u>The Great Gatsby</u> not only a little story about an obsessed Army veteran and a Southern Belle, it is a classic love story like Lancelot and Guinevere, Romeo and Juliet, and Heathcliff and Cathy. <u>The Great Gatsby</u> is a work of Great Literature. It is character driven and appeals to universal themes. Because it is Great Literature, it is appropriate to teach in school.

The essay ends a little weakly, but this is probably attributable to lack of time. All in all, Chandra has made a compelling case. She clearly understands the assigned topic and the novel.

Analysis of Exam Essay

What is this writer's point? Chandra's point is that *The Great Gatsby* contains the qualities of being character driven and universal and can, therefore, be considered a work of literature. Marginally, she also asserts that, being a work of literature, the novel is appropriately studied in school.

In what way(s) does this thesis fulfill the requirements of the prompt? Her point is precisely what the prompt demands: *Consider the various views discussed this year of what constitutes a "literary work." Then, choose a full-length work from this year's syllabus and write a thoughtful, well-organized essay in which you demonstrate that the work meets some standard of literary quality and is, therefore, suitable for inclusion in a course curriculum.*

What information does the writer provide to demonstrate her understanding of the tested subject matter? Chandra presents information that demonstrates her understanding of both literary quality and *The Great Gatsby*, including:

- Gatsby's obsession and Tom's cruel possessive jealousy and how they motivate the plot from initiating incident through climax and conclusion

- an interpretation of the novel as not only the love story of Gatsby and Daisy, but also as the story of a generation, a social class, and in a broader sense, the corruption of the American Dream, possibly even the story of the wealthy's oppression of the poor and those who would join their ranks

- an interpretation of the novel as a classic, star-crossed love story on the level of Romeo and Juliet, *et al.*

What techniques has this writer used to present this information in a coherent, cohesive essay? Chandra has organized her essay according to a broadening of perspective, focusing first on individual characters and their impact on this specific plot, then looking at the social, cultural, and finally the literary relevance of the novel.

What type of score is this essay likely to receive? Why? This essay should receive a very high score. Chandra fully addresses the prompt, clearly understands the nature of literary quality—and provides enough explanation to demonstrate this to her scorer—and is also familiar with the novel. Not all of her discussions are equally strong, and she verges on a tangent in one part, but as scorers are generally instructed to reward what the student does well, the strengths of this fine essay should net Chandra a strong score.

TIME SPENT: 55 MIN—TIME REMAINING: 5 MIN

STEP 6: Review, Proof, and Edit (5 min out of 60)

Chandra clearly does not have time to take her essay into a complete second draft, but before she turns it in, she should give it one last quick read and correct any surface errors she finds that might reduce her score. Misspellings of key words or prominent people's names are especially damaging.

Chandra's essay above has already been corrected for surface errors—because we wanted to model correct conventions use for you—but here is a portion of her actual submission with its cross-outs and insertions:

> Another ^ character ~~that~~ makes the plot events seem inevitable is
>   *well-developed*   *who*
> Tom Buchanan. Tom is a bully. He is cruel, jealous, and possessive. Nick
> says that he knew Tom a little in college, and this establishes
>
> Tom's primary character trait^. It is Tom's cruelty and ~~posesive~~ nature
>   *s*   *possessive*
> that motivate his affair with Myrtle and his taunting of Wilson. It is his
> possessive nature that also makes him torment Gatsby. He probably does not
> love Daisy as much as he feels he owns her. And it is this sense of
> ownership that motivates him telling ~~George~~ that it was Gatsby's car
>   *his*   *Wilson*

that killed Myrtle, clearly suggesting that Gatsby killed Myrtle, and this

vengeance

motivates Wilson's revenge and Gatsby's death. So, the tragic end of the

strong

novel is presented as the inevitable result of the clash of two ^ characters.

in its characters and themes

    Great Literature also appeals to something universal ^. It might be the story of specific people in a specific time and place, but there is something in it that readers can identify with that makes it the story of everyone

everywhere. The Great Gatsby is truly the story of Nick ^ and Gatsby ^ and Tom, and Daisy on Long Island in the 1920s. But details of the "valley of ashes," the parties, the cars, and the drinking of bootleg liquor make it also the story of a generation, a period in United States history. References to the "Swastika" company suggest the beginning of the situation that led to World War II. Fitzgerald also makes comments about the irresponsibility of this generation of people and of the social class represented by Tom and Daisy. The characters are not simply individual

persons

people, they are symbols of a generation and a social class.

TIME SPENT: 60 MIN—TIME REMAINING: 0 MIN
Turn in your essay, or begin the next section.

PART IV:

The Research Projects

By now, you should know that the ability to learn something on your own, without taking a class or having an instructor stand over your shoulder will be crucial to you as you continue your education and enter your professional career. The ability to communicate what you've learned to someone else is equally important.

Consider the two chief reasons for communicating to someone else information you have learned independently:

1. You need to prove to an instructor, coach, or certification board or panel that you did in fact learn what you are claiming to know. Many students at the end of their Master of Arts, Doctor of Philosophy, or Doctor of Jurisprudence must defend their theses before panels of experts before they are granted their degrees.

2. You are addressing an audience that genuinely does not know this information, and you are instructing them.

Both of these reasons assume you have a thorough enough *knowledge* of the facts and a deep enough *understanding* of the issues associated with the topic, so that you might even be able to field questions asking about information or insights not included in your paper.

Both reasons also assume an understanding of what your audience is expecting from you. The certification panel does not want a mere recitation of facts and statistics. You will not impress them with a superb memory for trivia. Likewise, your reading audience is not going to want simply a rehash of research sources they can look at for themselves. Both audiences want to know what they can learn from *you*. What have *you* learned and realized, and what new insight can *you* bring to the table?

This is the new aspect we're introducing to your thesis—insight.

You know that your thesis cannot be mere fact: *Some breeds of dog are considered dangerous.*

You know that your thesis cannot be mere opinion: *Dangerous breeds of dog do not make very good pets.*

You know that your thesis must be *arguable*—rooted in fact but with room for interpretation and discussion: *Owners of dogs that are considered dangerous should take extra precautions to prevent their pets from injuring innocent people.*

Now consider that this arguable thesis should be, at least to some degree, a little *original*. It's not terribly original to try to argue that the owner of a dog that bites should keep the dog contained. Not many people are going to need to read *your* paper to accept that idea as valid. The search for evidence to support such a thesis won't be very interesting, nor will the paper that presents the evidence.

At this point in your education, no one expects you to discover a new star or the answer to Shakespeare's missing years, but you do need to make sure that, as you perform your research and gather your information, you always look for what your information is suggesting, what you might realize that others might not.

That new realization, then, is the purpose of your paper, much more so than the mere information that your reader could easily find for him or herself.

ASSIGNMENT 1:

Research Project—Non-English Language Arts

STEP 1: Select a Topic

Derek began his research online, and started to find possible topics from each category.

Medical Science:

— Invention of the germ theory—This one's both scientific and social/ historical, since it was widely resisted by the medical establishment at first. Doctors didn't even wash their hands before surgery.

> This could be a good selection for Derek, but he would need to find his own slant, a unique thesis, to make a paper that would read as more than mere historical research and reportage.

Technology:

— Invention of the microchip—This is what made modern computing possible, right up to smart phones and tablets. I could get into this one easily, but will a lot of other people choose it? Is it too obvious?

> This is a valid concern, but as long as Derek develops a thesis that is individual, unique, and well supported by research, there's no reason he couldn't write a superior paper on this topic.

Economics:

— Development of Keynesian Economic Theory—I can relate this one to the current economic crisis and find a lot of relevance to what's going on now. But it might be too easy to seem as if I'm editorializing or making my own statement, might come off as politically slanted.

> While being too overtly political in a research paper could be perceived as a fault, every paper and essay a student writes needs to have a point of view at the heart of its thesis. Keynesian economics may not be embraced across the political spectrum, but it is a historic theory that had definite impact on past history, and Derek could write a fine paper, *whether his thesis was pro-Keynesian or not.*

History/Social Studies:

— Impact of the Invention of the Elevator—It changed the face of cities, meant that buildings could be taller than just a few stories. Skyscrapers were possible because of it, the workforce and economy changed. My teacher is really keen on this one, he really emphasizes the social impact of technological advances in class. I could score some points there. The only problem is, <u>I'm not all that interested in it</u>, and I don't know how I'd make it interesting to the reader.

Derek is right to be concerned about his own lack of interest in a proposed topic, but perhaps he should keep searching for something else in this category that compels him more. He might be missing an opportunity.

Derek has several promising topics to choose from, and each of them can yield a number of interesting and worthwhile theses. He may do a preliminary Internet search and some casual reading about each one to find which will provide him with the richest research and most information and which he is most interested in pursuing. This is important; you want to be interested in, moved by, and compelled by whatever topic you choose. If the writer isn't compelled, he won't be able to compel the reader. And remember that you will be living very closely with this topic for several weeks—or maybe even longer.

STEP 2: Draft a Thesis

Early resistance to the germ theory by the medical establishment in the nineteenth century was not due only to scientific ignorance, but to social and religious attitudes of the period.

> This is a big assertion, I'd have to work hard and do an exhausting amount of research to prove it.

Social and religious attitudes of the nineteenth century were the major factor in resistance to the germ theory, more than scientific ignorance.

> Still a pretty big assertion, and I'm not sure it's provable.

Overcoming social and religious attitudes to gain wide acceptance, the germ theory marked a turning point in the medical establishment's perception of science and research.

> I'm still not happy with this, it's provable but not much of a statement.

The independent development of the microchip by Jack Kilby and Robert Noyce, and their subsequent rivalry and ultimate collaboration, helped propel their mutual invention toward its dominant place in technology and modern life.

> Wow, I'm overworking this one. It's long and awkward, and I don't know if I can really prove it. I think they would have had a rivalry early on, before their companies decided to merge their interests in the microchip, but I can't find much to support that in my online searches.

Jack Kilby and Robert Noyce's collaboration on the invention of the microchip pointed the way for subsequent advances achieved through cooperative efforts.

> That isn't really any better, I don't seem to be saying much with it. I think I should move on.

Keynesian Economics and Classical Economics, while opposing theories, have both had major impacts on history, as well as the present day economic debate.

> "Major impacts" sounds pretty weak to me, I need to make more of a statement, something more definite.

Keynesian Economics and Classical Economics, while solidly based theories, were both also formed by prevailing social and political attitudes.

> I may be getting closer here, but it still needs to be a little more of a unique statement. "Also" in addition to what?

Keynesian Economics and Classical Economics, and all their derivative theories, illustrate how economic theories are all intertwined with social and political attitudes.

> That might not be bad. I'm making an observation, and a statement, but not necessarily coming down on one side or the other.

The invention of the elevator had wide-ranging impact on urban development, business expansion, and social evolution.

> All of this is true, and I can prove it, but I just don't really care that much.

The invention of the elevator was the single-most influential technological advance in urban development.

> I guess this is more of a thesis, it makes more of a statement, but I'm still not really interested. I do like "single-most influential." I think that's <u>where</u> the argument is.

The invention of the elevator, which made skyscrapers and high-rise buildings possible, altered the face of cities for centuries to come.

> This is only getting worse. Isn't this a mere statement of fact? I'm not getting anywhere with this one, I think I should forget about it.

STEP 3: Draft a Preliminary Outline

Thesis: Keynesian Economics and Classical Economics, and all their derivative theories, illustrate how <u>economic theories are all intertwined with social and political attitudes</u>.

I. Introduction

  A. Brief description of Keynesian Theory

  B. Brief description of Classical Economic Theory

    1. Contrast with Keynesian Theory

    2. Contrast with current Free Market Theory

  C. Background of John Maynard Keynes and Adam Smith

    1. Contrast in their bios, schooling, and intellectual development

    2. How each saw the roles of government and markets

> Derek is planning his paper in a fairly typical manner, but he might be better advised to remember that the purpose of his paper is to support his thesis. He needs to allow his thesis and the demands of his reader to determine the extent of any introduction or exposition.

II. How each theory influenced history

    A. Smith's views and the Industrial Revolution in England

        1. Physiocratic School vs. Mercantilism

        2. Birth of Free Market concept

        3. Impact on society and business

    B. Keynes's views and The Great Depression

        1. Keynesian idea of what causes recessions and depressions

        2. Letter to Roosevelt

        3. Roosevelt changes from deficit reducer to Keynesian

        4. Political fallout

III. Political/Social Views, and how they impacted each theory

    A. Smith and The Theory of Moral Sentiments

        1. Contradictory or non-contradictory to Theory of Nations

        2. Influenced by views of Quesnay, Benjamin Franklin, etc.

        3. View of individual's role in society

        4. Embraced by conservatives and hard line capitalists

    B. Keynes and The General Theory of Employment, Interest and Money

        1. Increased role of Government and financial institutions

        2. Need for regulation

        3. View of national deficit as positive rather than negative in a down economy

        4. Embraced by liberals and unions

IV. Future Economic Theory

    A. Neo-Classicists

    B. Neo-Keynesian

    C. New Keynesian

    D. Monetarism

    E. Political/social influence on each

While Derek's outline at first glance looks well thought out and organized, there is one problem with it: in its present form, it does not sufficiently address his thesis.

STEP 4: Conduct Your Research

Taking notes is nothing new to a college- or career-preparatory eleventh grader. You've been taking some form of notes from your reading, viewing of and listening to electronic media, teachers' lectures, even class discussions.

You've been instructed in—and have practiced—taking notes from your sources in the form of direct quotation, close paraphrase, and brief summary and synopsis. You have (hopefully) learned to appreciate the need to take notes on your own ideas and insights and how they fit into the overall scheme of your paper.

Possibly most important of all, however, is to stick to your thesis and outline. Buy only the groceries you have on your shopping list. The twenty-first century has so far been called The Information Age, and it is more likely than not that you will be deluged with facts, opinions, interpretations, statistics, and so on and on… until you can't see or think straight. It's far too easy to be distracted by the interesting, the unique, and the scandalous, and far too many scholars have had their important research projects derailed by distractions and irrelevancies— not to mention just bad information from untrustworthy sources—for you to believe that you are immune.

You may indeed find you need to make the occasional substitution, or you may need to pursue a line of research you hadn't anticipated, but these occurrences are definitely more the exception than the rule. *And they are minor*.

Very, *very* rarely should you ever think it necessary to scrap all of your work up to this point and start over.

It is so important not to lose sight of the goal you set for yourself in the early stages of the process that this is the reason so many teachers and professors absolutely forbid changing directions or modifying the original plan without a conference and permission.

If you did the work you were supposed to do in the earlier steps, this step will be time-consuming, and the amount of information you will process might be baffling, but the entire project will not grind to a halt or become impossible to complete.

Just learn your material and take note of it in such a way that you'll be able to remember it when you need to and communicate it to someone else.

STEP 5: First Draft

Despite a flawed outline, Derek thinks he is ready to write his first draft.

Thesis: Keynesian Economics and Classical Economics, and their derivative theories, illustrate how economic theories are all intertwined with social and political attitudes.

In any in-depth discussion of economics, the names of John Maynard Keynes and Adam Smith are likely to be brought up. Both men, separated in time by more than a century, were the fathers of divergent, but equally influential theories of world economics. Each of these theories was influenced by the background, education and social experiences of each of these men, and by their political beliefs and affiliations.

In his opening paragraph, Derek wisely gets straight to his thesis, nicely laying the groundwork for the paper.

In the language of an economist, Keynesian Economics holds that the amount of money spent in the economy (which he terms the aggregate demand) does not necessarily equal the total productivity of the economy (which he terms the aggregate supply), and therefore is influenced by any number of outside factors, causing it to behave erratically and affecting production, employment, and inflation (Blanders). In practical terms, this means that, for the economy to be stable and robust, it needs to be a mixed economy, with the private sector taking the lead role, but with nevertheless a significant participation of government and public sector. In this view, the economy of a given country can be ill affected by a large proportion of firms and individuals taking steps that force the economy to operate below its potential growth rate, and a general glut (Stephens, 1998, p. 275)—an overage of supply owing to a want of demand—occurs. The result is unnecessarily high unemployment; the reaction of producers further damages the

Derek is using these terms correctly but awkwardly. The wording can be cleaned up in the following draft.

- 285 -

macroeconomic picture. Keynesian economics advocates a stabilization policy, to help control the business cycle; government investment, for instance in infrastructure, helps inject income into the economy, resulting in increased spending by consumers and companies (Stephens, p. 293).

This is in stark contrast to Classical or Neo-Classical economic theories, which hold that a free market will regulate itself, without any need of outside intervention, presumably from the government ("Classical Economics." [n.d.] In Wikipedia. Retrieved from http://en.wikipedia.org/wiki/Classical_economics). In the eighteenth century, when Adam Smith, along with his friend and mentor Francois Quesnay and several other emerging economists were beginning to form a new theory of assessing the wealth of nations, the Industrial Revolution was bringing vast changes to civilization. Capitalism was emerging from Feudalism, and Smith's concept was to measure national wealth not by the size of the king's treasury, but by the yearly national income, composed of wages, rent, and interest or profits produced by labor, land, and capital (Minkoff, 2008, p. 175). This was, in many ways, a revolutionary world view, influenced as it was by emerging new philosophies that flew in the face of many accepted beliefs, especially regarding monarchy, aristocracy, and religion. Quesnay had developed the Physiocratic School, the first true economic theory, which led directly to Classical Economics. Physiocratic Economics held that the wealth of nations derived solely from agricultural development, in opposition to mercantilism, which cited the ruler's wealth, the accumulation of gold, or the balance of trade as the measure of a nation's wealth (John M. Keynes in Library of Social Sciences).

Derek should be specific about who the "other emerging economists" were.

Derek has oversimplified the definition of the Physiocratic School and will have to clarify that in the next draft.

Smith's views, while not universally accepted at first, would come to have a profound effect on Industrial Revolution era England, which increasingly turned away from mercantilism and began, more and more, to embrace the free market theory. Open markets, free trade and laissez-faire policies arguably led to the meteoric rise of the British Empire, with rampant colonization and dramatically expanded trade leading to unprecedented wealth. Smith, in <u>The Wealth of Nations</u> (n.d.) had argued that the individual, seeking only to further his self-interest when engaging in trade or other forms of business, set in motion a chain of events that led to the betterment of the whole economic picture:

> As every individual, therefore, endeavours as much as he can both to employ his capital in the support of domestic industry, and so to direct that industry that its produce may be of the greatest value; every individual necessarily labours to render the annual revenue of the society as great as he can. He generally, indeed, neither intends to promote the public interest, nor knows how much he is promoting it. By preferring the support of domestic to that of foreign industry, he intends only his own security; and by directing that industry in such a manner as its produce may be of the greatest value, he intends only his own gain, and he is in this, as in many other eases, led by an invisible hand to promote an end which was no part of his intention. Nor is it always the worse for the society that it was no part of it. By pursuing his own interest he frequently promotes that of the society more effectually than when he really intends to promote it. I have never known much good done by those who affected to trade for the public good. (p. 47).

This is a big assertion, and Derek needs to back it up by citing some sources.

Here, Derek is wisely citing the source material to support his assertions. He will need to do more of this in the following draft.

Derek's making an interesting assertion here, and one that makes sense on the surface, but he needs again to back up his ideas with some concrete sources on "trickle down" and the Reagan era.

The "invisible hand" theory would become a widely cited concept right up to the present day; modern free market economists still assert that individuals pursuing self-interest indirectly benefit the public good by keeping prices low while building a demand for a wide array of goods and services—"Trickle Down" or Supply-Side Economics, put forward during the Reagan years, were a direct translation of the theory, though not necessarily one that Smith himself would have agreed with. For all his endorsement of free market ideals, Smith also warned of the dangers of an actual laissez-faire economy, which he believed would rapidly lead to the collusion of unscrupulous businesses against the consumer, and a resulting rise in prices to "whatever can be squeezed out of the buyers" (p. 53). In his earlier work, The Theory of Moral Sentiments, Smith had actually proposed a theory of sympathy, wherein the individual, observing the plight of others, becomes aware of the morality of his or her own behavior, and modifies that behavior accordingly. This seems to be a direct contradiction of the theories he states in The Wealth of Nations, and it has been the topic of much debate among economists and scholars. Some argue that there is no contradiction, that Smith was merely presenting different aspects of human nature that vary with the situation an individual might find themselves in. When considered alongside his statements on the danger of a completely unregulated business environment, it might seem that Smith was possibly more Keynesian in his philosophy than the greater number of his interpreters would like to admit.

Derek is making another interesting observation here, but he's doing it in a rather roundabout way, and once again, not giving enough sources for backup. He's also missing an opportunity to relate this section to his thesis.

John Maynard Keynes's greatest period of influence, unlike Smith's, was not during a period of economic upswing, but its very opposite—the Great Depression of the 1930s. In 1933, Keynes published The Means to Prosperity, outlining the policies he believed were necessary to reverse the economic decline that the U.S. and world found itself in. Keynes argued that public spending, not austerity measures to counter deficits, was key in lowering unemployment and jump-starting economic recovery. While copies of The Means to Prosperity were given to Franklin Delano Roosevelt and other prominent world leaders, it did not exert an immediate influence on policy other than in Sweden and Germany. Even letters and a direct meeting between Roosevelt and Keynes, while increasing the men's mutual regard for each other, did not result in Roosevelt putting forth a Keynesian plan for recovery. In 1936, Keynes published The General Theory of Employment, Interest and Money, in which he argued even more intensely for interventionist policies in confronting a recession. Pitting his theory in complete opposition to Neoclassical Economics, which he saw as outmoded, applying only to the special case of the previous century, Keynes advocated increased spending in public works, to spur growth and increase demand. As opposed to Classical Economists, who espoused the idea that supply creates its own demand, Keynes believed that demand was the central element that determines economic activity.

There is important information in the last paragraph, but it is not well organized and presented, probably owing to the flaws in Derek's outline. He is also not sticking especially well to his outline, which, imperfect as it may be, would give him some better idea of how to structure this paragraph.

Yes, but what is Derek's argument? He seems to sidestep making one in a misguided effort to seem impartial. He has also not addressed the core matter of his thesis, which seems to have gotten lost in the shuffle of the barrage of historical information he is presenting, and remains unproven. He needs, in the next draft, to point his outline more specifically toward his thesis, and to take a stand one way or another on what his own interpretation is on economic theory.

The future of economic theory will doubtlessly be affected by the work of both Smith and Keynes, along with the various interpretations of their ideas. In looking at Neo-Keynesian, Neoclassical, New Keynesian and Post-Keynesian and all other modern economic interpretations, it is evident that the same arguments persist, from Smith's time and Keynes's, and the debate continues to the present day, never in more heated terms. Whether one is arguing for interventionist policies, or for a laissez-faire approach, one could not form a persuasive theory without serious consideration of both Smith and Keynes, and an appreciation of what their individual effect was on history and economy.

References

Blanders, A. (n.d.) "Keynesian Economics." In Encyclopedia of Economics. Retrieved from Library of Social Sciences (http://www.encecon. com/EBchecked/topic/659723/keynesian).

Buchmann, J. (2006). The Life and Ideas of Adam Smith. Boston: W. W. Northrop & Sons.

"Classical Economics." (n.d.) In Wikipedia. Retrieved from http://en.wikipedia.org/ wiki/Classical_economics.

John M. Keynes. (n.d.) In Library of Social Sciences. Retrieved from http://www. socscilib.org/library/bios/Keynes.html.

Keynes, J. M. (1933, 1950). A Treatise On Money. New York: MacNaughton.

Keynes, J. M. (1936). The General Theory of Employment, Interest and Money. New York: MacNaughton.

Keynes, John. (n.d.) In Wikipedia. Retrieved from http://en.wikipedia.org/wiki/Keynesian_ economics.

Marshall, Alfred. (n.d.) In Library of Social Sciences. Retrieved from http://www. socscilib.org/library/bios/Marshall.html.

Minkoff, S. (2008). "John Maynard Keynes." Boston: McNally & Hill. First edition published by Concordia University Press, 1972.

"Origins of the Concept of Development: the Evolution of Capitalism." (n.d.) In The Center for International Finance and Development of Denver University. Retrieved from http://blogs.law.denver.edu/ebook/uicifd-ebook/origins-development

Smith, A. (n.d.). The Wealth of Nations. The Literature Network. Retrieved 29 November 2012. (http://www.online-literature.com/ adam_smith/wealth_nations/).

Stephens, K. (1998). The Keynesian Revolution. New York: Edwards Press.

Stockington, D. (1986). Political Triumphs: How the Reagan Economic Revolution Failed. Cleveland: Hipster & Rowe.

Analysis of First Draft

What is this writer's purpose? The writer's purpose is to show the impact of two divergent theories of economic analysis and how each one was formed in reaction to historical and political changes.

What is this writer's thesis? His thesis is that both Keynesian and Classical economics are intertwined with the prevailing political and social attitudes.

What key points has the writer identified to clarify the thesis? This is a major weakness in Derek's paper. He provides sources to back up the historical facts he is referencing, but fails to fully relate those facts to his thesis.

What key points has the writer identified to support the thesis?

- The impact of the Industrial Revolution on Adam Smith's thinking

- The Physiocratic School, and Quesnay's influence on Smith

- Smith's book *The Wealth of Nations* and its influence on economic theory

- Keynes's reaction to the Great Depression and how it affected his theories

- Keynes's books *The Means to Prosperity* and *The General Theory of Employment, Interest and Money*; how they codified his thoughts on interventionist policies and finally influenced Roosevelt

Does the writer effectively prove his thesis? The writer doesn't really prove his thesis; the thesis itself gets rather lost in the shuffle of historical, social, and political information that the author fails to fully relate to it.

NOW plan your own research paper, following the same process by which Derek arrived at his first draft.

STEP 1: Select a Topic

STEP 2: Draft a Thesis

Make sure your thesis is arguable—not merely fact, not pure opinion.

Make certain you have or know you can find sufficient evidence from a variety of sources to explain and support your key points.

STEP 3: Draft a Preliminary Outline

STEP 4: Conduct Your Research

STEP 5: First Draft

STEP 6: Peer Edit

What is this writer's purpose?

What is this writer's thesis?

What key points has the writer identified to *clarify* the thesis?

What key points has the writer identified to support the thesis?

Does the writer effectively prove the thesis?

STEP 7: Revised/Final Draft

Here are Derek's editor's comments and analysis as well as his responses:

- In his opening paragraph, Derek wisely gets straight to his thesis, nicely laying the groundwork for the paper.
- Derek is using these terms correctly but awkwardly. The wording can be cleaned up in the following draft.
- Derek should be specific about who the "other emerging economists" were.
- Derek has oversimplified the definition of the Physiocratic School and will have to clarify that in the next draft.
- This is a big assertion, and Derek needs to back it up by citing some sources.
- Here, Derek is wisely citing the source material to support his assertions. He will need to do more of this in the following draft.

- Derek's making an interesting assertion here, and one that makes sense on the surface, but he needs again to back up his ideas with some concrete sources on "trickle down" and the Reagan era.

- Derek is making another interesting observation here, but he's doing it in a rather roundabout way, and once again, not giving enough sources for backup. He's also missing an opportunity to relate this section to his thesis.

- There is important information in the last paragraph, but it is not well organized and presented, probably owing to the flaws in Derek's outline. He is also not sticking especially well to his outline, which, imperfect as it may be, would give him some better idea of how to structure this paragraph.

- Yes, but what is Derek's argument? He seems to sidestep making one in a misguided effort to seem impartial. He has also not addressed the core matter of his thesis, which seems to have gotten lost in the shuffle of the barrage of historical information he is presenting, and remains unproven. He needs, in the next draft, to point his outline more specifically toward his thesis, and to take a stand one way or another on what his own interpretation is on economic theory.

> Okay, my outline was not all that great apparently, and not only do I not prove my thesis, it somehow gets lost. And I guess I need to not back off from taking a position and standing behind it.
>
> I think I need to go back to the outline first and rework that before I go on to the next draft.

Analysis of First Draft

What is this writer's purpose? The writer's purpose is to show the impact of two divergent theories of economic analysis and how each one was formed in reaction to historical and political changes.

> *Well, at least I got that point through. I must have something here.*

What is this writer's thesis? His thesis is that both Keynesian and Classical economics are intertwined with the prevailing political and social attitudes.

> *I need to keep going back to that; I somehow forgot about it with all the historical research and background I had to do.*

What key points has the writer identified to clarify the thesis? This is a major weakness in Derek's paper. He provides sources to back up the historical facts he is referencing, but fails to fully relate those facts to his thesis.

> *So I really need to go back to the outline and rework that first.*

What key points has the writer identified to support the thesis?

- The impact of the Industrial Revolution on Adam Smith's thinking

- The Physiocratic School, and Quesnay's influence on Smith

- Smith's book *The Wealth of Nations* and its influence on economic theory

- Keynes's reaction to the Great Depression and how it affected his theories

- Keynes's books *The Means to Prosperity* and *The General Theory of Employment, Interest and Money*; how they codified his thoughts on interventionist policies and finally influenced Roosevelt

> *It looks like I've got enough background here to choke a horse. I just need to use it better.*

Does the writer effectively prove the thesis? The writer doesn't really prove his thesis; the thesis itself gets rather lost in the shuffle of historical, social, and political information that the author fails to fully relate to it.

> *Again, I just need to keep coming back to the thesis and make sure what I'm doing relates directly to it.*

Here is Derek's revised draft. Because his peer editor said his outline was not structured sufficiently to serve his thesis, he revised the outline before he wrote his second draft.

Thesis: Keynesian Economics and Classical Economics, and their derivative theories, illustrate how economic theories are all intertwined with social and political attitudes.

Derek is now structuring his outline with much more of an eye on how the information he has to present will relate to his thesis. This is a promising beginning.

I. Introduction

    A. Brief description of Keynesian Theory

        1. Keynes's schooling and background

        2. His social and philosophical ideas, their basis

    B. Brief description of Classical Economic Theory

        1. Adam Smith's schooling and background

        2. His social and philosophical ideas, their basis

II. Political/Social Views, and how they impacted each theory in detail

    A. Smith and <u>The Theory of Moral Sentiments</u>

        1. Contradictory or non-contradictory to <u>Theory of Nations</u>

        2. Influenced by views of Quesnay, Benjamin Franklin, etc.

        3. View of individual's role in society

        4. Embraced by conservatives and hard-line capitalists

    B. Keynes and <u>The General Theory of Employment, Interest and Money</u>

        1. Increased role of Government and financial institutions

        2. Need for regulation

3. View of national deficit as positive rather than negative in a down economy

4. Embraced by liberals and unions

III. How each theory influenced history

A. Smith's views and the Industrial Revolution in England

1. Physiocratic School vs. Mercantilism

2. Birth of Free Market concept

3. Impact on society and business

B. Keynes's views and The Great Depression

1. Keynesian idea of what causes recessions and depressions

2. Letter to Roosevelt

3. Roosevelt changes from deficit reducer to Keynesian

IV. Future Economic Theory

A. Neo-Classicists

B. Neo-Keynesian

C. New Keynesian

D. Monetarism

E. Political/social influence on each, <u>and why each is flawed</u>.

Note that Derek has flipped sections II and III, putting the political/social impact of each theory ahead of how they influenced history. This is a choice that will help him relate his paper more fully to his thesis and aid him in proving it.

It looks as if Derek is going to finally give himself the freedom to have a point of view on the subject. This is an important step, and a central one in writing a successful paper. The author should express a point of view on the subject and be prepared to back that point of view up. The paper should be a persuasive argument, not merely a report.

Thesis: Keynesian Economics and Classical Economics, and their derivative theories, illustrate how economic theories are all intertwined with social and political attitudes.

Derek is wise to retain this opening paragraph. Now he needs to follow up on its promise.

This is an important "add" for Derek because it places what he will eventually tell his reader about Keynesian economics in the context of what previous ideas helped form it.

In any in-depth discussion of economics, the names of John Maynard Keynes and Adam Smith are likely to be brought up. Both men, separated in time by more than a century, were the fathers of divergent, but equally influential theories of world economics. Each of these theories was influenced by the background, education and social experiences of its creator, and by his political beliefs and affiliations.

John Maynard Keynes was the son of John Neville Keynes, an economist and lecturer in moral sciences, and Florence Ada Keynes, a social reformer (Blanders). Attentive and supportive, Keynes's parents encouraged him to pursue his education vigorously. He received a degree in mathematics from Cambridge University, where he would remain for another year to study monetary policy under the influential economists Alfred Marshall and Arthur Pigou (Stephens, 1998, p. 275) Marshall came to economics as a direct result of his study of ethics and social science, and he saw the study and refinement of economic theory as a method of improving the lot of the working class. He believed that economics were bound up with prevailing social, ethical, and political attitudes, and that no economist could ignore these (Stephens, p. 293). Pigou forged the concept of externalities, meaning a positive or negative result of an individual action, and advocated governmental intervention in terms of subsidizing positive externals (to encourage education, for instance) or taxation on a negative external (such as pollution) (Stephens, p. 306). The exposure to both of these important economists and teachers must have impacted Keynes's own ideas and concepts on both economics and its impact on social and ethical issues. He would publish <u>Treatise on Money</u>, in which he stated, in agreement with Marshall and Pigou, that the way to stabilize a shaky economy was to stabilize the price level, and that the Central Bank must lower interest rates to achieve this (Minkoff, 2008, p. 175). It was a theory that Keynes would later disavow, when unemployment in Britain remained high between the two World Wars. He would then publish <u>The General Theory of Employment, Interest and Money</u>, which would revolutionize economic theory by introducing the concept of aggregate demand.

Derek is now relating his opening section much more directly to his thesis by examining Keynes's background and early influences.

It was with this theory, which substantially broke away from the concepts of his mentors, Marshall and Pigou, that Keynes defined his own brand of economics. Keynesian Economics holds that aggregate demand (the spending capacity of the economy) does not necessarily equal aggregate supply (the total productive capacity of the economy), and therefore is influenced by any number of outside factors, causing it to behave erratically and affecting production, employment, and inflation (John M. Keynes in <u>Library of Social Sciences</u>). In practical terms, this means that, for the economy to be stable and robust, it needs to be a mixed economy, with the private sector taking the lead role, but with nevertheless a significant participation of government and the public sector. In this view, the economy of a given country can be ill affected by a large proportion of firms and individuals taking steps that force the economy to operate below its potential growth rate, and a general glut (Keynes, 1950, p. 52)—an overage of supply owing to a want of demand—occurs. The result is unnecessarily high unemployment; the reaction of producers further damages the macroeconomic picture. Keynesian economics advocates a stabilization policy, to help control the business cycle; government investment, for

Derek has reworked the wording here, and the result is clearer and less clunky.

instance in infrastructure, helps inject income into the economy, resulting in increased spending by consumers and companies (Blanders).

Like Keynes, Adam Smith also found his way to economic theory through advanced and rounded studies. Attending Glasgow University, he initially devoted his attentions to moral philosophy, under the tutelage of Francis Hutchison, a preeminent figure in the Scottish Enlightenment. Like the European Enlightenment, the Scottish Enlightenment embraced a humanist and rationalist view of the primacy of human reason and individual freedom. This view affected every discipline of the time, from philosophy to agriculture, chemistry, sociology—and economics. Hutchison, probably the most influential thinker of this movement, defined virtue as whatever provides "the greatest happiness for the greatest numbers" (Origins). This is not very far removed from the economic theory Smith would profess in his most influential book, The Wealth of Nations; in fact, it seems indistinguishable from the concept of free markets and laissez-faire policy.

In the latter part of the eighteenth century, when Smith, along with his friend and mentor Francois Quesnay and his friend David Hume were beginning to form a new theory of assessing the wealth of nations, the Industrial Revolution was bringing vast changes to civilization. Capitalism was emerging from Feudalism, and Smith's concept was to measure national wealth not by the size of the king's treasury, but by the yearly national income, composed of wages, rent, and interest or profits produced by labor, land, and capital (Keynes in Library of Social Sciences). This was, in many ways, a revolutionary world view, influenced as it was by emerging new philosophies that flew in the face of many accepted tenets, especially regarding monarchy, aristocracy, and religion. Quesnay, developed the Physiocratic School, the first true

Derek is sticking more closely to his outline here than in the previous draft, and it is working well for him.

Note that it is much better to list a specific figure or event than to use a generalization, as Derek had in the previous draft when citing "several other emerging economists."

economic theory, which led directly to Classical Economics. Physiocratic Economics held that the wealth of nations derived solely from agricultural development (Classical Economics), or in other words, from productive work, in opposition to mercantilism, which cited the ruler's wealth, the accumulation of gold, or the balance of trade as the measure of a nation's wealth.

Smith's views, while not universally accepted at first, would come to have a profound effect on Industrial Revolution era England, which increasingly turned away from mercantilism and began, more and more, to embrace the free market theory. Smith had sharply criticized mercantilism, with its monopolistic tendencies and high tariffs, as a barrier to true economic growth, and advocated the reduction of oppressive governmental interventions (Buchmann, 2006, p. 43). Open markets, free trade, and laissez-faire policies arguably led to the meteoric rise of the British Empire, with rampant colonization and dramatically expanded trade leading to unprecedented wealth (Buchmann, p. 56). In <u>The Wealth of Nations</u>, Smith had argued that the individual, seeking only to further his self-interest when engaging in trade or other forms of business, set in motion a chain of events that led to the betterment of the whole economic picture:

> As every individual, therefore, endeavours as much as he can both to employ his capital in the support of domestic industry, and so to direct that industry that its produce may be of the greatest value; every individual necessarily labours to render the annual revenue of the society as great as he can. He generally, indeed, neither intends to promote the public interest, nor knows how much he is promoting it...By pursuing his own interest he frequently promotes that of the society more effectually than when he really intends to promote

Derek has beefed this section up a bit and found some supporting sources to cite. It's improved, but could still be expanded on.

Derek has retained the quote, but edited it down somewhat, to good advantage. This amended version brings the reader more immediately to the point.

it. I have never known much good done by those who affected to trade for the public good. (p. 47)

The "invisible hand" theory would become a widely cited concept right up to the present day; modern free market economists still assert that individuals pursuing self-interest indirectly benefit the public good by keeping prices low while building a demand for a wide array of goods and services. "Trickle Down" or Supply-Side Economics, put forward during the Reagan years, and defined as a "laissez faire" approach, was a translation of the theory, though not necessarily one that Smith himself would have readily embraced, as it related more directly to tax cuts for the wealthiest class, rather than supply and demand of the marketplace (Stockington, 1986, p. 128). For all his endorsement of free market ideals, Smith also warned of the dangers of an actual laissez-faire economy, which he believed would rapidly lead to the collusion of unscrupulous businesses against the consumer, and a resulting rise in prices to "whatever can be squeezed out of the buyers" (p. 437). In his earlier work, <u>The Theory of Moral Sentiments</u>, Smith had actually proposed a theory of sympathy, wherein the individual, observing the plight of others, becomes aware of the morality of his or her own behavior and modifies that behavior accordingly. This would seem to be in direct contradiction to the theories he puts forward in <u>The Wealth of Nations</u> and has been the source of much debate among economists and scholars. Some argue that there is no contradiction, that Smith was merely presenting different aspects of human nature that vary with the situation an individual might find him- or herself in. When considered alongside his statements on the danger of a completely unfettered business environment, it might seem that Smith was possibly more Keynesian in his philosophy than the greater number of his

Derek's assertion in this section has been expanded and a backup citation added. Much improved from the previous draft, and it leads nicely into the next section.

interpreters would like to admit. As different as their approaches to economic theory may seem on the surface, there is a common theme to their work that links them closely: they compose theories in response to social, political, and ethical realities of the world as they perceive it, with the motive of benefiting the greater good, not merely the upper class and aristocracy.

Derek has done a good job of both relating this section to his thesis and in making a cohesive, persuasive argument.

John Maynard Keynes's greatest period of influence, unlike Smith's, was not during a period of economic upswing, but its very opposite—the Great Depression of the 1930s. In 1933, Keynes published The Means to Prosperity, outlining the policies he believed were necessary to reverse the economic decline that both the U.S. and Europe found themselves in. Keynes argued that private sector decisions can sometimes lead to inefficient outcomes that drag down the macroeconomic picture and require a policy response from the public sector. Therefore, public spending, not austerity measures to counter deficits, was key in lowering unemployment and jump-starting economic recovery. This was a controversial position in its own day, and remains controversial to the present. While copies of The Means to Prosperity, were given to Franklin Delano Roosevelt and other prominent world leaders, it did not exert an immediate influence on policy other than in Sweden and Germany. Even letters and a direct meeting between Roosevelt and Keynes, while increasing the men's mutual regard for each other, did not result in Roosevelt putting forth a Keynesian plan for recovery. In 1936, Keynes published The General Theory of Employment, Interest and Money, in which he argued even more intensely for interventionist policies in confronting a recession. Pitting his theory in complete opposition to Neo-Classic Economics, which he saw as an outmoded, nineteenth-century school of thought, Keynes advocated increased spending in public works to spur growth and increase demand. As opposed to Classical Economists, who espoused the idea that supply creates its own demand, Keynes believed that demand was the central element that determines economic activity. It is a "bottom-up" rather than a "top-down" view of how the economy works, and dovetails to Keynes's social and political bent.

This paragraph has been improved in its structure and now supports his thesis nicely, with Derek's interpretive comment making a fine point.

The future of economic theory will doubtlessly be affected by the work of both Smith and Keynes, along with the seemingly endless interpretations, reinterpretations, and refutations of their ideas. In looking at Neo-Keynesian, Neoclassical, New Keynesian and Post-Keynesian, and all other modern economic interpretations, it is evident that the same arguments persist, from Smith's time and Keynes's. The debate continues to the present day—never in more heated terms—as to the proper role of government in economic policy, and even the proper role of government to the individual. Neither Smith nor Keynes could have envisioned the present global economic reality and the present crisis. From the ripple effects of communication technology, to the housing and banking crises and trade deficits, the pressures on the present-day world economy are unprecedented and require new economic philosophies to counter their effects and bring employment and prosperity back to past levels. As both Smith and Keynes knew, no economist can ignore the social, political, and ethical realities of the time in forming an economic theory; but as they both also knew, neither can that theory be formed solely as a political tool and have any chance of benefiting the many rather than the few.

Derek is embracing a point of view and an actual argument here, and he's doing it quite effectively. He should think about expanding this section in a third draft, citing some outside sources and building his case even more persuasively.

References

Blanders, A. (n.d.) "Keynesian Economics." In Encyclopedia of Economics. Retrieved from Library of Social Sciences (http://www.encecon.com/EBchecked/topic/659723/keynesian).

Buchmann, J. (2006). The Life and Ideas of Adam Smith. Boston: W. W. Northrop & Sons.

"Classical Economics." (n.d.) In Wikipedia. Retrieved from http://en.wikipedia.org/wiki/Classical_economics.

John M. Keynes. (n.d.) In Library of Social Sciences. Retrieved from http://www.socscilib.org/library/bios/Keynes.html.

"John Keynes." (n.d.) In Wikipedia. Retrieved from http://en.wikipedia.org/wiki/Keynesian_economics.

Keynes, J. M. (1933, 1950). A Treatise on Money. New York: MacNaughton.

Keynes, J. M. (1936). The General Theory of Employment, Interest and Money. New York: MacNaughton.

Marshall, Alfred. (n.d.) In Library of Social Sciences. Retrieved from http://www.socscilib.org/library/bios/Marshall.html.

Minkoff, S. (2008). "John Maynard Keynes." Boston: McNally & Hill. First edition published by Concordia University Press, 1972.

Origins of the Concept of Development: the Evolution of Capitalism. (n.d.) In The Center for International Finance and Development of Denver University. Retrieved from http://blogs.law.denver.edu/ebook/uicifd-ebook/origins-development.

Smith, A. (n.d.). The Wealth of Nations. The Literature Network. Retrieved 29 November 2012. (http://www.online-literature.com/adam_smith/wealth_nations/).

Stephens, K. (1998). The Keynesian Revolution. New York: Edwards Press.

Stockington, D. (1986). Political Triumphs: How the Reagan Economic Revolution Failed. Cleveland: Hipster & Rowe.

Analysis of Revised Draft

What is this writer's purpose? The writer's purpose is to show the influence of historical and political changes on all economic theories, especially Keynesian and Classical economics, and how both of these theories have inherent virtues and flaws.

What is this writer's thesis? His thesis is that both Keynesian and Classical economics are intertwined with the prevailing political and social attitudes.

Has the writer's new draft strengthened his point? Yes, decidedly so. This draft not only has more supporting material for Derek's assertions, but he takes an actual point of view on the issue of economic theory.

What new details, facts, etc., have been included to make this a more potent assessment of the book or article?

- The background and education of both Keynes and Smith
- The influence of Alfred Marshall and Arthur Pigou on Keynes's early ideas
- How Keynes eventually broke away from the theories of Marshall and Pigou to form his own school of economic theory
- An effective comparison of "laissez faire" and "trickle-down," or "supply-side" economics
- An even more effective comparison of Keynes and Smith, not only for their differences, but for what they have in common

Does the writer effectively prove his thesis to any greater degree than the previous draft? Yes, emphatically—and he's made a substantial improvement on the previous draft in that he actually takes a point of view on the subject, makes an argument, and supports that argument.

Now write your final draft.

ASSIGNMENT 2:

Research Project—English Language or Literature Topic

While exploring different critical literary theories, **Eleanor** was particularly interested in the New Historicist view that examines a work in the context of the cultural, social, and political background in which the work was created—both the impact of the background on the literature and the impact of the literature on the culture. When her teacher formalized her second-semester research project, Eleanor knew that she wanted to do something on the interplay of politics and art.

STEP 1: Select a Topic

Eleanor now needs to narrow down a list of possible topics for her paper that will address her interest and fulfill the requirements of the assignment.

Impact of literature on culture or society...

- To Kill a Mockingbird...probably everyone's going to do that one. And, really, how influential was that book when compared to the whole Civil Rights movement?

- Uncle Tom's Cabin...that's possible...there's that neat Lincoln quote from when he met her: "You're the little lady who started this big war..." or something like that.

- The Jungle...that's another one probably everyone will do...and some people around here don't like the book because of its socialist themes, and I don't want to be graded down for that.

- A lot of Dickens' stuff...but I haven't really read any of it except A Christmas Carol...could I do something about how Dickens and that other guy on that History of Christmas DVD "invented" the modern Christmas?

Eleanor is referring to Washington Irving and his fictional travelogue, *Old Christmas*, also published as *Old Christmas and Bracebridge Hall*.

Impact of background on literature...
- Shakespeare and his portrayal of Richard III

- McCarthy's blacklist of writers

> This is not really an accurate summary of the issue, but Eleanor is early
> enough in her process that, if she chooses this topic, she can correct her
> misstatement and oversimplification.

- wasn't The Crucible about McCarthyism?

- there was something about Arthur Miller and some movie maker...
they were friends and then Miller got blacklisted or something

> Again, if Eleanor chooses this topic, she can clarify and elaborate on points
> she is not certain of.

- In The Brady Bunch, Carol Brady was supposed to be a divorced
woman, but the producers were afraid audiences would judge her
harshly.
- I think Mary Richards (The Mary Tyler Moore Show) was
originally going to be divorced as well.

> Some of these more pop-culture topics might be interesting but might
> not lend themselves to academic research or be as acceptable to some
> teachers as others.

Eleanor has several good (and a few not-as-good) topics to choose from. She
may do a preliminary Internet search and some casual reading about each one
to find which will provide her with the richest research and most information
and which she is most interested in pursuing. This is important; you want to
be interested in, moved by, and compelled by whatever topic you choose. If the
writer isn't compelled, she won't be able to compel the reader. And remember
that you will be living very closely with this topic for several weeks—or maybe
even longer.

STEP 2: Draft a Thesis

Because divorce was still a taboo subject in American society, and divorced people were generally looked down upon, many television shows of the 1960s and 1970s portrayed female characters who were either widowed or single, but not divorced.

> Even as I was writing this, I realized it was a dumb statement and didn't say what I wanted to say.

Two of the era's most popular and enduring television programs, The Brady Bunch and The Mary Tyler Moore Show, reflect the way art is not created in a vacuum, but against a vast tapestry of social, political, and cultural values that impact the art.

> Okay, I see that, except for listing the shows and the difference between divorced women and a widow and a broken engagement, there's not a lot here.

Writers are sometimes thought to be separate from, or above, the petty politics of their day, but one of playwright Arthur Miller's greatest works, The Crucible, was written as a form of political protest.

> Well, I do like this better, but I think it's too specific, too factual.

Eleanor may be having trouble coming up with a thesis, but she is doing a wonderful job diagnosing problems in her attempts.

Two powerful persons in the theatre world, Arthur Miller and Elia Kazan, were great friends and collaborators until they were torn apart by their differences in handling their involvement in the McCarthy witch hunts.

> I think I'm getting there, but this doesn't address their literature at all, only their friendship.

- 309 -

Deciding that she is interested in the friendship and then alienation of Miller and Kazan, Eleanor decides to walk away from her thesis for a few days to do some additional preliminary research. She has a vague sense of what she hopes to find but does not have the language to articulate it without some additional, specific information.

To see how works of literature are shaped by the circumstances in which they are written, one needs only to look at work produced by onetime friends and collaborators Arthur Miller and Elia Kazan...

Elia Kazan's <u>On the Waterfront</u> and Arthur Miller's <u>A View from the Bridge</u> illustrate both how these onetime friends differed in their response to the McCarthy witch hunts and how artists can transform painful personal and political experiences into significant work.

> I think this is more like it; it's specific and gives an interesting slant on the subject matter.

STEP 3: Draft a Preliminary Outline

Thesis: Elia Kazan's <u>On the Waterfront</u> and Arthur Miller's <u>A View from the Bridge</u> illustrate both how these onetime friends differed in their response to the McCarthy witch hunts and how artists can transform painful personal and political experiences into significant work.

> I think I'll present this thematically rather than chronologically; the history needs to be illustrating the thesis, rather than becoming the main focus.

I. Introduction—Miller and Kazan's friendship and collaboration, the basic facts of the rift, leading up to my thesis

II. HUAC; Miller and Kazan's differences, how it relates to their subsequent work

III. Compare the main characters of <u>On the Waterfront</u> and <u>A View from the Bridge</u>; show how they relate to Kazan's and Miller's different ideas about informing.

IV. How Kazan and Miller actually ended up working together years later on <u>After the Fall</u>, and what that points up about their relationship

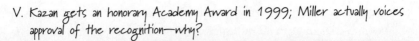

V. Kazan gets an honorary Academy Award in 1999; Miller actually voices approval of the recognition—why?

> This outline will ultimately prove to be insufficient as Eleanor has not given her-self a plan for how to present the information gathered during her research.

STEP 4: Conduct Your Research

As we've already suggested, taking notes is nothing new to a college- or career-preparatory eleventh grader. You've been taking some form of notes from your reading, viewing of, and listening to electronic media, teachers' lectures, even class discussions.

You've been instructed in—and have practiced—taking notes from your sources in the form of direct quotation, close paraphrase, and brief summary and synopsis. You have (hopefully) learned to appreciate the need to take notes on your own ideas and insights and how they fit into the overall scheme of your paper.

Possibly most important of all, however, is to stick to your thesis and outline. "Buy" only the "groceries" you have on your "shopping list." The twenty-first century has so far been called The Information Age, and it is more likely than not that you will be deluged with facts, opinions, interpretations, statistics, and so on and on…until you can't see or think straight. It's far too easy to be distracted by the interesting, the unique, and the scandalous, and far too many scholars have had their important research projects derailed by distractions and irrelevancies—not to mention just bad information from untrustworthy sources—for you to believe that you are immune.

You may indeed find you need to make the occasional substitution, or you may need to pursue a line of research you hadn't anticipated, but these occurrences are definitely more the exception than the rule. *And they are minor*.

Very, *very* rarely should you ever think it necessary to scrap all of your work up to this point and start over.

It is so important not to lose sight of the goal you set for yourself in the early stages of the process that this is the reason so many teachers and professors absolutely forbid changing directions or modifying the original plan without a conference and permission.

If you did the work you were supposed to do in the earlier steps, this step will be time-consuming, and the amount of information you will process might be baffling, but the entire project will not grind to a halt or become impossible to complete.

Just learn your material and take note of it in such a way that you'll be able to remember it when you need to and communicate it to someone else.

STEP 5: First Draft

Eleanor is now ready to write her first draft.

There is some important information packed into the second sentence, and it's far too long. Eleanor should consider breaking it down into two or even three sentences.

Another overlong sentence. The reference to Miller's refusal to use his screenplay as a vehicle for anti-Communist propaganda leans toward her thesis, but Eleanor needs to establish her thesis now.

In April of 1952, a great artistic collaboration and a great friendship ended. Arthur Miller, one of America's preeminent playwrights, sundered his professional and personal relationship with Elia Kazan, one of the most successful theater and film directors of the day, over Kazan's decision to testify at the House Un-American Activities Committee (HUAC) and name the names of friends and contacts who had been members of the Communist Party in the 1930s, when Kazan had been a member of the Group Theatre. Kazan had directed Miller's greatest successes on Broadway, including <u>Death of a Salesman</u> and <u>All My Sons</u>; the two had also been planning to collaborate on Miller's screenplay <u>The Hook</u>, about waterfront workers in the Red Hook section of Brooklyn, which they had been unable to sell to Columbia pictures because of Miller's refusal to recast corrupt union officials as Communist conspirators. Three years later, Kazan would win a second Academy Award for directing <u>On the Waterfront</u>, a film with distinct similarities to Miller's unsold screenplay <u>The Hook</u>, and Miller would write what would later be seen as one of his best plays, <u>A View from the Bridge</u>. The two pieces both had central characters

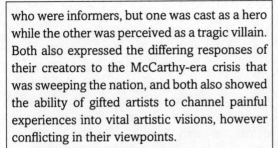

who were informers, but one was cast as a hero while the other was perceived as a tragic villain. Both also expressed the differing responses of their creators to the McCarthy-era crisis that was sweeping the nation, and both also showed the ability of gifted artists to channel painful experiences into vital artistic visions, however conflicting in their viewpoints.

Unlike Kazan, Miller had refused to name names when he testified before HUAC; he was fined and sentenced to jail time for his defiance. The two men, in their memoirs, differ substantially in the recounting of this period, even to when Kazan told Miller of his decision to inform; Kazan maintains he met with Miller before his testimony, and Miller states the meeting took place afterward (Bernstein). Miller, in his autobiography <u>Timebends</u>, recalls Kazan's defense of his actions: "Listening to him I grew frightened. There was a certain gloomy logic in what he was saying: unless he came clean he could never hope, in the height of his creative powers, to make another film in America, and he would probably not be given a passport to work abroad either. If the theatre remained open to him, it was not his primary interest anymore; he wanted to deepen his film life, that was where his heart lay, and he had been told in so many words by his old boss and friend Spyros Skouras, president of Twentieth Century Fox, that the company would not employ him unless he satisfied the Committee..." (276).

Eleanor has finally come to her thesis, but again, it's a bit overwritten, overlong, and even awkward. She'll need to address this in her next draft.

Eleanor must be careful not to lose her reader with brief references to important historical events without sufficient background information. Since the two films speak to the country's anti-Communist sentiment (the political aspect), she needs to make sure her reader understands the connections among HUAC, informing, not informing, the men's friendship, and their art.

An examination of the characters of Terry Malloy and Eddie Carbone reveals a clear contrast, but their similarities are apparent, too. Malloy may ultimately be seen as the hero for informing on his corrupt bosses, but he is hardly pure; under his brother's influence, he has made moral compromises for much of his life, and his decision to finally make an ethical choice can be seen as driven as much by his passion for Evie as by principal. Carbone is also driven by passion, but that passion itself is ethically compromised, as it is centered on his seventeen-year-old niece, whose every move he jealously watches, ultimately driving him to betray the young immigrant she has fallen in love with. Both pay a price for their actions; Malloy is beaten nearly to death by the henchmen of the boss he has exposed, and Carbone, his betrayal having made him a pariah, is killed in a knife fight with Marco, one of the immigrants he has <u>informed on</u>. But Malloy is triumphant at the end, and Carbone is defeated utterly; there can hardly be a more dramatic illustration of how Kazan and Miller viewed the act of informing and its consequences.

It is interesting to note that, while Kazan was metaphorically defending his decision to inform to the HUAC, he did not request Schulberg to change the mobsters in the screenplay to Communist infiltrators, as Columbia chief Harry Cohn had requested of Miller for the screenplay of <u>The Hook</u>; Kazan was perhaps more comfortable with metaphor than with a literal defense of his actions. It is also interesting to contrast Miller's characterization of Carbone with the inquisitors of his more politically charged play, <u>The Crucible</u>; the sanctimonious judges of Salem are, each and every one, without redeeming human qualities, while Carbone is portrayed as a flawed, tragic figure—if not a hero, then his own victim. In a 2005 biography of Kazan, Richard Schickel states that the play is a "metaphor about betrayal and its consequences,"

Eleanor has made a common word-choice error, confusing *principal* (person or most important thing) and *principle* (value or ideal).

While the "act of informing" is the clearly the crux of the issue for Eleanor, she could probably make it clearer to her reader that the two men's treatment of informers is the "McCarthy" element of her thesis.

Although Eleanor has mentioned this earlier, at this point, she should cite her source.

Certainly, a discussion of *The Crucible* would help Eleanor support her thesis, but this brief reference can only confuse a reader who is not familiar with the play.

rather than a political condemnation (366). In a New York Times article about the 2010 Broadway revival of the play, director Gregory Mosher says that, in Miller's view, informing "is an act of self-betrayal," losing Eddie his place in the community, his self-respect and finally, his life (Taylor 58). Had Miller's feelings toward Kazan softened between 1952 and 1955? Was he now seeing his former friend and collaborator as the victim of his own nature, rather than as the hard-nosed, opportunistic, and selfish turncoat that much of the left-wing theater community believed Kazan to be? It is plain that the two men had a complicated relationship, but however Miller felt toward Kazan at this point, it is also plain that he did not see him in the same light as he saw Terry Malloy; for Miller, that metaphor didn't play. But over time, it did seem that Miller had some degree, if not of forgiveness, then of understanding toward Kazan. In his memoir Timebends, Miller writes "...it came down to a governmental decree of moral guilt that could easily be made to disappear by ritual speech: intoning names of fellow sinners and recanting former beliefs. This last was probably the saddest and truest part of the charade, for by the early 1950s there were few, and even fewer in the arts, who had not left behind their illusions about the Soviets" (355). For his part, Kazan remained unyielding in his defense of his actions throughout his life, stating firmly, "I did what I did because it was the more tolerable of two alternatives that were, either way, painful, even disastrous, and either way wrong for me. That's what a difficult decision means: Either way you go, you lose" (475).

Like Eddie Carbone, Kazan really was treated as a pariah by most of the left-leaning, intellectual theater community that had once embraced him so closely. Along with Miller, Kazan was shunned and even vilified by Lillian Hellman, Dalton Trumbo, and even some of the Hollywood community, who had...

Eleanor is overusing the rhetorical question.

A reader who is not familiar with the two stories might find it difficult to keep track of all of the characters. Eleanor needs to find some way to remind the reader who, for example, Terry Malloy is.

Eleanor should go deeper into Kazan's justifications for his actions here.

Unlikely as it would seem, a decade later Miller and Kazan would work together again, this time on <u>After the Fall</u>, at the suggestion of producer Robert Whitehead, who was shepherding an ambitious plan to create a repertory theater company as part of the then new Lincoln Center. The play would be the inaugural production of the company; the opportunity to be a part of so significant a new cultural institution must have been tempting to both men, despite their history. "Once brought together, Art and I got along well—even though I was somewhat tense in his company, because we'd never discussed (and never did discuss) the reasons for our 'break,'" Kazan would later reflect in his autobiography (465).

<u>After the Fall</u> was Miller's most autobiographical piece, in which he portrayed his family's financial ruin in the stock market crash, the HUAC hearings and rift with Kazan, and most controversially, his relationship with his second wife, Marilyn Monroe. Kazan and Miller worked very closely, Kazan even having input on the script itself. Miller insisted that he'd intended no relevance to real life events and figures. "'The play,' he said at the time, 'is a work of fiction. No one is reported in this play. The characters are created as they are in any other play in order to develop a coherent theme, which in this case concerns the nature of human insight, of self-destructiveness and violence toward others'" (<u>New York Times</u>, Miller obituary). This time, it was Miller's objection that was failing to convince. Critics were excoriating when <u>After the Fall</u> opened, and most especially scornful of Miller's transparent portrayal of Monroe in the form of Maggie, a blond and beautiful pop singer (instead of a blond and beautiful movie star) with

Another long and unwieldy sentence.

This quotation is a nice touch, but Eleanor might find something a little more penetrating about the two men deciding to work together after such a long period of estrangement.

The way Eleanor has worded this sentence is misleading. The characters' names and a few other key details are changed, so the play is not, strictly speaking, "autobiographical."

emotional demons and chemical dependencies. Miller was particularly criticized for seeming to exploit his relationship with Monroe, revealing her secrets and portraying her in a less than flattering light. The playwright was taken aback by the response; "I was totally surprised to hear him say that everyone would of course reduce Lorraine, renamed Maggie, to a portrait, purely and simply of Marilyn. I was sure that the play would be seen as an attempt to embrace a world of political and ethical dilemmas, with Maggie's agony perhaps the most symbolically apparent but hardly the play's raison d'etre" (Timebends 378). Ironically, now it was Miller who was seen as the informer, having betrayed his former wife, who had also had a relationship with Kazan before meeting Miller. The two men were now once again linked, in a way neither could have expected or envisioned.

As was the case with *The Crucible*, Eleanor should provide a little more description of this play to help her reader, who might be unfamiliar with it.

This is a fascinating piece of history, well written and presented, but Eleanor needs to work harder to relate it to her thesis.

Decades later, in 1999, it was announced that Kazan would be receiving an honorary Academy Award for lifetime achievement. The news found a Hollywood as divided on the director and his actions as it had been over forty-five years earlier; hundreds of protesters were present outside the Dorothy Chandler Pavilion on the night of the presentation. Many held signs and placards decrying both the Academy and Kazan; both the director's supporters and detractors were highly vocal from the time the award was announced. When Kazan came onstage to accept the Oscar, the reaction shots of the star-studded audience were as notable for those not applauding as those who did applaud (Abel). Interestingly, when asked about his opinion on Kazan's recognition by the Academy, Miller was supportive. "My feelings toward that terrible era are unchanged, but at the same time history ought not to be rewritten. Elia Kazan did sufficient extraordinary work in theater and film to merit acknowledgement," he would write in a letter to The Los Angeles Sentinel. Despite recriminations, perceived betrayal, and ethical differences, the playwright and director were still linked by their professional respect, regard for one another's work, and passion for theater. The friendship may have died, but the collaboration endured.

A good concluding paragraph, but again, Eleanor needs to work harder at tying it in with her thesis that the rift fed both men creatively.

Works Cited

Abel, Theodore. "The Politics of Forgiveness," America Today, 22 March 1999: AL 17. Print.

Bernstein, Robert. "Long, Bitter Debate From the '50's: Views of Kazan and His Critics," The New York Times, 3 May 1988.

Kazan, Elia. A Life. New York: DaCapo Press, 1997.

Miller, Arthur, Letter. The Sentinel, 3 March 1999: A 19. Print.

Miller, Arthur. Timebends. New York: Penguin Books, 1995.

Navasky, Victor S. Naming Names. New York: The Viking Press, 1980.

Schickel, Richard. Elia Kazan, a Biography. New York: Harper Books, 2005.

Schreckler, Eileen. The Golden Age of McCarthyism: Defusing the Red Menace in Hollywood. Kingston, Jamaica: San Trope Press, 1997.

Taylor, Tate. "Death of a Friendship, Birth of a Play," The New York Times. 5 January 2010.

The New York Times, Miller obituary, 11 February 2005.

Analysis of First Draft

What is this writer's purpose? The writer's purpose is to illustrate how the impact of the political atmosphere created by the McCarthy witch hunts affected the friendship and the art of two preeminent figures in American theater and film.

What is this writer's thesis? Her thesis is that the conflict between Arthur Miller and Elia Kazan over Kazan's decision to name names when testifying before HUAC may have ended their friendship, but it fed both men creatively, and their subsequent work illustrates the differences in their views and ethical codes.

What key points has the writer identified to clarify her thesis? This is a weakness in Eleanor's paper. She does not provide sufficient information to make it clear what exactly the political atmosphere was, what Elia Kazan did that angered Arthur Miller so, and how that had an impact on the film and play discussed in the paper.

What key points has the writer identified to support the thesis?

- The differing ways each man portrayed the events in their respective memoirs
- Miller's account of how Kazan told him he was going to testify
- The contrasting characters of Terry Malloy and Eddie Carbone, and how they relate to Miller and Kazan's differing viewpoints
- The abortive collaboration between them on Miller's screenplay for *The Hook*, and its similarities to *On the Waterfront*
- The two men's collaboration again, a decade later, on Miller's play *After the Fall*

Does the writer effectively prove the thesis? On balance, she proves her thesis, but her support of the thesis is more implicit than explicit throughout the paper. She frequently does not provide enough important background information or draw clear connections between the information she is providing and the point she is arguing.

NOW plan and write your own English language arts research paper, following the same process by which Eleanor arrived at her first draft.

STEP 1: Select a Topic

STEP 2: Draft a Thesis

Make sure your thesis is arguable—rooted in the text of the story, not pure opinion.

Make certain you have or know you can find sufficient evidence in the text of the story to explain and support your key points.

STEP 3: Draft a Preliminary Outline

STEP 4: Conduct Your Research

STEP 5: First Draft

STEP 6: Peer Edit

What is this writer's purpose?

What is this writer's thesis?

What key points has the writer identified to clarify the thesis?

What key points has the writer identified to support the thesis?

Does the writer effectively prove the thesis?

STEP 7: Revised/Final Draft

Here are Eleanor's editor's comments and analysis as well as her responses:

- There is some important information packed into the second sentence, and it's far too long. Eleanor should consider breaking it down into two or even three sentences.

- Another overlong sentence. The reference to Miller's refusal to use his screenplay as a vehicle for anti-Communist propaganda leans toward her thesis, but Eleanor needs to establish her thesis now.

- Eleanor has finally come to her thesis, but again, it's a bit overwritten, overlong, and even awkward. She'll need to address this in her next draft.

- Eleanor must be careful not to lose her reader with brief references to important historical events without sufficient background information. Since the two films speak to the country's anti-Communist sentiment (the political aspect), she needs to make sure her reader understands the connection between HUAC, informing, not informing, the men's friendship, and their art.

- Eleanor has made a common word-choice error, confusing *principal* (person or most important thing) and *principle* (value or ideal).

- While the "act of informing" is clearly the crux of the issue for Eleanor, she could probably make it clearer to her reader that the two men's treatment of informers is the "McCarthy" element of her thesis.

- Although Eleanor has mentioned this earlier, at this point, she should cite her source.

- Certainly, a discussion of *The Crucible* would help Eleanor support her thesis, but this brief reference can only confuse a reader who is not familiar with the play.

- Eleanor is overusing the rhetorical question.

- A reader who is not familiar with the two stories might find it difficult to keep track of all of the characters. Eleanor needs to find some way to remind the reader who, for example, Terry Malloy is.

- Eleanor should go deeper into Kazan's justifications for his actions here.

- Another long and unwieldy sentence.

- This quotation is a nice touch, but Eleanor might find something a little more penetrating about the two men deciding to work together after such a long period of estrangement.

- The way Eleanor has worded this sentence is misleading. The characters' names and a few other key details are changed, so the play is not, strictly speaking, "autobiographical."

- As was the case with *The Crucible*, Eleanor should provide a little more description of this play to help her reader, who might be unfamiliar with it.

- This is a fascinating piece of history, well written and presented, but Eleanor needs to work harder to relate it to her thesis.

- A good concluding paragraph, but again, Eleanor needs to work harder at tying it in with her thesis that the rift fed both men creatively.

Apparently I don't get to my thesis soon enough? Or it's not clear enough or something? I think I understand the comment about giving more background information about McCarthyism and the HUAC and what the issue of informing was all about.

Same thing, I guess, with my mentions of The Crucible and After the Fall. I talk about the plays as if my reader already knows them as well as I do.

Analysis of First Draft

What is this writer's purpose? The writer's purpose is to illustrate how the impact of the political atmosphere created by the McCarthy witch hunts affected the friendship and the art of two preeminent figures in American theater and film.

> Okay, so that's clear.

What is this writer's thesis? Her thesis is that the conflict between Arthur Miller and Elia Kazan over Kazan's decision to name names when testifying before HUAC may have ended their friendship, but it fed both men creatively, and their subsequent work illustrates the differences in their views and ethical codes.

> Good, so far.

What key points has the writer identified to clarify her thesis? This is a weakness in Eleanor's paper. She does not provide sufficient information to make it clear what exactly the political atmosphere was, what Elia Kazan did that angered Arthur Miller so, and how that had an impact on the film and play discussed in the paper.

> Okay...this goes along with what was said above: that I need more background information on McCarthyism, the whole issue of informing, and maybe even the other Arthur Miller plays I mention.

What key points has the writer identified to support the thesis?

- The differing ways each man portrayed the events in their respective memoirs

- Miller's account of how Kazan told him he was going to testify

- The contrasting characters of Terry Malloy and Eddie Carbone, and how they relate to Miller and Kazan's differing viewpoints

- The abortive collaboration between them on Miller's screenplay for *The Hook*, and its similarities to *On the Waterfront*

- The fact that the two men actually collaborated again, a decade later, on Miller's play *After the Fall*

> So these are all right, and they're not saying I don't have enough.

Does the writer effectively prove the thesis? On balance, she proves her thesis, but the support of her thesis is more implicit than explicit throughout the paper. She frequently does not provide enough important background information or draw clear connections between the information she is providing and the point she is arguing.

> Okay...got it.

Here is Eleanor's revised draft. Because her peer editor initially told her that her outline was too general and underdeveloped, she revised the outline before she wrote her second draft.

Thesis (revised): Elia Kazan's <u>On the Waterfront</u> and Arthur Miller's <u>A View from the Bridge</u> illustrate how an apparently distant and unrelated political movement, like the trials that are often called the McCarthy witch hunts, can have a profound effect on the personal life of an artist and on the work he or she creates.

I. Introduction—Miller and Kazan's friendship and collaboration

   A. HUAC: what it was and why it was started

   B. What it meant if someone informed or "named names"

     1. to the informer

     2. to the person informed on

   C. What it meant if someone refused to inform

     1. to the informer

     2. to the person informed on

   D. Why did Elia Kazan turn informer?

     1. Miller's account

     2. Kazan's account(s)

II. The two artists' stories of informers

   A. compare characters

     1. Kazan—Terry Malloy

       a. unfortunately influenced by others

       b. motivated by passion or love

    2. Miller–Eddie Carbone

        a. highly flawed (attraction to niece)

        b. motivated by envy

  B. compare endings

    1. <u>On the Waterfront</u> = inspiring

    2. Malloy is cheered as a hero.

    3. <u>View from the Bridge</u> = alarming

    4. Carbone is beaten to death.

III. Relate characters and endings to authors' views

  A. Kazan apparently believed himself to be the put-upon hero, simply wanting to live his life, forced into an impossible position by forces beyond his control.

  B. Miller obviously saw Kazan as immoral and selfish; if Kazan couldn't have something, he would make sure others didn't have it as well.

IV. McCarthy witch hunts were the cause of the crisis.

  A. Anti-Communist propaganda as in <u>The Hook</u>.

  B. Parallels between Carbone, Malloy, Kazan, Miller, and HUAC testimony

  C. Writers air personal views in public performances

V. Reconciliation and redemption

  A. How Kazan and Miller actually ended up working together years later on <u>After the Fall</u>

  B. Something here about writers no longer support Soviet Union

  C. Honorary Academy Award in 1999

In April of 1952, a great artistic collaboration and a great friendship ended. Arthur Miller, one of America's preeminent playwrights, sundered his professional and personal relationship with Elia Kazan, one of the most successful theater and film directors of the day. Miller's reason was Kazan's decision to testify before the House Un-American Activities Committee (HUAC) and name the names of friends and contacts who had been members of the Communist Party in the 1930s. Kazan had directed Miller's greatest successes on Broadway, including <u>Death of a Salesman</u> and <u>All My Sons</u>. The two had also been planning to collaborate on Miller's screenplay, <u>The Hook</u>, about waterfront workers in the Red Hook section of Brooklyn. Columbia pictures had refused to purchase the screenplay, because they wanted Miller to recast corrupt union officials as Communist conspirators, and he refused.

Eleanor has made this introduction clearer by separating the sentences and editing out some information not relevant to the point here.

The anti-Communist sentiment then prevalent in the United States lay at the center of Miller and Kazan's parting. In Washington, D.C., thousands of miles away from Hollywood, Joseph McCarthy, a Republican senator from Wisconsin, was rising to fame on a tide of sensationalism and fear-mongering. According to McCarthy, there were Communists everywhere, especially in Hollywood. In response to this frenzy, and to ease the fears of American citizens, the House of Representatives convened the House Un-American Activities Committee (HUAC) and charged it with rooting out Communists from every aspect of American society. Those who were called to testify before the HUAC were either known or suspected Communists. They were asked, under oath, to admit their own Communist leanings, and they were asked to name other people they knew to be Communists.

To be called before the HUAC was like a curse. Writers, directors, and actors who refused to give names were blacklisted and prevented from working in their professions. Those who were named in someone else's testimony were likewise blackballed. Only those who gave in to the committee and gave names were spared, allowed to continue working. But they were often seen as cowards and "tattletales" by their colleagues, especially those whom they had named to the committee.

When Elia Kazan was called to testify, he named names.

Four years later, when Arthur Miller was called to testify, he refused to cooperate.

Three years after his testimony and subsequent break with Miller, Kazan would win a second Academy Award for directing <u>On the Waterfront</u>, a film with distinct similarities to Miller's unsold screenplay <u>The Hook</u>. Miller would write what would later be seen as one of his best plays, <u>A View from the Bridge</u>. The two pieces both had central characters who were informers, but one was cast as a hero, while the other was perceived as a tragic villain. Both also expressed the differing responses of their creators to the McCarthy-era crisis. Both also showed the way writers, even writers with different viewpoints, often translate their own experiences into artistic visions.

The two men, in their memoirs, differ substantially in the recounting of this period, even about when Kazan told Miller of his decision to inform. Kazan maintains he met with Miller before his testimony, and Miller states the meeting took place afterward (Bernstein). They also differ in their accounts of Miller's reaction to Kazan's decision. In his autobiography, Kazan

This is just the type of background information Eleanor was told she needed, but now she is presenting it too early in her paper. The reader does not even know her thesis yet.

In cleaning up the language of her thesis, Eleanor may have lost some of its strength. How are the differing viewpoints relevant to the ability to translate personal experience into art?

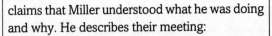

claims that Miller understood what he was doing and why. He describes their meeting:

> "Walking back to the house…[Miller] put his arm around me…and said, 'Don't worry…Whatever you do will be okay with me. Because I know your heart is in the right place.'…There was no doubt that Art meant it and that he was anxious to say this to me before we separated." (461)

By contrast, Miller recalls the anger he felt even before arriving at his friend's home, knowing what Kazan was about to tell him: "[I felt] anger rising, not against [Kazan], whom I loved like a brother, but against the Committee" (332). Miller repeats later that his anger was not personal:

> I was experiencing a bitterness with the country that I had never even imagined before, a hatred of its stupidity and its throwing away of its freedom. Who or what was now safer because this man [Kazan] in his human weakness had been forced to humiliate himself? What truth had been enhanced by all this anguish? (334)

It even seems as if Miller does forgive Kazan when he writes, "Listening to [Kazan] I grew frightened. There was a certain gloomy logic in what he was saying: unless he came clean he could never hope, in the height of his creative powers, to make another film in America, and he would probably not be given a passport to work abroad either. If the theatre remained open to him, it was not his primary interest anymore; he wanted to deepen his film life, that was where his heart lay, and he had been told in so many words by his old boss and friend Spyros Skouras, president of Twentieth Century Fox, that the company would not employ him unless he satisfied the Committee…" (276).

Eleanor has fixed one of the biggest problems with her first draft—lack of historical context—but she now has a problem with organization and flow of information.

But the play he wrote in response to Kazan's self-justifying <u>On the Waterfront</u> makes the issue seem all too personal.

An examination of the characters of Terry Malloy and Eddie Carbone reveals a clear contrast, but their similarities are apparent, too. Malloy may ultimately be seen as the hero for informing on his corrupt bosses, but he is hardly pure. Under his brother's influence, he has made moral compromises for much of his life, and his decision to finally make an ethical choice can be seen as driven as much by his passion for Evie as by principle. Carbone is also driven by passion, but that passion itself is ethically compromised, as it is centered on his seventeen-year-old niece, whose every move he jealously watches, ultimately driving him to betray the young immigrant she has fallen in love with. Both pay a price for their actions; Malloy is beaten nearly to death by the henchmen of the boss he has exposed, and Carbone becomes a pariah and is killed in a knife fight with one of the immigrants he has betrayed. But Malloy is triumphant at the end, and Carbone is defeated utterly. Clearly, if one can infer a writer's attitudes from his work, Kazan believed himself to be something of a put-upon hero, punished for doing the right thing, but ultimately victorious.

Miller, on the other hand, clearly saw informing as a crime and the informer as lower than blatant lawbreakers. When called to testify before the HUAC in 1956, rather than emulate his own despicable character, Miller refused to name names. He was found in contempt of Congress, fined, and sentenced to a brief term in jail (Navasky 199).

It is interesting to note that, while Kazan was obviously justifying his decision to inform to the HUAC, he did not request Schulberg to change the mobsters in the screenplay to Communist infiltrators, as Columbia chief

Harry Cohn had requested of Miller for the screenplay of <u>The Hook</u> (Schreckler 782). Perhaps Kazan did not want to make his defense of his actions too obvious. It is also interesting to contrast Miller's characterization of Carbone with the judges of his more politically charged play, <u>The Crucible</u>. Written in 1952 as a condemnation of the HUAC's tactics, <u>The Crucible</u> tells the story of the infamous Salem witch trials. As portrayed by Miller, the sanctimonious judges of Salem, who condemn innocent men and women to be tortured and hanged unless they confess to a crime they did not commit, are all without redeeming human qualities.

Carbone is more fully developed and receives more of the audience's sympathy, even as they reject his actions.

In a 2005 biography of Kazan, Richard Schickel states that <u>A View from the Bridge</u> is a "metaphor about betrayal and its consequences," rather than a political condemnation (366). In a <u>New York Times</u> article about the 2010 Broadway revival of the play, director Gregory Mosher says that, in Miller's view, informing "is an act of self-betrayal," losing Eddie his place in the community, his self-respect and finally, his life (Taylor). Perhaps Miller's feelings toward Kazan had softened between 1952 and 1955. Perhaps he was now seeing his former friend and collaborator as the victim of his own nature, rather than the hard-nosed, opportunistic, and selfish turncoat that much of the left-wing theater community believed Kazan to be. He himself suggests this in his autobiography, when he writes, "Certainly, I felt distaste for those who groveled before this tawdry tribune of moralistic vote-snatchers, but I had as much pity as anger toward them" (329).

This is a much clearer reference to *The Crucible*.

It is plain that the two men had a complicated relationship, but however Miller felt toward Kazan at this point, it is also plain that he did not consider Kazan to be a hero like Terry Malloy was. But over time, it did seem that Miller had some degree, if not of forgiveness, then of understanding toward Kazan. In his memoir he writes

> ...it came down to a governmental decree of moral guilt that could easily be made to disappear by ritual speech: intoning names of fellow sinners and recanting former beliefs. This last was probably the saddest and truest part of the charade, for by the early 1950s there were few, and even fewer in the arts, who had not left behind their illusions about the Soviets. (355)

For his part, Kazan remained unyielding in his defense of his actions throughout his life, stating firmly, "I did what I did because it was the more tolerable of two alternatives that were, either way, painful, even disastrous, and either way wrong for me. That's what a difficult decision means: Either way you go, you lose" (Kazan 465). Time and again, apparently whenever anyone seemed willing to listen, Kazan justified his decision to turn informer: "'Everyone must do what his conscience tells him to do' [Kazan] said. 'I've got to think of my kids'" (Navasky 202).

Like Miller's Eddie Carbone, however, Kazan was treated as a pariah by most of the left-leaning, intellectual theater community that had once embraced him so closely. Along with Miller, Kazan was shunned and even vilified by Lillian Hellman, Dalton Trumbo, and even some of the Hollywood community, who had...

Unlikely as it would seem, a decade later Miller and Kazan would work together again, this time on Miller's <u>After the Fall</u>. The play would be the inaugural production of a new repertory theater company established as part of the new Lincoln Center. The opportunity to be a part of so significant a new cultural institution must have been tempting to both men, despite their history. Kazan would later reflect in his autobiography, "Once brought together, Art and I got along well—even though I was somewhat tense in his company, because we'd never discussed (and never did discuss) the reasons for our 'break'" (465).

Apparently unable to relate the information to her thesis, Eleanor has cut the entire section about Miller's portrayal of Marilyn Monroe in *After the Fall*.

Decades later, in 1999, it was announced that Kazan would be receiving an honorary Academy Award for lifetime achievement. The news found a Hollywood as divided on the director and his actions as it had been over forty-five years earlier; hundreds of protesters were present outside the Dorothy Chandler Pavilion on the night of the presentation. Many held signs and placards decrying both the Academy and Kazan; both the director's supporters and detractors were highly vocal from the time the award was announced. When Kazan came onstage to accept the Oscar, the reaction shots of the star-studded audience were as notable for those not applauding as those who did applaud. Interestingly, when asked about his opinion on Kazan's recognition by the Academy, Miller was supportive. "My feelings toward that terrible era are unchanged, but at the same time history ought not to be rewritten. Elia Kazan did sufficient extraordinary work in theater and film to merit acknowledgement," he would write in a letter to the <u>Los Angeles Sentinel</u>. Despite recriminations, perceived betrayal, and ethical differences, the playwright and director were still linked by their professional respect, regard for one another's work, and passion for theater. The friendship may have died, but the collaboration endured.

Despite her peer editor's comment, Eleanor has not revised her conclusion, so the reader is still unclear how successfully she has established her thesis.

Works Cited

Abel, Theodore. "The Politics of Forgiveness," America Today, 22 March 1999: AL 17. Print.

Bernstein, Robert. "Long, Bitter Debate From the '50's: Views of Kazan and His Critics," The New York Times, 3 May 1988.

Kazan, Elia. A Life. New York: DaCapo Press, 1997.

Miller, Arthur, Letter. The Sentinel, 3 March 1999: A 19. Print.

Miller, Arthur. Timebends. New York: Penguin Books, 1995.

Navasky, Victor S. Naming Names. New York: The Viking Press, 1980.

Schickel, Richard. Elia Kazan, a biography. New York: Harper Books, 2005.

Schreckler, Eileen. The Golden Age of McCarthyism: Defusing the Red Menace in Hollywood. Kingston, Jamaica: San Trope Press, 1997.

Taylor, Tate. "Death of a Friendship, Birth of a Play," New York Times. 5 January 2010.

The New York Times, Miller obituary, 11 February 2005.

Analysis of Revised Draft

What is this writer's purpose? The writer intends to demonstrate that Arthur Miller's play *A View from the Bridge* and Elia Kazan's film *On the Waterfront* were artistic responses to both a political crisis in the United States and the personal pain that resulted from the loss of their friendship.

What is this writer's thesis? The thesis is: Elia Kazan's *On the Waterfront* and Arthur Miller's *A View from the Bridge* illustrate how an apparently distant and unrelated political movement, like the trials that are often called the McCarthy witch hunts, can have a profound effect on the personal life of an artist and on the work he or she creates.

Has the writer's new draft strengthened her point? To the extent that Eleanor has now provided some essential historical background information about the McCarthy Era, the proceedings of the House Un-American Activities Committee, and so on, she has strengthened her point. Her discussion of how these two works illustrate her thesis is still weak.

Has the rewrite strengthened the case for her thesis? Again, Eleanor does provide a much clearer context for her comparison of the two works and what each means on a metaphoric level. She does not, however, establish the personal pain aspect of her thesis.

What new details, facts, etc., have been included to make this a more potent assessment of the works in question?

- The dates and circumstances of the two men's testimonies before the HUAC

- Other historians' and biographers' reactions to both Kazan and Miller and to their responses to HUAC

Does the writer effectively prove her thesis to any greater degree than in the previous draft? Unfortunately, not really.

NOW write your final draft.

POSSIBLE STEP 8: Rewrite Opportunity

Not fully satisfied with the analysis of her second draft, Eleanor has decided to take one final look at her thesis and revise her paper a second time. This will be her third and absolutely final draft.

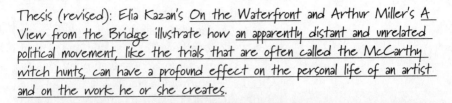

Thesis (revised): Elia Kazan's <u>On the Waterfront</u> and Arthur Miller's <u>A View from the Bridge</u> illustrate how <u>an apparently distant and unrelated political movement, like the trials that are often called the McCarthy witch hunts, can have a profound effect on the personal life of an artist and on the work he or she creates.</u>

So Eleanor is going to keep her thesis but be vigilant in her essay to discuss the works as direct results of the political movement.

In April of 1952, a great artistic collaboration and a great friendship ended. Arthur Miller, one of America's preeminent playwrights, sundered his professional and personal relationship with Elia Kazan, one of the most successful theater and film directors of the day. Miller's reason was Kazan's decision to testify at the House Un-American Activities Committee (HUAC) and name the names of friends and colleagues who had been members of the Communist Party in the 1930s. Kazan had directed Miller's greatest successes on Broadway, including <u>Death of a Salesman</u> and <u>All My Sons</u>. The two had also been planning to collaborate on a screenplay by Miller that Columbia Pictures had refused to purchase for purely political reasons; Columbia wanted to use the film to add to the growing body of anti-Communist propaganda being presented to the American public, and Miller refused to cooperate. This seemingly minor act, a singular incident in the career of one of the nation's most prominent playwrights, turned out to be a sign of a deeper ideological conflict: whether one should acquiesce to someone else's political demands or stand firm in one's own beliefs, even at the risk of personal and professional hardship. When Elia Kazan was called to testify before the HUAC and told Miller he intended to give the committee names, the path the

Eleanor makes her reason for mentioning *The Hook* clearer. She also focuses more on Kazan's decision to inform and a little less on simply the writing of the plays.

two had followed together split in two, and it would be decades before they would speak and work together. Elia Kazan's and Arthur Miller's most famous post-testimony works, On the Waterfront and A View from the Bridge, illustrate how an apparently distant and unrelated political movement, like the trials that are often called the McCarthy witch hunts, can have a profound effect on the personal life of an artist and on the work he or she creates.

Miller's screenplay, The Hook, was to be about corruption and union violence among the waterfront workers in the Red Hook section of Brooklyn. Seizing on the nation's Cold War and the rampant fear of Communists everywhere, Columbia Pictures wanted Miller to recast corrupt union officials as Communist conspirators. Miller refused, not wanting a well-researched and authentic story to become mere propaganda (Saffron). To make such a refusal in Hollywood in the 1950s could be a dangerous move. In Washington, D.C., thousands of miles away from Hollywood, Joseph McCarthy, a Republican senator from Wisconsin, was rising to fame on a tide of sensationalism and fear-mongering. According to McCarthy, there were Communists everywhere, especially in Hollywood. In response to this frenzy, and to ease the fears of American citizens, the House of Representatives convened the House Un-American Activities Committee (HUAC) and charged it with rooting out Communists from every aspect of American society. Those who were called to testify before the HUAC were either known or suspected Communists. They were asked, under oath, to admit their own Communist leanings, and they were asked to name the names of other people they knew to be Communists.

To be called before the HUAC was like a curse. Writers, directors, and actors who refused to give names were blacklisted and prevented from working in their professions. Those who were named in someone else's testimony were likewise blackballed. Only those who gave in to the committee and gave names were spared, allowed to continue working. But they were often seen as cowards and "tattletales" by their colleagues, especially those whom they had named to the committee.

When Elia Kazan was called to testify, he named names.

Four years later, when Arthur Miller was called to testify, he refused to cooperate.

It is obvious from each man's biography that the break in friendship that resulted from Kazan's testimony was painful to both of them. In A Life, Kazan comments sadly on how he learned of his friend's disapproval of his testimony:

> It would have been nice if Art, at this moment, while expressing the strong disapproval he felt, had acknowledged some past friendship - or even written me a few words, however condemnatory. But he didn't, not a word ... (471)

Instead, Kazan learned that his friendship with Miller was over by reading it in the newspaper ("HUAC and the Rise of Anti-Communism"). Elaborating on how he felt about Miller's rejection, Kazan concluded, "I've been perplexed and angry at him, as he, I must believe, has been disgusted and mad at me... But I like Miller; I wouldn't even mind being cast away on a desert island with him" (530).

Miller seems to have been likewise saddened by the breach and, even from the first, tried to find understanding and maybe even forgiveness for his friend. Kazan certainly remembers feeling as if Miller understood and forgave. He writes of the day he told Miller that he had decided to cooperate with the Committee:

> Walking back to the house...[Miller] put his arm around me...and said, 'Don't worry... Whatever you do will be okay with me. Because I know your heart is in the right place,'...There was no doubt that Art meant it and that he was anxious to say this to me before we separated. (530)

Miller, however, recalls anger, but not directed toward Kazan: "[I felt] anger rising, not against [Kazan], whom I loved like a brother, but against the Committee" (<u>Timebends</u> 330). Miller repeats later that his anger was not personal:

> I was experiencing a bitterness with the country that I had never even imagined before, a hatred of its stupidity and its throwing away of its freedom. Who or what was now safer because this man [Kazan] in his human weakness had been forced to humiliate himself? What truth had been enhanced by all this anguish? (332)

Clearly, even though Miller might thoroughly disagree with Kazan's action, he understands the human frailty that would allow a man of principle to make a mistake and do the wrong thing, thinking it to be right.

It even seems as if Miller does forgive Kazan when he writes:

> Listening to [Kazan] I grew frightened. There was a certain gloomy logic in what he was saying: unless he came clean he could never hope, in the height of his creative powers, to make another film in America, and he

Eleanor has done several good things in this revision so far. 1. She has shifted the focus of this section away from the creation of the works to the men's human reactions to the loss of their friendship. 2. While she is presenting essentially the same information from her earlier drafts, she is pausing to reflect on her quotations, to lead her reader to appreciate how the quotation supports her point.

would probably not be given a passport to work abroad either. If the theatre remained open to him, it was not his primary interest anymore; he wanted to deepen his film life, that was where his heart lay, and he had been told in so many words by his old boss and friend Spyros Skouras, president of Twentieth Century Fox, that the company would not employ him unless he satisfied the Committee … (334)

Three years after Kazan's testimony and the subsequent break, both artists would present to the public different treatments of a similar theme—what is the man who betrays his friends? Kazan would win a second Academy Award for directing On the Waterfront, a film with distinct similarities to The Hook. Miller would write what would later be seen as one of his best plays, A View from the Bridge. The two pieces both had central characters who were informers, but one was cast as a hero, while the other was perceived as a tragic villain. Both also expressed the differing responses of their creators to the McCarthy-era crisis. Both also showed the way writers, even writers with different viewpoints, often translate their own experiences into artistic visions.

Again, notice how Eleanor has very subtly shifted the focus away from the works themselves to the fact that the works illustrate each man's reaction to the situation.

By simply reminding her reader that Malloy is Kazan's character, Eleanor reinforces the notion that Kazan is casting a heroic hue on his own actions.

An examination of the characters of Terry Malloy and Eddie Carbone reveals a clear contrast, but their similarities are apparent, too. Kazan's Malloy may ultimately be seen as the hero for informing on his corrupt bosses, but he is hardly pure. Under his brother's influence, he has made moral compromises for much of his life, and his decision to finally make an ethical choice can be seen as driven as much by his passion for Evie as by principle. Carbone is also driven by passion, but that passion itself is ethically compromised, as it is centered on his seventeen-year-old niece, whose every move he jealously watches, ultimately driving him to betray the young immigrant she has fallen in love with. Both pay a price for their actions; Malloy is beaten nearly to death by the henchmen of the boss he has exposed, and Carbone becomes a pariah and is killed in a knife fight with one of the immigrants he has betrayed. But Malloy is triumphant at the end, and Carbone is defeated utterly. Clearly, if one can infer a writer's attitudes from his work, Kazan believed himself to be something of a put-upon hero, punished for doing the right thing, but ultimately victorious.

It is important to note, however, that one of the complaints levied against Miller's portrayal of the informer was moral ambiguity or ambivalence. Victor Navasky notes that one critic complained that Miller "tried simultaneously to understand and condemn the informer" (199). Miller is at the height of his anger. He wants more than anything to disparage the informer, but he cannot pretend he does not understand the human fear and confusion that lay beneath the surface.

Decades later, in 1999, when it was announced that Kazan would be receiving an honorary Academy Award for lifetime achievement, the news found a Hollywood as divided on the director and his actions as it had been over forty-five years earlier. Hundreds of protesters were present outside the Dorothy Chandler Pavilion on the night of the presentation. Many held signs and placards decrying both the Academy and Kazan. When Kazan came onstage to accept the Oscar, the reaction shots of the star-studded audience were as notable for those not applauding as those who did applaud. Miller, however, was supportive: "My feelings toward that terrible era are unchanged, but at the same time history ought not to be rewritten. Elia Kazan did sufficient extraordinary work in theater and film to merit acknowledgement," he would write in a letter to the Los Angeles Sentinel. Despite recriminations, perceived betrayal, and ethical differences, the playwright and director were still linked by their professional respect, regard for one another's work, and passion for theater. Their lives and careers had taken significantly different directions, but as evidenced by their contemporaneous works, On the Waterfront and A View from the Bridge, their opinions differed, but their understanding of one another might never have really died.

In her earlier drafts, Eleanor treated this as a curious fact-in-passing. Now, it is more the point of the paragraph.

This is a much better conclusion than Eleanor's previous attempts. It brings the reader right back to the central issue that she has been trying to establish.

Works Cited

Abel, Theodore. "The Politics of Forgiveness," America Today, 22 March 1999: AL 17. Print.

Bernstein, Robert. "Long, Bitter Debate From the '50's: Views of Kazan and His Critics," The New York Times, 3 May 1988.

"The HUAC and the Rise of Anti-Communism in America." Citizen of the World. n. p. n.d. Web 5 April 2012.

Kazan, Elia. A Life. New York: DaCapo Press, 1997.

Miller, Arthur, Letter. The Sentinel, 3 March 1999: A 19. Print.

Miller, Arthur. Timebends. New York: Penguin Books, 1995.

Navasky, Victor S. Naming Names. New York: The Viking Press, 1980.

New York Times, Miller obituary, 11 February 2005.

Saffron, Iris. "Commies and Commie-Haters: A Compendium of American Cold War Film Literature" U.S. History in Film. n. p. 26 Aug. 2007. Web. 12 March 2012.

Schickel, Richard. Elia Kazan, a Biography. New York: Harper Books, 2005.

Schreckler, Eileen. The Golden Age of McCarthyism: Defusing the Red Menace in Hollywood. Kingston, Jamaica: San Trope Press, 1997.

Taylor, Tate. "Death of a Friendship, Birth of a Play," The New York Times. 5 January 2010.

Analyze Eleanor's final draft. Has she successfully met the demands of the assignment and established the validity of her thesis?

What is this writer's purpose?

What is this writer's thesis?

Has the writer's new draft strengthened her point?

Has the rewrite strengthened the case for the thesis?

What new details, facts, etc., have been included to make this a more potent assessment of the works in question?

Does the writer effectively prove the thesis to any greater degree than in the previous draft? Why or why not?

APPENDIX

Samples of APA and MLA Citation and Documentation

Remember that all citation and documentation formats serve the same purpose: to give appropriate credit to the sources from which you got information and ideas and to give the information and insight you provide the credibility of expert authority.

Remember also that there is nothing to be gained by memorizing a documentation style. Through the course of your education and career, you will most likely need to use several forms, and the forms themselves are frequently changed, updated to reflect changes in the ways information is distributed and retrieved. It is more important that you instead learn how to follow a style sheet.

In his paper on Keynesian economics, Derek used **APA (American Psychological Association)** style documentation because this is the form most commonly used in the social sciences like psychology, education, and economics.

Here is a review of the APA-style samples Derek consulted when formatting his parenthetic citations and "References" page:

Parenthetic citations essentially provide the reader with enough information to identify the source on the References page and then to locate the specific information in the cited source. The basic form provides the author's name, copyright date, and page number:

> In the language of an economist, Keynesian Economics holds that the aggregate demand does not necessarily equal the aggregate supply **(Minkhoff, 2008, p. 111)**.

If you name the author in the text:

> **According to Minkhoff (2008)**, Keynesian Economics holds that the aggregate demand does not necessarily equal the aggregate supply **(p. 111)**.

If you refer to a website:

> **The Library of Economics and Progress provides** groundbreaking ideas from the most prominent economists in the Western world **(http://www.socscilib.org/)**.

To refer to a specific page or chapter:

Nobbs and Hendricks (1994, p. 62) note that ...

In another troubling but thought-provoking study, most *Laissez-faire* economists seem to support both Capitalism and anarchy **(Molloy & Malachi, 2002, chap. 5)**.

If there is no stated author, include the first few key words from the title:

The authors of *Ethics of economics* **(1999, p. 20) assert**, "Economists must remember ... and livelihoods."

"Economists must remember ... and livelihoods" **(*Ethics of economics*, 1999, p. 20)**.

The References list provides all the information the reader will need if he or she chooses to verify your information and how you handle it.

Formats for books. The necessary punctuation has been **increased in size and bolded** for emphasis:

Author last name, First and middle initials**.** (copyright date)**.** *Title***.** City of publication**:** Publishing Company**.**

Buchmann, J**.** (2006)**.** *The life and ideas of Adam Smith***.** Boston**:** W. W. Northrop **&** Sons**.**

Books with more than one author:

1st author last name, First and middle initials, **&** 2nd author last name, First and middle initials**.** (copyright date)**.** *Title***.** Publishing information as above**.**

Terrapinski, L., **&** Ostler, B. (2009). ...

1st author last name, First and middle initials, 2nd author last name, First and middle initials, **&** 3rd author last name, First and middle initials**.** (copyright date)**.** *Title***.** Publishing information as above**.**

Cunningham, D. B., Bunting, B., **&** Strauss, R. (2012). ...

Periodicals:

Last name, Initials**.** (Publication date)**.** Title of article**.** *Title of periodical*, *volume number* (issue number), page numbers**.**

Dorchester, M**.** (1977)**.** Modern economics revisited**.** *Economics Digest*, 78(5), 22-27**.**

Electronic Books:

Last name, Initials. (Date of publication). *Title of book*. **Retrieved from** URL

Smith, A. (n.d.). *The Wealth of Nations*. **Retrieved from** http://www.online-literature.com/adam_smith/wealth_nations/

Online electronic encyclopedia or dictionary:

Last name, Initials. (Date of publication). Article title. **In** *Name of online encyclopedia or dictionary*. **Retrieved from** URL

Blanders, A. (n.d.). Keynesian economics. (n.d.) *Encyclopedia of economics*. **Retrieved from** http://www.encecon.com/EBchecked/topic/659723/keynesian

"Article title." (Date of publication). *Name of online encyclopedia or dictionary*. **Retrieved from** URL

Economics can be fun. *Economics digest*. **Retrieved from** http://www.ecdig.com/DCchecked/topic/67923/childhood

Website:

Last name, initials. (Date of publication). *Title of document*. **Retrieved from** URL

John M. Keynes. (n.d.). Library of Social Sciences. **Retrieved from** http://www.socscilib.org/library/bios/Keynes.html

Because her Arthur Miller/Elia Kazan paper was on a literary topic and written for her English class, Eleanor used **MLA (Modern Language Association)** style documentation.

Here is a review of the MLA-style samples Eleanor consulted when formatting her parenthetic citations and Works Cited page:

The basic form for **parenthetic citations** essentially provides the author's name and page number:

(Pearson 87)

(Conchina 34)

(Dunnel C12)

If there is no stated author, then use an abbreviated form of the title, along with the page number:

(Kazan and the HUAC 35)

Notice that there is no comma or abbreviation for "page" in MLA.

There are only a few, relatively minor variations to the basic form:

If you name the author in the text:

> Miller insists that his anger was not personal, "I was experiencing … this anguish" **(*Timebends* 293)**.

If you name the author *and source* in the text:

> In his autobiography, *Timebends*, Miller insists that his anger was not personal, "I was experiencing … this anguish" **(293)**.

If there is no stated author:

> The period of the McCarthy witch hunts has been labeled the "saddest period for civil liberties in the history of the United States **("Why We Must Always be Vigilant" 75)**.

> RightsWatch.com's insightful article, "Why We Must Always be Vigilant," labels the era "the saddest period for civil liberties in the history of the United States" **(75)**.

The "Works Cited" page, like the APA References list, provides all the information the reader will need to verify your information and how you handle it.

Formats for books. The necessary punctuation has been increased in size and bolded for emphasis:

> Author last name**,** First and middle initials**.** *Title***.** City of publication**:** Publishing Company, copyright date**.**

> Kazan, Elia**.** *A Life***.** New York**:** DaCapo Press**,** 1997.

Books with more than one author:

> 1st author last name**,** First name**, and** 2nd First and last names**.** *Title***.** Publishing information as above**.**

> Schickel, Richard and Eileen Schreckler**.** …

Books with more than *three* authors.

> 1st author last name**,** First name, **et al.** *Title***.** Publishing information as above**.**

> Cunningham**,** Richard, **et al.** …

Periodicals:

Author(s). "Title of Article." *Title of Periodical* Day Month Year: pages. Medium of publication.

Dorchow, Matthew. "Politics and the Death of Friendship." *Dramaturge's Digest* 12 Nov. 1977: 22-27. Print.

Biklind, Paula and Jeremy Kent. "The Catastrophe that was the HUAC." *The Artist Politician* 20 Dec. 2005: n.p. Electronic.

Web Site:

Editor, author, or compiler name (if available). *Name of Site*. Version number (if available). Name of institution/organization affiliated with the site (sponsor or publisher), date of resource creation (if available). Medium of publication. Date of access.

Sapphire, Crysalline. *A Compendium of ShowBiz Gossip Old and New*. Crystal Sapphire, Inc., Web. 10 May 2006.